Beneath the Sands of Egypt

ADVENTURES OF AN
UNCONVENTIONAL ARCHAEOLOGIST

DONALD P. RYAN, PH.D.

HARPER

NEW YORK · LONDON · TORONTO · SYDNEY

HARPER

A hardcover edition of this book was published in 2010 by William Morrow, an imprint of HarperCollins Publishers.

HarperCollins books may be purchased for educational, business, or sales promotional use. For information please write: Special Markets Department, HarperCollins Publishers, 10 East 53rd Street, New York, NY 10022.

FIRST HARPER PAPERBACK PUBLISHED 2011.

Designed by Lisa Stokes

Library of Congress Cataloging-in-Publication Data has been applied for.

ISBN 978-0-06-173283-6

11 12 13 14 15   OV/RRD   10 9 8 7 6 5 4 3 2 1

For Sherry Lynn

CONTENTS

PREFACE

I'M A FORTUNATE FELLOW. Literally hundreds if not thousands of times, people have told me that I'm doing something they wish they could do. I'm living their dream, or part of it anyway, they tell me. I've never figured out a good response to such comments. I've gone to fantastic places, worked with fascinating people, and discovered, as Howard Carter once put it, "wonderful things." Sadly, society can't realistically sustain millions of archaeologists and Egyptologists, but I can at least attempt to share the adventure and perhaps educate, entertain, and even inspire.

In this book I hope to do all of these things, and if I'm lucky, I'll succeed in one or two of them. Yes, I've been involved in some pretty great stuff. Serendipity, coincidence, and meeting the right people have all played a role, but so have creativity, ingenuity, preparation, and initiative. "Nothing ventured, nothing gained," they say, and I hope you enjoy my sharing of some of my adventures, focused mostly on Egypt, which is without doubt one of the most intriguing of all lands on this gorgeous planet.

ACKNOWLEDGMENTS

GIVEN THAT THE CONTENT of this book spans decades, I could thank dozens upon dozens of people, but unfortunately a relatively short list will have to suffice, lest these acknowledgments become a chapter of their own. Appreciation is extended to the following: Sherry and Samuel Ryan, who patiently live in the midst of this explorer's life and tolerate its chaos; the late Thor Heyerdahl, a lifetime hero and inspiration; Dr. Zahi Hawass and the Supreme Council of Antiquities in Egypt, who have allowed me to conduct my work, and the American Research Center in Egypt, which facilitates my projects; my various scholarly associates, including Barbara Mertz, Dennis Forbes, Nick Reeves, Edmund Meltzer, Jonathan Elias, Ray Johnson, David Lorton, Ted Brock, Otto Schaden, Sir Christopher Frayling, and the members of "The Dinosaur Club"; T. G. H. James and the curators and staff of the Egyptian department at the British Museum; the Kon-Tiki

Museum; Fred Duerr and the Kona Village Resort *'ohana*; and the various members of my expeditions, including Brian "Gordy" Holmes, Paul Buck, John Rutherford, Larry Berman, Barbara Aston, Salima Ikram, Darrell Baker, Adina Savin, Denis Whitfill, Tito Valencia, Jerry Cybulski, Lisa Vlieg, Mojka Jereb, Katie Hunt, Dr. Rick Reanier, and Stephanie Steinke, along with my antiquities inspectors and local workmen in Egypt. I would like to thank my loyal supporters, including James D. Ryan and Patricia Armstrong, Lester and Shirley McKean, Jane Ho, Jane Hayes, the Heyerdahl family, Jeffrey Belvill, Hugh Crowder, Joshua Alper, Joe and Joanne Attaway, and Mark Glickman; my many fine colleagues at Pacific Lutheran University; and my editors at HarperCollins, Jennifer Brehl, Emily Krump, Maureen Sugden, and Dale Rohrbaugh. Very special thanks to Maurice and Lois Schwartz, Dorothy A. Shelton, Albert Haas, Jerry Vincent, Liisa and Richmond Prehn, and Tom and Kelly Ott for their gracious generosity, and to Professor Robert J. Wenke, who gave a young man a chance to visit Egypt for the first time. Sadly, some of my distinguished colleagues have passed away during the last few years, including T.G.H. James, Gary "Termite" Lindstrom, Mark Papworth, Daris Swindler, Lawry Gold, David Hansen, Doug Esse, and Michael Dennett. May their memory survive as inspiration to those who follow.

Beneath the Sands of Egypt

ONE

THE TOMB

THE HAUNTING MELODY of a Beethoven piano sonata played softly in the background as I gazed into the slit of darkness evolving before my eyes. I handed another small stone to Achmed, who in turn handed it up the ancient white steps to be added to the growing pile of rubble. Beethoven would no doubt have been incredulous that his *Appassionata* served as the sound track for such a remarkable scene: the opening of an ancient Egyptian tomb, in the famed Valley of the Kings. It was actually a reopening of this particular tomb, myself being perhaps the fourth person to have done so, I reckoned, over a period of over three millennia.

As I carefully removed the stones, I marveled at the situation in which I found myself. Here I was, in the most famous archaeological site in the world, following in the footsteps of earlier explorers who were likewise entranced by this ancient place. The vertical lime-stone walls of the valley soared nearby, their golden hues becoming increasingly lighter due to the same intense summer sun that baked us as we worked in the vanishing late-morning shade. What tales these cliffs could tell, having borne witness for centuries to episodes of passionate human drama, the sweat of ancient workmen, the tears of the bereaved, and, now, the drama of modern archaeological discovery.

A view looking down the Valley of the Kings.

Approximately thirty-four hundred years ago, one of the most powerful men on the planet, the mighty pharaoh, Lord of Upper and Lower Egypt, Akheperkare Thutmose, commanded that a secret tomb be constructed for his burial in the arid Theban mountains. Unfortunately, the pyramids of his predecessors now stood only as towering beacons calling out to the treasure-minded and had proved to be utter failures when it came to protecting the remains of those considered to be god-kings. Thutmose had instigated a new strategy in the hope of better ensuring his eternal security by building a hidden tomb carved deep into the bedrock in a remote desert valley unseen by the masses with an immense peak hovering nearby, whose natural shape provided a symbolic pyramid over the royal grave. Thutmose's tomb would initiate the "Valley of the Kings" as the burial place for three dynasties of rulers during the historical period referred to as the New Kingdom, which would span approximately five hundred years, from about 1500 to 1000 B.C. It was this royal cemetery that was the stage for our unfolding tomb opening. Just a few minutes' walk from where we were lies the tomb of the famous warrior pharaoh Rameses II and, not far beyond, that of Tutankhamun, the obscure, short-lived king whose virtually intact tomb brought him lasting immortality in the modern world. And just a few dozen yards from our dig is the original tomb of Thutmose I, a deep, dangerous subterranean sepulcher, expanded and later utilized by his daughter, the remarkable female pharaoh Hatshepsut.

The early tombs in the valley were well hidden, often in fissures in the cliffs or in other places easily concealed. Those of the later pharaohs typically boasted large, obvious entrances carved into the valley's limestone. The magnificently painted corridors that followed led to an imposing stone sarcophagus holding the mummy of the king. Like the pyramids, the Valley of the Kings, too, in the long run, would prove to be a failure in guarding against the greedy. Many of its tombs would be robbed even while the cemetery was still in use.

As early as the third century B.C., several of the tombs were tourist attractions to Greek and Roman sightseers who came to marvel at the remains of the past, much as we do today. Many of them even left evidence of their visit in the form of graffiti, which can still be seen and read today scrawled on the walls of several tombs.

A view of the general vicinity of KV 60. The man in the photo stands above the location of the tomb. The entranceway to KV 19 was cut directly over KV 60, and its door is situated to the right. Just above, in the shadow of the cliffs, is KV 20, the royal tomb of the pharaoh Hatshepsut.

Some of the valley's tombs would later serve as austere housing for reclusive Christian hermits, and some would suffer the devastations of flash floods and other natural and human indignities. Ultimately, few of the pharaohs survived in their intended final resting places. Most of their ravaged mummies were gathered up by ancient priests, rewrapped, and stowed in secret caches where they have been rediscovered during the last century or so.

Like most archaeology in Egypt, the Valley of the Kings has a rich history of exploration. Although the location of the valley was long known to European travelers, it wasn't until the arrival of Giovanni Belzoni in 1816 that excavations actually began in our modern era (more on him in another chapter). Then, in 1827, John Gardner Wilkinson wandered about the valley with a container of paint, boldly numbering each known tomb as he went along and establishing a numbering system that provided a ready frame of reference for the scholars and archaeologists who followed. Although Wilkinson got only as far as the number 21, the system would eventually extend to 63, the number that has been assigned to the last new tomb discovered as of this writing, a bizarre cache of mummyless coffins uncovered in 2006.

While the Valley of the Kings is certainly one of the most celebrated sites of antiquity on earth, most people (archaeologists included) are unaware that among the thirty or so beautifully decorated royal tombs lie an approximately equal number of typically small and uninscribed tombs, whose very presence in the valley actually bespeaks some sort of great importance. Some consist merely of a shaft leading to a single rectangular burial room, while others contain a corridor or two and steps that eventually lead to a final chamber. These tombs, whose blank walls routinely render their deceased occupants anonymous, were until recently considered of little interest to Egyptologists. Readily identifiable art and writing on the walls of the bigger royal tombs are certainly alluring and have long attracted the majority of scholarly attention.

The particular tomb we were currently excavating was nameless. It was simply known as Tomb 60—or KV 60, to use the "Kings' Valley" prefix commonly appended by Egyptologists to designate a tomb in the valley rather than tombs in other ancient Egyptian cemeteries. When English archaeologist Howard Carter stumbled across this tomb in the spring of 1903, he was unimpressed by its size, its lack of decoration, and its looted interior. Carter was looking for bigger and better things: large royal tombs, for instance, with painted walls and nicely preserved artifacts. Nineteen years later Carter would hit the archaeological jackpot when, on just the other side of the valley, he discovered the burial rooms of someone who has since become one of the world's great ancient celebrities, Tutankhamun—"King Tut." Just as they did in 1922, people flock to see Tut's tomb, but few among them have heard of KV 60, or the many others of the small and undecorated sort.

My own first visit to the Valley of the Kings was on a scorching-hot July afternoon in 1981, eight years before I would encounter Tomb 60. I rented a dilapidated bicycle on the west bank of the Nile across from the modern town of Luxor and traveled a road headed straight west along green fields before turning north past two immense seated stone statues, which are most of what is left of the mammoth mortuary temple to the great pharaoh Amenhotep III. Pedaling by the village of Qurna, with its mud-brick houses built among the tombs of an ancient cemetery, I biked a long uphill stretch through a dry, winding ravine. The heat reflecting from the asphalt road added to the strenuous misery of the ride, but eventually I reached the narrow entrance to the valley. Rows of closed souvenir kiosks reminded me that this remote place was very well known to tourists, who had abandoned the scene earlier in the day to seek the cool refuge of their luxury hotels on the opposite side of the river. At midday the valley was empty except for a few tomb guards, *gaffirs*, napping in the shade.

Tutankhamun's tomb was at the top of my agenda, and I walked immediately to the stone wall surrounding its entrance, so familiar to me from years of studying photographs. I wanted to experience the tomb as Howard Carter would have. As I entered the enclosure, a *gaffir* clad in dark robes sat up from his prone position and checked my ticket before resuming his slumber. I remember counting the steps, sixteen, as I descended to the spot where Carter had stood and observed an ancient door closed with plaster and stamped with the seal of the ancient necropolis, a jackal recumbent above nine bound and kneeling captives. Carter would have then sent a telegram to his sponsor in England, Lord Carnarvon, and patiently awaited his arrival before the two breached the door together to find a tunnel filled with rubble guarding another sealed door. I walked down this corridor and paused at the second doorway. Here is where Carter would have taken his first peek into the tomb that would make archaeological history. When Carnarvon asked if he could see anything through the small hole poked through the plastered door, Carter was said to have replied, "Wonderful things."

A prominent American Egyptologist, James Henry Breasted, who visited Tut's newly opened tomb, admits that he was "utterly dazed by the overwhelming spectacle. . . . The gorgeousness of the sight, the sumptuous splendor of it all, made it appear more like the confused magnificence of those counterfeit splendors which are heaped together in the property-room of some modern grand opera than any possible reality surviving from antiquity."

During my own visit, I saw that what Carter had found choked with a remarkable assortment of royal grave finery were only four tiny rooms, their small size a sobering dose of reality to many who visit the tomb for the first time. Since I had already personally viewed the magnificent assortment of artifacts retrieved from the tomb spread out over large halls in the Egyptian Museum in Cairo, it boggled my mind to think of this minuscule space housing them all. Off to the right of the room, a railed fence kept tourists back from the sunken burial chamber in which a golden coffin, the outermost of Tut's nesting three, could be seen under a pane of glass. I have no idea how long I gazed at this token remainder of a dismantled royal burial. I wasn't aware of it at the time, but the pathetically damaged mummy of the young pharaoh remained hidden from view inside that very coffin as I looked on, stripped of its jewelry and other burial accoutrements by well-meaning archaeologists in the name of science. The naked remains lay in a tray of sand, a severed head and limbs placed in their proper anatomical position, as if to soothe the embarrassment of the mummy's exuberant investigators.

The rest of the afternoon was spent investigating some of the larger tombs in the valley accessible to tourists, empty royal tombs with painted, carved walls that dazzle the imagination and confound the uninitiated with their esoteric symbolism. As closing time neared, I mounted my bike for the exhilarating brakeless ride down the valley road to the fertile river plain.

I returned to the valley a couple of years later, with a map in hand showing dots here and there accompanied by tomb numbers. My goal during this second visit was to see as many of the tombs as possible—if not to enter their interiors, then at least to locate their exteriors. After noting the obviously visible tombs with their wide, gated doors, I spun my map about in confusion, wondering where many of the others might lie. To my surprise, about half of the tombs were identifiable only by little shafts or holes, while others could not be seen at all.

I went yet again to the valley the following year, this time well equipped with a comprehensive knowledge of the area as a whole.

My preparation had been a magnificent research volume titled *The Royal Necropoleis of Thebes,* written by an Egyptologist named Elizabeth Thomas in 1966. The book had never been formally published, but its single-spaced typewritten pages had been printed and assembled into a mere ninety copies to be found in scattered libraries. Thomas had collected nearly every known tidbit of information on the valley and other royal cemeteries in the region. There was very little that she missed, and her footnotes contain many references to archival notes by explorers and archaeologists. Something of interest can be found on every page, and I was struck not only by what was known but by what was not. Each tomb had something special and fascinating about it, and I discovered details of the obscure tombs that had piqued my interest from my previous tour of the valley. In the old days of Egyptian archaeology, finding a tomb or more a day might be de rigueur, and a robber-ravaged burial with nothing of artistic value was hardly worth a yawn. Yet the very existence of these many unpainted tombs speaks of their significance.

Since the discovery of the tomb of Tutankhamun, very little archaeological excavation had taken place in the Valley of the Kings. While there had been studies of the funerary texts on the walls of the some of the large royal tombs, the assumption seemed to be that there was little left to be found. An expedition from the Brooklyn Museum broke that trend in 1977 by spending a few years excavating a huge shaft in the tomb of Rameses XI and conducting some useful conservation studies. A dozen years later, I would apply to investigate a series of the "anonymous" tombs located behind a prominent hill in the valley. They seemed to form a group, and the information I had about each was truly compelling. Each had its number—21, 27, 28, 44, and 45—and all but 21 were visible as shafts, open or otherwise. The general area of 21, the largest of the five, could be discerned from a map, but its specific location was paved over by rubble most likely brought by a combination of flash floods and dumping on the site by early excavators.

I wrote to Elizabeth Thomas with my idea of investigating these small, ignored tombs, and she presented me with a suggestion. As I would be working in the vicinity, why not see if I might be able to locate an enigmatic, undecorated grave known as tomb KV 60? It was supposed to be located in the vicinity of KV 19, which belonged to a Twentieth Dynasty prince by the name of Montuhirkhopeshef. I had no interest. There were four tombs with known locations to keep me plenty busy, in addition to uncovering and studying Tomb 21. Besides, the location of Tomb 60 was nowhere immediately apparent. It was, however, a very interesting burial. The discovery was made in the spring of 1903 as described briefly by Howard Carter in an article published the following year:

> A small uninscribed tomb, immediately in the entrance
> of No. 19 (tomb of Ment-hi-khopesh-ef). It consists of
> a very rough flight of steps leading down to a passage
> of 5 metres long, ending in a low and rough square
> chamber, about 4 x 5 metres, which contained the
> remains of a much destroyed and rifled burial. Nothing
> was in this tomb but two much denuded mummies of
> women and some mummied geese. One of the mummies
> was lying in the lower portion of its coffin (lid missing),
> the other on the floor beside it. Their heads were fairly
> well preserved and had long hair of a golden colour. I
> should say that they must have been elderly people. The
> burial had probably been robbed by the workmen when
> making the tomb of Ment-hi-khopesh-ef. The portion of
> the coffin containing the mummy had been stripped of its

outer moulding, possibly on account of its being gilded, and the only inscription of value that could be made out was the following name and title: the royal nurse, In. Mr. Newberry was present at the opening, and he thinks that possibly these were the mummies of the nurses of Thouthmes IV. I reclosed the tomb, only removing the geese.*

In retrospect the description of the tomb would seem sufficient to cause any modern archaeologist a major twinge of excitement, yet Carter's comments suggest almost a casual disinterest in this remarkable discovery. The tomb description appears as a couple of paragraphs in a lengthy article in which Carter describes his work in Upper Egypt for the years 1902–3. During that time he also excavated at the mortuary temple of Rameses II ("the Ramesseum"), inspected the work of various archaeologists, made repairs to temples, excavated the dangerous tomb of Thutmose I and Hatshepsut in the Valley of the Kings, discovered the marvelous royal tomb of Thutmose IV, and oh, yes, an undecorated tomb of minor interest in the vicinity containing two female mummies.

Carter, at the time, had been contracted to do some archaeological work for the eccentric American millionaire Theodore Davis. Davis, an amateur archaeologist, hired Carter to conduct excavations on his behalf in the Valley of the Kings. Davis had the concession to dig wherever he chose in the sacred valley, and despite his armchair background he was exceedingly successful in uncovering some wonderfully provocative tombs. He was also responsible for finding a cache of embalming materials belonging to a then-obscure

---

* The ancient Egyptian name "Ment-hi-khopesh-ef" can be spelled several ways, including "Mentuherkhepshef" and "Montuhirkhopeshef," the latter being that preferred by this author.

pharaoh named Tutankhamun, a discovery that provided evidence that the king's burial was yet to be found somewhere in the valley. When a small tomb was discovered in 1907, Davis concluded that this must be the woefully robbed tomb of the little-known king and moved on, although Carter himself remained skeptical.

If Howard Carter's notes regarding KV 60 are brief, Theodore Davis himself has even less to say about the experience: "During the season of 1904–5, Mr. Carter, while excavating for Mr. Davis, dug a trench across the entrance to this tomb, and discovered a tomb of the XVIIIth Dynasty, over which the tomb of Mentuherkhepshef had been cut. This earlier burial he found to contain the mummies of two women. The tomb had been plundered and contained nothing of interest."

The words "nothing of interest" certainly confirm the early-twentieth-century attitude about these smaller tombs, an attitude so blasé that the wrong year was given in Davis's description of the find.

Just a month or two before he encountered Tomb 60, Howard Carter discovered in the same vicinity the large, decorated, and looted tomb of the great Eighteenth Dynasty pharaoh Thutmose IV. In fact, an old rope, likely used by robbers three thousand years ago, was found tied to a pillar in order to facilitate the crossing of a deep shaft, and a large ancient cursive graffito records an inspection of the tomb after the robbery. Though the tomb was robbed in antiquity, there was an impressive residual collection of battered burial debris found along with the pharaoh's magnificent stone sarcophagus, sans mummy, that dominated the spacious burial chamber.

Given the prevailing outlook of the day and the continual search for more "significant" discoveries, it is not surprising that Tomb 60 drifted quickly into obscurity. Carter closed the tomb, probably filling it with the debris of continuing excavations, but its history was far from over. The tomb was likely entered three years later, in 1906, by another excavator, Edward Ayrton, while he was in the process of excavating KV 19. We know of this visit only indirectly, through a handwritten notation in the Egyptian Museum's inventory catalog, the *Journal d'Entrée*, which records the acquisition of a coffin with a mummy, "recognized by Carter as having been found by him near Menthuherkhepeshef in 1903. It was brought away later by (Ayrton?)." No mention was made of the second mummy in the tomb, found lying on its floor. Might it and other burial remnants still remain within? Sometime, perhaps immediately, after this second modern visit to the tomb, KV 60 became once again buried and its specific location lost, destined to remain obscure for another eighty years.

As Carter noted, the mummy in Cairo retrieved by Ayrton was initially identified by hieroglyphs on the coffin in which she lay, yet later research revealed that she was *not* the nurse of pharaoh Thutmose IV but rather served that role for Hatshepsut, the controversial woman who ruled over Egypt for about twenty years. Her name was Sitre (Daughter of the god Re), and her nickname was "In" (Fish). A shattered statue of this woman was discovered at the site of Hatshepsut's temple, on the other side of the cliffs from the valley, and depicts her seated with the young queen/pharaoh-to-be seated on her lap. The location of Tomb 60 would perhaps seem to make sense, then, because the closest royal tomb of the appropriate date was indeed that of Hatshepsut nearby.

Out of respect for Elizabeth Thomas, I added KV 60 to my list of requests to be submitted for approval to the Egyptian antiquities authorities. If the situation presented itself sometime during the next few years, perhaps I would spend a moment contemplating the location of this long-missing tomb. The scenario as it played out, however, would be quite different.

It was late June 1989 when we arrived in Luxor to begin our work on the valley's undecorated tombs, and the intense summer heat had already arrived a couple of months before. We spent a day getting established, negotiating a reasonable long-term rate with our hotel manager, and rounding up the supplies we would need to begin work. I was accompanied by one of my former professors, Mark Papworth, a brilliant thinker and the unsung co-instigator of a major theoretical revolution that swept through American archaeology in the 1960s and '70s. We were also joined by Hisham Hegazy, an inspector with the Antiquities Service who worked as a freelance archaeologist from time to time. I had met him the year before, while spending a few weeks on an excavation in the Nile Delta directed by another former professor. Handsome, charming, and with a reasonably good command of the English language, Hisham was a wonderful asset with his knowledge of local archaeology *and* the system that governs it.

The morning of June 26 had been spent making sure all was in order with the local authorities, and by the time that had been dealt with, the solar inferno was in full effect. We set off to the valley that day to orient ourselves to our work site and drop off a few brooms, hoes, and buckets. The ride up the valley was especially searing, even with the windows of our rented car wide open. Our driver pulled up as close to the entrance as possible, the souvenir dealers having already locked up their little trinket kiosks and disappeared for the day. It was exciting to be in the valley on official business, not merely as a tourist. We rounded the corner by the old rest house, heading toward the valley's eastern cliff, passing the remarkable tombs of Rameses I and Seti I. The well-maintained path soon ended as we walked a bit farther up a small path to the only visible shade at the entranceway of Tomb 19, the beautifully painted corridor tomb of Prince Montuhirkhopeshef. We put the tools down in a heap. "We're here, let's take a look around," I offered, and we took a little stroll down the small wadi that contained the tombs in our concession: KV 21, 27, 28, 44, 45, and, lost somewhere in the area, 60.

The environment was virtually unchanged from what I had observed in years before, a handful of shafts filled with rubbish, a small breeze blowing an odd bit of paper over the mixed surface of silt, rock, and stone chips. These last were the result of the carving of tombs by ancient workmen, whose detritus had been redistributed by Western excavators in the last couple hundred years. Some of the earlier excavators used a technique perhaps best described as "the human bulldozer." Large numbers of local workmen, sometimes in the hundreds, were employed to clear portions of the valley, or other archaeological sites, to the bedrock. As they went from one spot to the next, earth and stones were removed by hoe and hand, placed into baskets, passed elsewhere, and dumped as the clearers surged forward. Some unfortunate later excavators were met with the task of removing the piled debris of their predecessors in order to conduct new excavations. A mountainous pile of stone chips, the result of Carter's digging, overlooked the area where we would be working. From its level top, we had a commanding view of the tombs below, and we nicknamed it "the Beach" for its flat and sunny demeanor.

The entrance of Tomb 21 was completely buried, but a small dimple in the overlying flood debris suggested a likely place to investigate. The other tombs—minus 60, of course—were all identifiable by visible shafts, each of which was filled with a variety of natural and human debris. Our initial inspection didn't take long, and on the way back toward Tomb 19 I brought up the matter of the lost Tomb 60. Carter's notes sprang to mind: "immediately in the entrance of Tomb 19." Looking to the left and right, I saw nothing that seemed even likely as a place for locating a tomb. The entranceway to Tomb 19 had been cut in ancient times through a rock spur, with a gently downward-sloping ramp and vertical sides approaching a square door that had three decorated jambs. In many ways it resembles a modern single-car garage, but with a high ceiling and pharaonically painted walls. The ramp was covered with several inches of windblown sediment, and when I spied a broom in our tool pile, an idea came to mind. Why should I doubt Carter? If he said immediately in front of Tomb 19, why shouldn't I look?

With the broom I began to sweep away several inches of loose sediment down to the bedrock starting just a few yards east from Tomb 19's door. Hisham helped, and without much difficulty we were able to make progress, with a new swath cleared about every meter. The rock beneath glared white as it was exposed, and after less than a half hour's work I noticed something unusual: a linear deformity in the bedrock. I continued to sweep along the break and found that this crack, of sorts, stretched horizontally nearly all the way across the entrance ramp of Tomb 19. One end disappeared underneath a rock wall to the south, while the northern end made a sharp turn to the west. At that point I removed my trowel and traced the edge of what appeared to be a pit or depression in the rock that was filled level with the white limestone chips and light brown sediment characteristic of the valley.

None of us said much, but it soon became clear we were on to something. A few photos were taken from the hillside above, and afterward I hoed out a few centimeters in a small area in one of the corners. "Well, we'll have to give this more attention, won't we?" I concluded. Both Mark and Hisham were reserved yet hopeful, and although we optimistically discussed the possibility that maybe we had just stumbled across the long-lost Tomb 60, we dared not let ourselves get overexcited lest we become disappointed should our prospect turn out to be nothing more than a shallow pit or a natural feature.

The next couple of days were spent excavating the pit. A few odd artifacts were beginning to turn up—some mummy wrappings and a couple of beads—but no immediate signs of a tomb. Two things changed that situation in short order. On the south end of our pit, a small stone shelf resembling a step began to appear, and on the north I noticed a few stones sinking downward as I worked my trowel, its metallic surface producing a characteristic high-pitched ringing sound with every scrape across the white limestone chips. A few more passes with the trowel revealed a tiny black slit, which proved to be a gap at the very top of a wall of boulders, blocking the entrance to some sort of corridor beyond. We were indeed on to something.

As we progressed, it became necessary to move a modern stone retaining wall to get at the top of what was now revealed to be a buried, steep, and crudely hewn staircase carved into the pit and leading down to a blocked door. Miscellaneous bits of ancient burial debris continued to turn up in our pit and from behind the wall. Could some of this stuff, including a resin-coated wood fragment bearing gold leaf, actually be fragments of ravaged burial equipment from the nearby anciently plundered royal tombs of Montuhirkhopeshef or possibly Thutmose IV? Or were they from Tomb 60 itself?

With excavating now well under way, we had to hire a small crew of workmen to assist in digging, moving stones, and hauling off the material. Our government-appointed antiquities inspector, Mohammed El-Bialy, recruited an assorted group of young men from the village of Qurna. Dressed in long gallabeyas and plastic slippers, they appeared strong, if not enthusiastic, and in the long run proved to be both, despite the hot Egyptian summer. The *reis,* or foreman, was a sturdy fellow named Nubie, a law student on a break from his studies.

As the work picked up, we realized we needed some sort of work space to store our tools and to study and catalog the artifacts that were beginning to accumulate. El-Bialy suggested a traditional solution utilized by generations of archaeologists working in these old cemeteries. We could use a nearby tomb as an office of sorts, providing that we exercised the utmost care. The closest tomb was KV 19, of course, with its large gated, locked entrance. It was a simple structure except for the paintings on its walls, which included scenes of Prince Montuhirkhopeshef presenting offerings to the gods, with accompanying hieroglyphic text. The tomb was at the time considered "off the beaten track" and not available for public viewing. We exercised our privilege seriously and took great pains to see that our presence in no way harmed the physical integrity of the tomb. We outfitted Tomb 19 with some chairs and a small desk, along with a worktable put together from a couple of sawhorses topped with a large sheet of plywood. It was a cozy, magnificent office, and our respect for the artisans of old increased daily as we gazed in wonder at our surroundings.

Small objects continued to appear from our excavation of the pit, and Papworth dutifully registered each in a notebook. With stairs leading downward, it was clear that in all likelihood we were excavating the long-lost KV 60. So our escapades with the broom seemed to be paying off. Another expedition had recently been working in the vicinity, experimenting with a variety of sophisticated remote-sensing devices to test their efficiency in locating lost or new tombs. Ground-penetrating radar, magnetometers, and electrical-resistivity methods all have proved somewhat effective at other archaeological sites, but none seemed ideal in the royal cemetery, due to the nature of the valley's bedrock and stony debris. An even earlier project, in the 1970s, tried using sound waves to test the possibility of locating unknown artificial voids in the bedrock and similarly produced uneven results. Our simple broom, purchased for a couple of dollars in Luxor, accomplished what tens of thousands of dollars' worth of high-tech equipment struggled to do. Thus, one example in which simple tools proved superior to expensive and complex gadgetry. The broom, however, was not acting on its own. Since we'd done our homework in advance (reading the notes of our predecessors in the valley) and considered those notes in the context of the physical terrain before us, a whimsical experiment had provided wonderful results.

From the very first realization that we had found some sort of blocked doorway, I decided that I would not venture a peek to see what lay beyond it until everything was ready for a formal opening. It certainly would have been easy; it would have involved only removing a few small stones and shining a flashlight through the hole. But as we cleared the pit to reveal more and more of the boulder-blocked door, I took pains to ensure that all would remain a surprise until the proper moment. This sort of attitude may seem surprising, but think of a nicely wrapped gift. The size and shape of the box and the color of the wrapping paper all invite speculation and fuel a great sense of excitement in the anticipation. But once the box is opened and its contents are revealed, the surprise is over. The gift might be well appreciated for many years, but its initial sense of mystery has been lost. Such can be said, too, about the finding of a tomb or some similar discovery, but in the case of the archaeologist the end of the initial surprise means the beginning of a whole lot of work. Howard Carter worked nearly ten years before he was finished with his efforts in Tutankhamun's tomb, and its contents and findings still remain only partially published even today.

Over a week had passed since we'd located the pit. It was July 4, a mere coincidence to myself and Mark Papworth. There would be no fireworks or family barbecues across the river in Luxor; opening a tomb at 10:00 A.M. would have to suffice for us. It was already brutally hot in the late-morning sun, although the fleeting shade from the valley's walls above provided some minor relief. I arranged a small group of our workers on the tomb's steep and narrow steps, whose bright limestone surface now glared vibrantly in the sun. Hisham and our inspector, Mohammed El-Bialy, were there, of course, as were a couple of the benefactors of another project operating in the vicinity, and a few other folks who had wandered up to watch the unfolding events.

To brighten things up, on a nearby wall I hung the flag lent to me by the Explorers Club of New York. It was the very same flag that had flown from the mast of the famous *Kon-Tiki* raft in 1947, skippered by my boyhood hero, the Norwegian explorer and archaeologist Thor Heyerdahl. The irony of this totem barely fazed me; the flag that once traversed the rolling waves of the Pacific now celebrated the opening of a timelessly static tomb in a bone-dry desert. In an attempt to make the moment even more special, I felt that some quiet music might add to the occasion. Unfortunately, modern archaeologists from Egypt, America, Europe, and elsewhere are unable to reliably reconstruct the long-lost melodic funeral dirges that accompanied the rites of the pharaonic dead. This being the case, I chose to foster a somewhat calming and dignified atmosphere and selected to accompany our work three Beethoven sonatas softly broadcast from a portable tape player. The melodies of the *Moonlight*, *Pathetique*, and *Appassionata* sonatas served as a kind of tribute, although clearly European, to a tomb from a mostly extinct culture.

I descended the pit's crudely carved stairs and proceeded to dismantle the wall of stones, rock by rock, and passed them upward. As the stones from the top of the blocked entrance became larger and heavier, the light began to reveal the beginning of the expected corridor beyond. A few boulders were rolled outward into the pit, and a gap large enough to stoop through was created. The sense of excitement was nearly overwhelming. I ditched my hat, and both El-Bialy and I made sure our flashlights were operational. In just a few minutes, we crouched to enter the tomb, stepping onto a short, downward-sloping pile of stone rubble. We lingered hunched down just inside the doorway for a few moments until our eyes could adjust from the blinding glare outside to the murky darkness beyond. Peering into the distance, we could begin to make out a square door at the end of the irregularly fashioned eight-meter-long corridor with its rubble-strewn floor.

The crudely carved steep steps leading down
to the blocked entrance of KV 60.

Just inside the door on each side of the corridor was a roughly carved niche containing the shattered remains of wooden grave goods. The majority resembled broken-up sticks of fresh kindling. Most striking among this debris was a chunk of wood that even in its ruinous state was readily identifiable as a face piece from a coffin. It had been badly smashed, its inlaid eyes torn out. A few flecks of gold still clung to the once-gilded wooden surface, which also bore telltale adze marks. We would later find specks of gold flakes in the dust nearby. It seems that ancient tomb plunderers may have done some of their damage close to the tomb's entrance, where there would be more light to allow them to accomplish their devious work. The gold could be scraped off gilded objects, collected, and then melted down, thus rendered anonymous and leaving future buyers clueless that their purchase was "recycled" from a royal cemetery.

Along the walls of each niche, we noticed some coarsely drawn graffiti featuring the protective "Udjat" eye of the god Horus, one looking into the tomb and one looking out. If such an eye *ever* had any power, it had long ago been lost and was pathetically ineffective. Outside, I could hear Mark Papworth calling in a comedic voice imitating Lord Carnarvon at the opening of Tut's tomb, "What do you see? What do you see?" "Broken things" would have been an appropriate answer, but I was too occupied and intrigued to reply.

Our tour of the tomb progressed down the corridor, and El-Bialy and I were careful to avoid stepping on the assorted bits and pieces of artifacts haphazardly strewn about on the floor. Halfway along the passage, we were greeted by a raised square aperture on the right wall, leading into a tiny room. Some small, stained, linen-wrapped mummy bundles lay scattered in the vicinity, including what looked like a section of desiccated beef ribs. These appeared to be food provisions left for the spiritual satisfaction of the deceased. Traces of mud plaster around the door of this little chamber indicated that it had once been sealed shut, and the mud bricks that once blocked the way had been trampled on the corridor floor. This curious chamber was an unexpected surprise. It had not been mentioned in Howard Carter's notes. In its center lay a large pile of yellowed mummy wrappings with a few broken potsherds littered across the floor. Against one wall was a large mummified cow's leg, perhaps another food offering or the remnant of a known ancient funeral ritual during which such a leg was often presented to the human mummy.

A view down the corridor of KV 60 toward
the square opening leading to the burial chamber.

Continuing our exploration of the tomb, we moved toward the square doorway that loomed at the end of the corridor. Beyond, no doubt, was the burial chamber we anticipated. We carefully stepped through the door and into a room about 5.5 by 6.5 meters (18 by 21 feet), whose odd, unsymmetrical shape provided further indication that this tomb had been hastily carved. Unlike the corridor behind, whose floor was sullied with smashed mud bricks and rocky debris that had seeped in from the outside, the surface of this chamber was clean and bright except for random scatterings of tomb wreckage.

A view into the burial chamber from its entrance,
featuring a pile of wrapped food provisions.

Directly across from the door was another collection of wrapped food provisions. They had been assembled on the floor in a peculiar little pile, causing me to wonder whether this had been the work of the earlier archaeologists. Such questions are relevant for the entire tomb. How much of what we were seeing was still in its ancient context, and how much had been shuffled around by more recent visitors? This matter of uncertainty continues to lurk in the back of my mind to this day. In one spot there were fragments of a smashed pot with the probable remains of its ancient contents adhering to the floor in the form of a patch of a dark, rubbery, speckled substance. Near one wall stood a large, thick, curved piece of wood, which appeared to be the isolated head end of a coffin box. Perhaps the fragments of the face piece found near the entrance were associated components.

The floor of the burial chamber of KV 60 as encountered in 1989. Note the mummy in the foreground and a large coffin fragment near the wall.

It was eerily quiet, and I was conscious of both my breathing and my heartbeat. The air in the tomb was warm, still, and relatively odorless. Although my research had taught me what to expect, I was not prepared for the sight that greeted the limited beam of my flashlight as it scanned the floor. A mummy, flat on its back, rested there, as if stiffly napping in an eternal closed-eye stare at the ceiling. It was a woman and was no doubt the uncoffined female that Carter had described and Ayrton had abandoned. The wrappings had been stripped off most of her body in an ancient grab for treasure. Even the toes had been bared in a search for the golden caps that often covered such appendages in elite burials. It was an almost embarrassing sight to witness, tragic in its indignity.

The mummy's face was quite striking. The embalmers had done an extraordinary job. Her nose had been packed with linen to preserve its shape, and her slightly parted lips revealed well-worn teeth. The ears retained their shape, and a smattering of reddish blond hair lay on the floor at the base of her nearly bald head. It was readily apparent that his individual had been quite obese in life, and a pampered existence was suggested by fingernails painted red and outlined in black.

The mummy encountered on the floor of the
burial chamber in KV 60. Her bent left arm and clenched
left fist suggest an Eighteenth Dynasty royal female.

While the quality of mummification was indeed remarkable, the most striking aspect of this noblewoman was her pose. Her right arm lay rigid against her side, but her left was bent at the elbow with a clenched fist as if grasping a scepter or other ceremonial object. This is a rare pose that seems to be confined primarily to royal females of the Eighteenth Dynasty.

The striking profile of the mummy from KV 60.

Mohammed and I spoke little as we spent a few more minutes examining everything around us, and we soon decided that it was time to return to the land of the living. We carefully retraced our steps, and as we emerged into the light and fresh air, we were bombarded with questions from the others, who were anxious to hear the news. "Give us a minute or two to regain our composure, please," I requested as El-Bialy and I took seats in a couple of wooden chairs, drenched in sweat and breathing in the fresh air. The whole experience had been overwhelming, and when we were ready to talk, we expressed both our wonder and our dismay. We were saddened by the violent treatment this burial had endured. On the other hand, we were intrigued by the perplexing archaeological puzzle that the tomb now presented. What was the *real* story behind this simple little tomb, and who might this regal lady be who lay so undignified on its floor? Little could I imagine at the time that such questions would soon prove to be both provocative and disturbing. Or that years later the solution would become a world sensation.

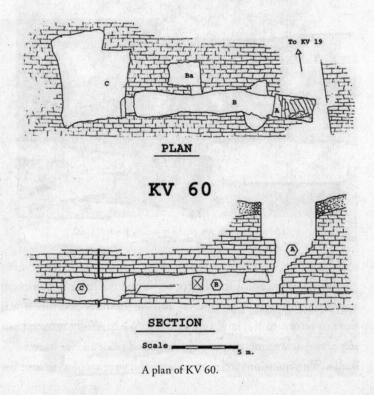

A plan of KV 60.

TWO

FROM HERE TO THERE

O NE DOESN'T JUST ARRIVE in the Valley of the Kings and begin to unearth mysteries. My activities there are the result of a long journey. I grew up in the town of Covina in Southern California, a pleasant place not far from the foothills of the San Gabriel Mountains and a short distance from the Pacific Ocean and downtown Los Angeles. With parents who traveled the world, I was constantly exposed to foreign lands and cultures. I eagerly awaited their return, the accompanying stories, photographs, and, of course, souvenirs.

My first sparks of a serious interest in the past can be traced to *The How and Why Wonder Book of Dinosaurs,* which provided no end of fascination to me when I was in first grade. Not only were these bizarre creatures captivating, but the notion of the discovery and reconstruction of their remains was equally compelling. More books followed, and my growing collection of plastic dinosaur figures often posed as actors in prehistoric, action-filled scenarios, complete with enthusiastic sound effects. My attempts to successfully assemble plastic scale models of dinosaur skeletons were usually quite miserable, so the little faux bones would often be buried in the yard for systematic excavation a day or two later, an early taste of the thrill of a dig.

Repeat visits to the Natural History Museum of Los Angeles County fueled my interest, and I was one of the younger members of the Museum Alliance that supported that institution. I was especially grateful when my handwritten letter about digging up some old cow bones in my backyard was personally answered by one of the curators. Dr. J. R. MacDonald, a prominent vertebrate paleontologist, not only encouraged my interest but invited my father and me for a private tour of the museum's fossil collections.

Luckily, in another part of Los Angeles there was another site of equal allure, the famed La Brea Tar Pits, located in a park right off Wilshire Boulevard, in one of the busiest parts of the city. The tar pits are sticky black oil seeps where untold thousands of prehistoric creatures became literally stuck in the muck, only to be exploited by other hungry creatures, which in turn became entrapped. Excavations there in the early twentieth century recovered millions of bones, including those of my favorite extinct beast, *Smilodon californicus,* the famed saber-toothed cat.

National Geographic magazine introduced me to ancient Egypt, and stories of discoveries quickly became a favorite of mine. Articles with such alluring titles as "Fresh Discoveries from Egypt's Ancient Sands" and "Yankee Sails the Nile" were read and reread. My father had a subscription, but we set out to collect all the back issues, searching weekend swap meets for the yellow-bordered volumes.

There were children's books as well, one favorite being Hans

Baumann's *World of the Pharaohs;* and at a very early age I read Howard Carter's *Tomb of Tutankamen* cover to cover, its accompanying photographs begging me to imagine what it must be like to discover and examine such a place. The book *Kon-Tiki* by the Norwegian explorer Thor Heyerdahl likewise had a profound impact on my youthful dreams, which, like my fascination with the Valley of the Kings, would fortunately play out years later. After a while ancient Egypt and paleontology became side-by-side obsessions.

As a teenager I developed a passion for mountain climbing, which provided me with a physical outlet for my yearning for adventure and helped me to overcome the curse of asthma. Given climbing's potential hazards, my parents tried to increase the odds of my survival by sending me through a comprehensive mountaineering course up on Mount Rainier, which taught me the skills to climb steep snow and ice and ascend glacial slopes. The fresh mountain air and a new driving motivation to exercise changed me from a bookworm who lived vicariously through others' adventures into someone who had the potential of being actively involved.

THERE ARE MANY WAYS one might choose a university. Sometimes it's by price, by proximity to home, or by a reputation for excellence. I perused the various catalogs, some offering programs in anthropology and archaeology. But ultimately I wanted to be close to the Cascade Mountains—Mount Rainier in particular, where I had learned to climb and where I hoped to mix my college career with a life of adventure. Pacific Lutheran University in Tacoma, Washington, proved to be a wonderful choice.

After a summer of climbing and hiking in the mountains of the Northwest, the transition to university life was dramatic. My first weekend as a freshman, I was asked to assist in leading a hiking excursion up to Mount Rainier's high camp—from then on I was involved in outdoor leadership at the university. I averaged about two weekends per semester on campus over the next four years. The rest of the time, I was either leading student outdoor excursions or involved in my own mountaineering challenges. I even organized an expedition to climb the highest peak in North America, Mount McKinley/Denali up in Alaska.

That first weekend at the university also set the stage for the future. Assisting that trip on the slopes of Rainier was a girl named Sherry from a small town in western Montana, whom I would marry four and a half years later. Apart from my action-filled lifestyle, I actually attended classes. The university required that students take a variety of courses in different fields to expose them to a breadth of knowledge, the hallmark of a liberal-arts education. I enjoyed *something* in nearly every subject, but the anthropology courses at the time were uninspiring. There was also no archaeology offered, and at least one of my professors was more intent on discussing contemporary radical politics than anything resembling a survey of cultures. At one point we were urged to "declare a major," and, having been disappointed by anthropology, I chose political science, as I had taken courses in that department taught by an outstanding professor of international relations. The classes, covering everything from American foreign policy to international organizations, were extremely challenging and as a result forced me to elevate my standards of scholarship until they finally met the excellence demanded by my professor.

Touching on history, geography, philosophy, foreign cultures, and languages, the study of international relations was a fascinating and wonderful avenue for a broad-based education, but during my senior year a visitor came to town who revived my interest in the past. In nearby Seattle, King Tut arrived in the form of a block-buster exhibition that has yet to be surpassed. Sherry and I waited in a long line and eventually were led into a magical display of some of the most exquisite pieces of ancient art imaginable. At the centerpiece of the exhibition was the gold funerary mask of Tut-ankhamun, arguably the most enchanting and stunning surviving piece of art from Egypt, if not all of antiquity. Gazing into its face was a revelation that completely reinvigorated my long interest in archaeology and in Egypt particularly.

Ancient Egypt, the Valley of the Kings, and Tutankhamun's tomb . . . A flame was fanned into a fire. The question then became, what do I do about it? Surprisingly, I found it relatively easy to convince another brilliant member of the PLU faculty to assist me in my interests. Dr. Ralph Gehrke was a professor of religion, well versed in the Old Testament and the ancient Near East, and he was able to facilitate a rigorous independent study of ancient Egyptian history and culture for me. The reading list was extensive, often intense, and it laid a nice foundation for future study on the subject.

The one thing lacking, though, was instruction in the ancient language. Although Professor Gehrke could effortlessly read the Scriptures and ancient texts in Hebrew and Greek, he had not for-mally studied Egyptian. This was something I would initially have to investigate on my own. I soon became acquainted with one of the classic works on the subject, Sir Alan Gardiner's *Egyptian Grammar*. Gardiner's hefty tome became a persistent companion, its blue covers with a gold embossed title on the spine guarding the secrets to ancient Egypt's language and hieroglyphic script. I was intrigued by the hieroglyphs and their picturesque quality, challenged by the unfamiliar grammar, and I tackled several of the book's initial chapters on my own.

Graduating with my degree in political science, I had no particular plans other than taking the ambiguous "year off" before graduate school to dedicate to climbing. I got a job at a local store selling outdoor equipment. I eventually worked for some mountaineering schools and guide services, where I spent my late-spring and summer days teaching all manner of people how to climb rocks, ice, and glaciers. I was naturally enthusiastic about sharing my favorite outdoor activity *and* getting paid to do so. Plus, I loved the challenge of taking folks into a potentially dangerous environment and bringing them back safely and happy for the experience.

The mountaineering crowd I hung out with in the late seventies and eighties was a wild bunch. A number of them boldly proclaimed that if they were still alive by age thirty, they hadn't lived life extremely enough. Money was of little concern, other than for facilitating their climbing habit, and living for months at campsites, in vans, on floors, and even under overhanging rock outcrops was not uncommon. Levels of difficulty were being continuously pushed in those days, and impressive new routes up peaks and rock walls were being established at a steady rate.

Some of us participated in the high-risk game of climbing unroped—"free soloing"—that required utmost audacity, confidence, and focus. The consequences of failure were dire, but the rewards of successfully surviving the experience were intense personal satisfaction and, occasionally, status among one's climbing peers. But it was addictive. I recall one particular day when mind, body, and spirit perfectly coalesced into an almost trancelike state during which I found myself free soloing a dozen rock climbs, some of which had previously scared me even when accompanied by a partner and a rope. It was magical, but when it was over, I shook in awe and fear for hours.

My obsession with climbing nurtured certain traits that are

useful in archaeology. It developed a physical toughness required for fieldwork, especially in remote locations where accommodations are often minimal and the environment unpleasant to humans. In fact, I learned not only to tolerate such situations but to savor them. Years of searching for the next hand- and footholds also bring an eye for subtlety, and an explorer will always benefit from a zeal to see what lies behind the next corner or over the next ridge. In practical terms, too, mountaineering offered me a skill set that can enable one to explore places where the average scientist or archaeologist cannot or will not go, whether it's up, down, or sideways in dangerous terrain.

While my climbing fanaticism lasted for years, I eventually toned it down a bit. As I eventually began doing serious research in archaeology and Egyptology, I found that scholarship had its own form of satisfaction, even without physical adversity. I loved studying in libraries and exploring archives and museum collections where new discoveries lurk in exciting, unexpected places. It certainly couldn't replace the joys of the outdoors, but it came in a close second.

I was also becoming disenchanted with the realities of big-mountain expeditions. I had been invited on a few in the Himalayas, but circumstances at the time didn't allow me to participate. I have no regrets. The price tag for such expeditions sometimes reaches hundreds of thousands of dollars, with little gained other than a few minutes on a summit such as Everest, a mountain that has now been climbed by several thousand people and has turned back many more due to weather or illness. Or if you're really unlucky, you don't return alive. And it's usually all over in less than three months.

As I began putting together my own archaeological projects for a fraction of the money required for mountaineering expeditions, my enthusiasm for giant peaks waned. More important, I was thrilled to have something to show for my more academic efforts. Scholarship and scientific projects provided something to share, and occasionally inspire, in the form of original contributions to human knowledge rather than just a good feeling and a hook for motivational speaking. ("Pursue your dreams, whatever they may be, one step at a time, just like when I was the 2,467th person to climb Everest," etc.)

Finally, the birth of my son, Samuel, also convinced me to tame some of my more reckless activities. My child needs his father, and though I'm still physically capable, I now use a rope and take a climbing partner more often than not. I've also replaced some of the physical and mental addiction of mountaineering with other activities that are much safer, like long-distance running on wilderness trails, mountain biking, and the occasional game of croquet.

The author climbing with his son, Samuel, on a peak near Mount Rainier.

In retrospect, archaeology probably saved my life. Anyone who has participated seriously in climbing for a decade or more can recite the names of several acquaintances and friends who didn't survive the experience. I personally quit counting after two dozen. Of eight people I worked with at one climbing school, only half of us are still alive, including one who had a leg nearly torn off by a falling rock. None were killed while working as professional guides, where our attention to client safety is foremost. Each perished pushing his own personal limits, often extreme, all of them doing what they loved to do.

After I'd completed my undergraduate career and spent a fun summer following graduation, fall arrived with its accompanying poor weather in the Northwest. In short order I found myself increasingly bored and wishing I had applied directly to graduate school. Scrambling in an attempt to make up for lost time, I managed to get admitted to two great schools in Southern California beginning in January, for the beginning of their winter quarters. One was a program in international relations and the other in Egyptology. I attended each for a week and dropped out of both. I learned quickly from the former that I didn't have the obsession or dedication to pursue a professional career in the very real and often ugly world of Cold War politics. Many of the professors at the school were presidential advisers or other prominent individuals, and the subject matter was immediately current and very, very serious. The career path seemed to be directed toward positions in the State Department, policy institutes, or university-level teaching. It wasn't political science per se that attracted me as an undergraduate, but the history surrounding it. I was more interested in its fascinating past than in its frightening present.

I had very different misgivings about the Egyptology program, mostly logistical, but my turning away from it was ultimately for the best. Somewhat trackless, I spent the rest of the spring climbing, returned to the Northwest, married the ever-patient Sherry, and directed a climbing school for the summer. In the meanwhile I applied to a graduate archaeology program at a very large institution that I will hereafter refer to as Big University.

FROM THE VERY BEGINNING, it was clear that my new graduate school would require some major adjustment. The campus was huge, and I was just one of thirty thousand students, about ten times more than my previous university. PLU had spoiled me. When I was an undergraduate, each of my professors knew me by name and was genuinely concerned about my academic progress and personal welfare. At the new school, I felt like just another face in the crowd, another herring in the ocean, a number just like the one I was issued.

My first quarter at Big University was like taking a plunge off a high board into unfamiliar and deep waters. There were two required classes that were seemingly designed to flush out the less-than-serious student. The first class dealt with archaeological theory. Behind the shovels, pots, and other physical manifestations of the archaeological practice, there is a level of abstraction that provides a theoretical framework for the organization and interpretation of the work. That particular class was taught by a quirky and eccentric archaeological version of Professor Kingsfield, the arrogant trainer of law students in the book, movie, and TV series *The Paper Chase*. Like Kingsfield, this professor was intent upon training our mush-filled heads into ones that could think critically.

Our massive reading list for the course consisted of 147 articles and books to be read and, more important, comprehended. During our first meeting, class was immediately dismissed for a week so that we could prepare with twenty-one of these readings, five of which were complete books. Needless to say, we left class that day in shock as we scrambled to the library. Even four years of undergraduate study had not prepared us for this level of intensity, but the only option was to get used to it and get used to it quickly.

Despite his numerous intimidating eccentricities, our theory professor was absolutely brilliant. The required courses taught by this pedagogue from Hades involved the critical examination of major theoretical issues in archaeology, including classification (how does one organize what is found?) and explanation (how does one interpret what is found?). Quotes scribbled in the margins of my notes from his classes retain the flavor of the experience. Classification, for example, is necessary for order in this world so "you can tell your grandmother from your dog" and so that "you can tell a round red rubber ball from an apple, the consequences of a mistake being gastric distress."

The professor also maintained a highly critical view of the study of the human past. "We're no worse off than alchemy!" he would declare after enlightening us with the hidden foolhardiness of the very subject we were devoted to studying. Very importantly, though, he urged us to develop the ability to analyze the theories, books, and journals in the field critically no matter how prestigious the author or pompous the prose. He insisted that we not be afraid to call a spade a spade (no archaeological pun intended). "Free yourself from the tyranny of the written word!" he would orate. "Don't be afraid to say, 'This is crap!'" In some of his classes, we were assigned a cutting-edge scientific article and asked to deconstruct it to reveal its basic theoretical flaws. The process was certainly surprising, as we discovered that a lot of what initially impressed us as quality archaeological methodology really was defective (and some of it still is!). In short, he taught us to think in new and different ways, something that might come in handy, for instance, in finding such things as lost Egyptian tombs.

Another class to be taken by new students during our first quarter was on the subject of "paleoenvironmental reconstruction," in which we were to study how to make sense of the greater world in which ancient people lived. After all, it's not only manufactured artifacts and human bones that are uncovered by archaeologists. Humans are just one component of a greater picture of the planet's past, which also includes plants and animals and variables such as landforms, landscapes, and climate. The class was at least as demanding as that of our theory professor and required us to read and summarize the hundred or so items on the reading list. We then had to give a critical presentation of a prominent article or book to be critiqued by our peers.

This, however, was no ordinary class on how to reconstruct the past. The professor was an outstanding specialist in "faunal analysis," and much of our work involved learning the fine art of animal bone identification. Every class period new bones of the mammalian skeleton would be introduced, and we were expected to learn their major features and be able to identify them in whole or fragmentary form. Boxes of disarticulated cat skeletons served as the basic model, supplemented with the remains of other creatures large and small. It wasn't so bad; I happen to like bones. Apart from their obvious anatomical necessity, they are a striking form of art in nature, worthy of admiration and wonder.

To check our progress, "bone quizzes" were held on a regular basis and consisted of a series of small cardboard boxes that held bone fragments for our identification. We lined up along the tables spaced throughout the room that held the bone-filled boxes while a teaching assistant held a stopwatch; every thirty seconds we were required to shuffle over to the next box. A calm demeanor and nerves of steel were helpful, and attention to detail was essential. Our anxious hands would quickly grab the bone, spinning it rapidly to take note of any distinguishing features. Is it a sliver of a left distal humerus or a battered chunk of a right proximal radius? An answer was hastily jotted down before we were promptly moved to the next box.

The number of bones we were required to know intimately grew with each class, so at the end we were to have a cumulative knowledge of the two hundred plus bones in the skeleton. Our proficiency would be tested at the end of the course with the much dreaded "FBQ," or "Final Bone Quiz." We were taunted by veterans of previous classes with stories of the horrors ahead, including one about a rat skeleton's being placed in a blender, from which fifty fragments would be randomly selected for our identification. Ultimately, a pureed rat might have been preferable, as the bones during the final were an amazing assortment of bizarre bits and pieces from peculiar creatures. I had never seen such odd bones. With the phrase "You may begin," a living nightmare ensued: the intense concentration, the rapidly spinning bones, and, as in the song by Jacques Brel, the horror of the word "Next!" called out every thirty seconds . . . the sea-lion scapula . . . the fragment of the antelope metatarsal . . . the fractured rabbit tibia . . . and box number 50.

We had heard that the final box could go one of two ways: If the professor were in a happy mood or liked the class, we might find something on the order of a rubber-squeaky-toy dog bone. On the other hand, the box might contain a bone sent from hell, whose identification would boggle even the most discriminately trained eyes. Unsurprisingly, the latter was the case—something from a manatee, perhaps—and the Final Bone Quiz left us exhausted. One young lady fled the room in tears; she had somehow written her answers out of order during the shuffle around the room, completely fouling her entire test. After it was all over, I knew a lot about methods to reconstruct ancient environments and a whole lot about bones.

I also studied human bones with a wonderful professor named Daris Swindler. His love of the subject permeated his teaching, and his lectures were a sunny light in an otherwise terse and frantic graduate-school existence. My having already studied the bones of dead cats and assorted mammals certainly aided the process, and given other circumstances I might have become one of those forensic anatomists with whom television currently seems so enamored.

When I enrolled at Big University, I had heard that a professor in the archaeology program had just conducted his first excavation in Egypt. Dr. W had previously worked in Iran, but with the recent revolution there his research investment was essentially terminated. With generous private funding, however, he was able to gain a fresh start in another ancient land. I sought out Dr. W on my very first day of graduate school. Nervously knocking on his office door, I interrupted the young professor typing away at a document. I quickly introduced myself as a new student, explained my deep interest in Egypt, and acknowledged that I was aware of his recent work there. I eagerly stated that I would be grateful to be involved in any opportunity to learn or participate in anything having to do with the subject. In what some might consider a profound coincidence, Dr. W was at that very moment typing a grant proposal to conduct an archaeological project in the Egyptian desert the following year. "Sign up as one of my advisees and I'll add you right in!" I did, and the very next summer a dream was realized as I traveled to the land of my childhood fantasies to participate in my first archaeological expedition.

THREE

FIRST IMPRESSIONS

I T WAS A VERY LONG first year in graduate school, and it seemed as if summer was ages away. Dr. W was successful in winning his grants, and the project would begin in June 1981. Egypt at the time was a politically tense place. Anwar Sadat, the president who boldly made peace with Israel, would be assassinated in Cairo in October of that same year. Despite the political complexities, we dealt with the problematic present by holding to our goal of addressing the past.

The expedition's objectives were fascinating. Everybody is aware of the grandeur of the pharaohs—their massive constructions, the hieroglyphs, and the opulence of royal tombs. But all these marvelous things, these manifestations of advanced "civilization" or what anthropologists call "societal complexity," didn't always exist, and they certainly didn't appear out of nowhere. People in fact lived in the Nile Valley for tens of thousands of years before there were any pyramids, sphinxes, or sprawling temples. Egyptologists and archaeologists tend to agree that what we might call "pharaonic civilization" began only about five thousand years ago, or around 3100–3050 B.C. Long before that, inhabitants of the place we now call Egypt were living off the land, hunting, fishing, and gathering natural produce. And at some time, between nine thousand and six thousand years ago, people in the Nile Valley started to grow their own crops and began the process of domesticating animals for their own benefit. Permanent villages became the norm, and food surpluses allowed for larger populations. Out of this situation, a "civilization" would arise with its relatively sophisticated characteristics, including monumental architecture, a writing system, craft specialists, political and religious bureaucrats, and a supreme ruler.

The transition from living off the land to manipulating the land is a topic of great anthropological mystery and discussion. It happened in many places, and here and there the notion spread through contact with those "in the know," but elsewhere processes of independent invention seem to be the case. The timing of this profound transition is suspicious; some of the earliest cases of the development of agriculture appear after the last ice age, and climate change may have played a major role. But however it may have happened, it was from this important cultural platform that most early civilizations evolved, not only in Egypt but in regions like Mesopotamia, the Indus Valley, and China. Dr. W's project would investigate this intriguing and somewhat shadowy transition period through archaeological exploration in a part of Egypt known as the Fayyum.

The Fayyum is a natural basin southwest of Cairo, its principal feature being a large lake known in Arabic today as the Birket Qarun, which has varied in size through the ages. In the

1920s two bold British scholars—archaeologist Gertrude Caton-Thompson and geologist Elinor Gardner—conducted some of the first archaeological surveys of the region and found evidence of early agricultural settlements in what is now desert, including baskets of grain well preserved in the dry sand and other essential clues. Certain portions of the region, including the north side of the lake and the deserts to the southwest, remained undeveloped and thus bore the potential of being excellent places to investigate Egypt's agricultural transition.

With June fast approaching, Dr. W presented me with an airline ticket that might as well have been a key to my future. I flew to London and from there to Cairo. I remember peering through the airplane window seeking any clue that we were coming close, and after a few hours the blackness of the Mediterranean yielded to a land punctuated by thousands of tiny lights. It was the Nile Delta in northern Egypt, and Cairo was but a couple of hundred miles away.

I arrived in Cairo after dark, and it was an experience right out of a very peculiar and restless dream. As we left the plane, large floodlights illuminated our every gesture and soldiers manning machine guns crouched behind small sandbag bunkers. The air was hot, and the unfamiliar sounds of Arabic added to an atmosphere of both wonder and excitement. And I was finally there! In Egypt! Land of the Pharaohs!

Outside the airport I hired a taxi, and thus began my pandemonic and fun introduction to the city of Cairo. A half hour high-speed career through the streets revealed a city still very much alive even at this late hour. I remember blurs of light, the rattling of the taxi and its various loose parts, the incessant horn honking, and the Egyptian music on the radio. Thanks to a couple of quick swerves, we avoided a donkey cart full of garbage while another dilapidated speeding car swung into our lane with only inches to spare. Eventually we arrived at the Garden City House, my eyes wide and my knees shaking.

Pronounce it like the Egyptians, "Garden See-tee House," I had been instructed by my friend Janet, who'd been in Egypt with Dr. W the year before. The Garden City House is located on the third and fourth floors of an aging building near the Nile. Its truly convenient location and its simple, inexpensive rooms have attracted many a scholar by word of mouth for years. Tired from my travels, I checked in, found my room, and attempted to sleep.

The first day's agenda was obvious. It had to be the famed Pyramids of Giza, including the Great Pyramid of Cheops and its two colossal neighbors, as well as the famous Sphinx along with fields of ancient cemeteries, all located just on the outskirts of the sprawling city. But before I began my adventure, I stepped outside the hotel and walked a short distance to gain my first glimpse of the legendary Nile River.

"Egypt is the gift of the Nile," stated the Greek historian Herodotus. That little quote appears in nearly every book ever written about Egypt, so there is no reason to break tradition and leave it out of this one. But it's true. The Nile is the undisputed life source for the country. In ancient times its annual flooding renewed the soil and produced an agricultural paradise that formed the foundation for the Egyptian civilization. It also served as a natural highway and easily facilitated the movement of people and their goods.

In antiquity the Nile was worshipped as a god and the people prayed for its benevolence: Too much flooding could be destructive, too little could bring about drought. The river, though, is no longer free to come and go as it once did. The immense dam at Aswan, built in modern times in the far south of Egypt, changed all that. While electricity is supplied for industry and floods are controlled, the new need for artificial fertilizers exhausts the soil, coastlines are eroded when sediments are trapped behind the dam, and the rise in water tables contributes to the deterioration of ancient monuments.

The Nile is quite impressive at Cairo, flowing smooth and wide. Too many bridges obscure the current panorama but are a necessity for a city whose growth knows no bounds. Travel just a few miles farther south of downtown, though, and the river flows unobstructed for great distances. River barges plow through the water, while local boats called feluccas hoist their sails to travel upstream with the north wind or track with the current toward the Mediterranean.

After taking in my fill of the majestic Nile, I located a taxi and settled in with great anticipation. The route to the pyramids crosses the river and then proceeds through the crowded suburb of Giza. Eventually we reached the Pyramids Road, a busy stretch of street whose opposing lanes are separated in part by occasional topiary bushes in symmetrical pharaonic shapes. A surprising number of garish discos were visible, but the ultimate culture shock came at the first sight of an indomitable American institution, Kentucky Fried Chicken. And also nearby was a Wimpy's hamburger outlet, a British chain. Dismayed, I found it best to stare straight ahead, keeping a lookout for pyramids. Soon the very edge of a distant, dusky shape could be seen lurking behind the onslaught of tall apartment buildings. The shape became increasingly more distinct until the first full view of the Great Pyramid hit with all its impact. The words that came to mind were "amazing," "incredible," and "stupendous."

In its pristine condition, the Great Pyramid stood around 480 feet tall—about fifty stories high—and it covers an area of about thirteen square acres. It is estimated that over 2 million stone blocks were necessary to construct the structure, with some of its interior chambers utilizing immense granite slabs transported from quarries located hundreds of miles away. In its day the exterior of the Great Pyramid was clothed with smooth limestone casing blocks that reflected the rays of the sun, creating a gleaming beacon, visible for miles.

I have often heard two opposing kinds of first impressions of the Pyramids of Giza from visitors. Some express a sort of disappointment, stating that "I thought they would be bigger!" while others are thoroughly overwhelmed at their immensity. But nearly all are impressed by the fact that these massive constructions were built by human ingenuity and manual labor thousands of years ago without the benefit of modern technology. They were just a little smaller than I anticipated, but unbelievably impressive nonetheless.

I had a similar experience when I first visited the famed ancient monument known as Stonehenge on the Salisbury Plain in England. From my reading and viewing of pictures, I had always imagined the celebrated megaliths as being truly gigantic in proportion, perhaps forty or fifty feet tall. Alas, had it not been for the security fence barring me, I felt that I could have run up and slapped the top of the standing stones. It was much the same with the Great Pyramid. And the closer one gets, the more apparent it becomes that the pyramids are no longer the smooth-sided models of geometrical virtue that they once were. Much of their outer casing blocks has been quarried away for quality building material in the millennia following their construction, when pyramids were no longer appreciated nor understood. A complete stroll around the perimeter of the Great Pyramid of Cheops, though, will cause even the disappointed to truly appreciate its tremendous size. The pyramid, like others in the vicinity, is still surrounded by a huge number of rectangular stone mastaba tombs and shaft graves of relatives and officials that are also remarkable and indicate that Cheops was served by an immense ancient bureaucracy.

One of the most impressive facts of the pyramids is their great age; they were built around forty-six hundred years ago, during the time period that historians refer to as the Old Kingdom. The pyramids were already well over a thousand years old when Tutankhamun, Rameses II, and even Moses were on the scene. By the time Herodotus allegedly visited Egypt as a tourist around 450 B.C., the Giza pyramids were already over two thousand years old. Herodotus includes an interesting chapter about Egyptian history and culture in his writings known as *The Histories,* and until the decipherment of the hieroglyphs in 1822, and even to some extent still, his commentary was a major source of information.

Herodotus reported many curious things about Egypt, some of which are so improbable that a number of scholars have questioned whether he actually visited the place. Others believe that he was merely a victim of misinformation or fanciful tales provided by local guides who themselves were very shaky on the true details. There is also speculation about a cultural and linguistic gap—after all, he was Greek in a foreign land. Whatever the circumstances, Herodotus relates the story that the Great Pyramid was built by hundreds of thousands of slaves under the orders of evil King Cheops. It took ten years to build a magnificent decorated track used to drag the stone blocks and twenty years to build the pyramid itself, using a system of levers to lift each block into place. When money for the construction ran short, the depraved Cheops prostituted his own daughter to obtain additional funds, according to Herodotus.

There is little to substantiate or confirm any of these notions. First of all, the use of slaves in the building of the pyramids is greatly disputable. (Despite the fantasies of Hollywood, Hebrews weren't on the scene for another thousand years!) One of the better theories suggests that the pyramids were not built with slaves but were great public-works projects whose labor force was supplemented by employing a huge number of idle farmers and other laborers during the time of the Nile's annual flood. Supporting this theory is the fact that the rising floodwaters would also allow for closer access to the building site by quarry barges. Although the actual building techniques are not fully known, it is more likely that some kind of system of earth ramps was used, rather than levers. Doubtless, huge numbers of workers were required, and some recent excavations in the vicinity of the Giza pyramids are revealing the barracks, bakeries, and other facilities necessary to keep a gigantic workforce in operation. As for Cheops—or, more accurately, Khufu, his ancient Egyptian name—there is little known about his life or personal disposition.

Until just a few years ago, when new regulations were put in place, walking around the pyramids wasn't always an easy or relaxing activity. It was never dangerous, unless you tripped on the uneven terrain, nor was it particularly strenuous, unless you met the intense summer sun as you traipsed through the sand. The difficulty began when the unsuspecting tourist encountered the enthusiastic local entrepreneurs who raised persistence to an art form.

Interactions generally went like this:

"'Scooz me, meester, want to ride a camel?" one of half a dozen or more hawkers would inquire, beckoning any and all approaching tourists. A simple no would never suffice and was countered by insistent pleading and a likely chase lasting up to several hundred yards.

"I'm a student, and I don't have any money," I'd insist within a few minutes of arriving at the Giza Plateau.

"No problem, my camel is a special student camel. Special price for you! No charge! Pay what you like!" If naïve travelers ever took the bait, they'd find that getting up on a camel could indeed be free, but getting back down from their awkward perches would cost plenty. After it became gradually clear to the entrepreneurs that a sale was not going to be made, the camel man would usually trot off on his bellowing, sandy-colored beast to seek out the next potential customer.

These camel men were clever. Many spoke several different languages conversationally and possessed a smattering of several more. I was often approached in German because of my blond hair, though they have accused me of being from a variety of other places. On other visits to Egypt, my friends and I would attempt to confuse our trailing camel man by claiming we were from Botswana, Lithuania, or some other land presumed to be outside his geographical awareness. After a few moments of contemplation, he might reply, "Ah! Botswana! I have a cousin who lives there!" And it would not have surprised me if he could speak a few words of a relatively obscure African tribal language.

The camel-riding industry was not the only occupation found amid the pyramids. Horse-buggy drivers, cola vendors, and peddlers of illustrated papyrus paper aggressively plied their trades against the backdrop of the grandest of pyramids. On more than one occasion, I was approached by a robed teenager who, after first looking about in all directions to see if anyone was watching or listening, would whisper, "Pssst! Meester! Come have a look! Quickly!" The boy then reached into his coat, slowly and carefully removing a small, suspicious-looking envelope. Drugs perhaps? Illicit antiquities? Still maintaining vigilance to keep his potential customer in suspense, he opened the envelope. "Look, meester! Ten postcards for one Egyptian pound!"

The cola vendors had their own tricks. They would appear out of nowhere in the hottest places with an ice-filled metal bucket in hand. These young entrepreneurs would grab a very warm bottle of soda from a nearby cache and secretly roll the outside of the glass on a block of ice before placing it in your hand. The unwitting foreigner would say, "Ice cold and refreshing! Give me two!" And then the smug young vendor would sit and wait for the return of the empty bottles as you tried to gag down at least one of the tepid, sickeningly sweet drinks.

Despite the constant interruptions from vendors on my first encounter with the "mountains of Pharaoh," I decided to hire a local "guide" to show me the area. The "guide," whom I contracted for a couple of hours and two Egyptian pounds, was an older man, perhaps in his early seventies, who offered to give me a tour of the Chephren (Khafre) Pyramid, the second-largest at Giza, along with some of the better small tombs in the area. He claimed to possess the keys to all the appropriate monuments.

Our trudge began in the severe noontime heat of June as the guide marched me across the sand of the Giza Plateau in a very roundabout fashion. Walking in the sand is tiring, and I was sure that I'd seen a paved road leading directly toward the Chephren Pyramid during my earlier stroll. Several stops for water later, I noticed that I was being followed by a camel driver who, it became apparent, was in collusion with the guide, presumably to garner a shared commission. The object of the game soon became clear: The guide was trying to wear me down in the sand and the heat until his friend would fortuitously appear to offer me a lift. "Forget it!" I exclaimed as I poured water over my head and shirt from my canteen and then continued my struggle as the water evaporated from my clothing in a matter of minutes.

As we arrived at our first destination, the guide said, "Well, here it is, the Chephren Pyramid, built by King Chephren. Come, I'll show you the palace of Cheops." He turned around and headed back across the sand in more or less the general direction of the Great Pyramid. I foolishly followed, the camel man once again trailing in my path.

At a convenient little dune, the guide stopped and pulled something "very old" from his robe. It was obviously a very cheap modern scarab—an amulet in the shape of a beetle—of the sort that are manufactured en masse for pennies apiece. "Special price for you, meester! America and Egypt, good friends. Look! Very, very old. For you? Fifty dollars!" I laughed and told him it was an obvious fake.

"I'm an archaeologist," I explained. "I study this kind of stuff!"

"Then you know it's old!" he replied. Not receiving the desired response, he continued his "tour" across the desert. "How about this so-called Cheops palace?" I asked incredulously.

"Just a moment," said he as we approached a group of dilapidated stone buildings. "This is the place! And here is Cheops's throne!" he exclaimed, pointing to a space on a low wall where several large stone bricks had been removed. "And over here is where Cheops ate his dinner every night, and if he wanted a drink of water, he came over here." The guide walked about the ruined walls pantomiming the activities as he described them. "And over here is where the king washed his hands after eating," he said, rubbing his hands together. I sat on Cheops's "throne," secretly enjoying the absurd antics, until I realized that we should see some of the nice smaller tombs before time ran out. "And let me show you Cheops's bathroom," he insisted. We rounded a corner to a small walled enclosure with dried human waste on the floor, obviously a latrine more recent than the time of Cheops. Sensing my frustration, the guide attempted to step over a low barbed-wire fence only to be rebuked by a cemetery guard.

"What happened to all your keys?" I inquired.

"This cemetery is closed for restoration today. I will show you another one." We proceeded down a path on the eastern side of the pyramid, passing numerous tombs, some with gates and locks. "How about this tomb?" I asked.

"Ah, it is not possible. The tomb is still full of gold, and inside there is the mummy of a small child." Of course this was just one of many excuses to disguise the fact that he possessed no keys whatsoever that would lead to anything of significance. A short distance further, we reached a small opening carved into the rock. "This is where they found the mummy of Rameses II. Take a look!" The tomb door was open, and its interior was full of modern rubbish, its ceilings and walls blackened by fire. Rameses II? Hardly likely! His mummy was actually discovered in the late 1800s in an amazing secret cache several hundred miles south of Giza!

Enough was enough. It wasn't worth debating the facts with my alleged guide. The novelty of this escapade had worn off, and I suggested that he be freed from his contract and that I would pay him. As I handed him two pounds along with a one-pound tip, he looked at the money and placed it back in my hands. "Seven pounds!" he yelled. I reminded him of our agreement, and he became furious. Seeing that I wasn't about to budge in this matter, he mentioned that he had a number of hungry children at home. Still finding no response from me, he insisted that seven pounds was the minimum amount he was entitled to by law for his services and that my failure to pay him would result in my incarceration. I wasn't buying it. He then threatened to call the police. As a last resort, he clutched his chest and began breathing heavily. Exasperated, I reached into my pocket and grabbed another pound note and forced it into his hand before stomping away. The guide counted the money, smiled, and yelled "Thanks, man!" I am now convinced that Herodotus visited Egypt. And he probably had a local guide, perhaps a direct descendant of my "well-informed" escort.

Shaking my head in disbelief at the performance I had just witnessed, I continued to walk about the area as the late afternoon brought cooler temperatures. It was a Friday, the weekly day of rest, and there were many Egyptian families sitting around the base of the pyramids enjoying picnics, music, and dancing with their friends. An uneventful taxi ride returned me to Garden City House and thus ended my first of many unforgettable days in a land that had filled my dreams for years.

Because the Fayyum expedition wouldn't be assembling for departure until Sunday, I had a second free day to spend as I pleased, and I wanted to see the Giza Plateau yet again, vowing that I would not be misled or otherwise relieved of my money. This time I took the bus, which was far cheaper and an adventure in and of itself. It deposited me close enough to my destination, and I walked up the hill to the pyramids' plateau, where the daily routines were already in progress. Turbaned heads popped up over walls and inquired about my desire for a camel, the clandestine postcard boy was making his rounds, and the cola-vending children were filling their buckets with warm bottles from the back of an old truck.

A ticket is required to go inside the pyramids, and as I approached the sales kiosk, I noticed a young English couple negotiating for an educational tour with my guide from the previous day. "Don't bother," I informed them. "He has no authority here, no keys to anything, and he doesn't know a thing. You're better off reading your guidebook." At this the guide became extremely angry, cursed vulgarly in English, and stalked off in a rage.

I purchased my ticket and approached the steps to a tunnel that led into the Great Pyramid. There a guard directed me inside through a crude passageway that led to an ascending ramp. The tunnel had been carved by early treasure seekers, who forced their way through stone blocks until they intersected an interior feature.

It has since become the most common means of entering the structure. As I learned from many subsequent visits, the ascent through the galleries to the burial or "King's" chamber can be relatively simple or quite hellish, depending on the number of tourists. The interior can be sweltering from the humidity brought on by the accumulation of human breath and perspiration, and certain passageways require one to bend over while descending groups pass by. The uncomfortable and variable climes mean that few people stay in the pyramid for long.

The King's Chamber is an incredible, smooth-walled granite room, empty except for a large stone sarcophagus. The body of Cheops likely lay here over several millennia ago, but, as is the case with all known Egyptian pyramids, his mummy never survived despite the incredible efforts to secure it for eternity.

The chamber is a draw for various and sundry New Age metaphysical persuasions, and their numbers can sometimes be seen wielding dowsing rods or pendulums in search of some sort of truth. Others come to meditate, to chant, or to "absorb the vibrations" there. Fortunately, pyramid explorers of any stripe were few during my initial visit, but I nonetheless left the pyramid drenched with sweat, thankful to be cooled by the light breezes outside. In moments it was time to run the gauntlet of vendors and camels again.

My second day in Egypt was as wonderful as the first, but carefree pyramid viewing was coming to an end, at least for a while, as the Fayyum expedition was about to begin the very next day. It must be mentioned that things are now much different on the Giza Plateau than they were during my first trip in 1981. Thanks to the Egyptian antiquities authorities, a serious archaeological site-management plan has been enacted for the long-term protection of the pyramids and for the greater enjoyment of tourists. The camel men and vendors are still around but are now confined to a specific locale well away from the monuments themselves. Their new venue is in an area that attracts tourists with a beautiful, commanding view of the site. And while the usual suspects are certainly there, their approach is much more low-key than before, and now the customers come to them.

WE HAD BEEN TOLD to meet at an appointed hour in front of the building that housed the American Research Center in Egypt (or ARCE). I recognized a few of my new colleagues from the Big University, but most I had never before met. It was an eclectic mix of Ph.D.'s, graduate students, a lively Egyptologist, an expert in bones, and a specialist in ancient plant remains. The students, too, provided an interesting collection of skills and personalities, from Lucy, a spunky, free-spirited Egyptology student, to "Blazo," a snooty know-it-all who tagged along as the archaeologist boyfriend of one of Dr. W's students. Despite our differences, we were now a team. We loaded up several jeeps and began our drive out of Cairo toward the Fayyum.

The road to the Fayyum passes the pyramids at Giza and heads straight out through the desert to the west of the Nile. The landscape then was rather bleak except for austere army outposts and an occasional long-abandoned vehicle. After dozens of miles, a few patches of trees began to appear on the sides of the road, and eventually the extensive ruins of an ancient Roman city, Karanis, gave way to the edge of a vast agricultural region, the modern Fayyum itself. This developed area skirts the southern edge of the now-brackish and shallow lake and extends west toward the Nile, which ultimately feeds a vast irrigation network.

The Fayyum region was populated throughout the time of the pharaohs, and the diminished remains of several pyramids can be found occasionally punctuating the landscape. Later Greeks and Romans extensively colonized the area, establishing industrious agricultural estates and many towns, most of which now exist only beneath well-plowed and irrigated fields. The warmth and the palm trees of the Fayyum reminded me of my California home, albeit with the addition of donkeys and camels, and the overall effect was one of a pleasant, hospitable, and productive land.

The journey to our "base camp" passed through lots of busy villages until we reached Qasr Qarun, just about a mile from the lake and a few miles from the very southwest end of the road terminating at the next village, Quta. Qasr Qarun was named for a nearby ancient temple that sits splendidly preserved at the desert's edge. Our accommodations were in a large two-story white house with a roof deck. Though impressive from the outside, the inside was a dusty mess, and there were no bathrooms and no electricity to pacify American tastes. A large ditch in an adjacent orchard temporarily served as a toilet, and water was collected from a village pump in many large plastic jerry cans. Eventually a generator was hooked up, and a rooftop water tank made our living quarters acceptable. Roommates were assigned by gender or relationship, and I shared the "Boys' Dorm" with a couple of male colleagues, where each of us had a small bunk rigged with mosquito netting hung from the sticks of stripped palm branches.

It was not long before our daily routine was established. We would awake at 4:00 A.M.; have a sleepy breakfast of tea, bread, and marmalade at 4:30; and depart for the desert at around 5:00. Our caravan of four vehicles would leave our little compound and travel down the dusty road through the village, which was just beginning to stir with the rising sun. At Quta the jeeps would then turn sharply south into the desert; a five-foot-wide canal separates the rich, verdant agricultural land from a desolate sea of sand that continues across Northern Africa to the Atlantic Coast. The difference is as stark as that between the moon and the earth, and without constant vigilance the green would succumb in short order.

The vehicles usually rode easily across the sand. Landmarks here consisted of dunes, an occasional looted grave, and a small police outpost. After a while a low ridge was reached, and our site of investigation was situated immediately behind in an empty stretch of desert. Apart from ourselves, the rare scrubby bush and a solitary lizard were usually the only obvious visible signs of life.

A view of the desolate desert region in the southwest Fayyum. In prehistoric times this area supported a lush environment and was home to some of Egypt's earliest agriculturists.

Despite the improbability that anyone would be living out in this remote wasteland, the evidence of human occupation was everywhere. The floor of the desert was virtually littered with ancient cultural debris. Flint tools, arrowheads, and, most abundant, the little stone chips left over from the manufacture of these tools could be found by anyone walking a few steps in any direction. Animal bones—many huge and fossilized—and gray rings of fire-cracked rocks from ancient campfires were scattered here and there. Large grinding stones and stone blades from sickles indicated that this was a site where early agriculture had been practiced. Incredibly, these remains still lay on the surface after many thousands of years, due to a natural process called deflation, in which the breath of the wind continuously blows the surface away from below the artifacts except for the occasional shifting dune that obliterates a section of the desert floor until it creeps on. During our time in the Fayyum, we were constantly reminded of the enormous environmental changes that had occurred since this material was originally deposited. The bones of fish and other animals indicated that this was once the very edge of a lake, now a fraction of its former size, and an area well occupied by people. With lush surroundings and an abundance of food, life was probably comfortable in the Fayyum six thousand years ago or so.

Given such a large area to investigate, we had to content ourselves with merely sampling the site. Thus we established a large grid system across the area with surveying devices, and from this base map, five-meter grid squares were physically laid out on the surface with string. Inside a selection of these squares, artifacts, bones, and whatever else remained were intensely documented and collected. That was pretty much the agenda for three hot months. Day after day, laying out the lines, laying out the squares, and collecting, collecting and bagging, bagging and tagging. As monotonous as it all might seem, there were sporadic moments of genuine excitement with the occasional discovery of an exquisitely fashioned ancient projectile point or flint knife, or perhaps the remains of an exotic beast from days long gone by. It often bordered on fun.

A lunch of bread, tuna fish, eggs, melons, and assorted items was consumed around ten o'clock, and work would stop by one. Did I happen to mention that it was hot? There was absolutely no shade to be had at our work site, other than that found beneath tarps stretched between the vehicles. Back at the house, a couple of hours of rest was followed by a few hours of lab work. There were always plenty of stone tools or bones to sort as well as artifacts to draw, and I tried a little of each. Each night's dinner was a welcome mystery, followed by our gathering to listen to news from "the outside" courtesy of BBC on the radio, and then the evening brought pleasant breezes and easy sleep.

The author's first archaeological fieldwork involved a detailed survey of prehistoric sites in the southwest Fayyum. Here, team members collect artifacts and bones from the desert surface.

It's hard to say what the villagers initially thought of the daily convoy of vehicles full of *howaga*s (foreigners) that snaked its way at odd hours through their little towns. Our dig-house compound was surrounded by a low mud-brick wall that proved to be no obstacle for the inquisitive locals, who seemed entertained by our every activity. Though somewhat an invasion of our privacy, their behavior was understandable. Imagine a large group of very peculiar people moving in next door. They speak an unfamiliar language, they appear to be quite wealthy, and they are in possession of all kinds of strange gear. For many weeks the mad fools travel at daybreak, accompanied by guards, to a shadeless, sandy hell in order to pick up rocks and old bones in a place generally unfit for human survival. They return hot, tired, and thirsty to spend the rest of the afternoon gawking at the insignificant refuse they collected during their daily efforts. After several months they pack up and return to their homes halfway around the world. No wonder the townspeople's curiosity was piqued, and we were the biggest show in town!

As perpetual novelties we were also targets for the irrepressible hospitality of the villagers. If we strolled a few yards from our compound, it would immediately evoke an invitation for tea, if not dinner. My first encounter with some of the citizens of Qasr Qarun was with our guards, who camped in the yard. They had noticed that I was at least as curious about them as they were about me and motioned me to join them. They made room for me on a flat woven mat, and a small fire was very cleverly and quickly built from local plant debris. A small copper kettle was filled with water, and a handful of tea was put atop it. (The Egyptians claim that if you drink hot tea on a hot day, it will cool you off.)

We could not understand one another's languages but made do with broad gestures to get our intentions across. Soon the tea was boiling, and one fellow produced a little paper cone from beneath his robe along with several small glasses for the tea. The cone contained sugar crystals, which were added to fill about a quarter of each glass. They passed me a glass, but the heat of it nearly caused me to drop it, so I set it down for a moment. The tea was hot, strong, and unbelievably sweet, and my initial urge was to run for my toothbrush, but after trying it several times I found that the experience grew on me, and it became a regular, enjoyable routine. Getting to spend time with my new friends was a wonderful way to occupy what little leisure we had. They were unflaggingly generous and willing to share anything they had. Our time together was also an excellent opportunity to learn Arabic from enthusiastic, patient teachers, and my vocabulary steadily grew. Appropriately enough, my first words referred to things I could point to in the immediate vicinity: "tea," "water buffalo," and "geese."

The hospitality of the Egyptians can't be underestimated. A trip to another Fayyum village one day to retrieve water was particularly insightful. We found a local well and began to unload our plastic water jugs. The containers were immediately snatched away from us and taken to the hand pump to be filled as dozens of villagers emerged to become involved in the process. They formed a human chain from the well to our jeep so that the full jugs could be passed along and easily placed in the vehicle. With memories of the Giza Plateau fresh in my mind, I began to search my pockets for change. My colleague did the same as we anticipated paying off every one of these gregarious, uninvited helpers. We scrounged up a small handful of money to present to the man who appeared to be organizing the operation, for distribution among his friends. When we approached him, however, he refused the money. Despite our insistence, he and his fellow villagers would not accept any money for their services. They were neither exploitive pyramid "guides" nor manipulative camel men; they were extremely hospitable, everyday people who were simply looking to be helpful, even to mysterious strangers.

Over the summer I learned many more lessons from my friends in the village. Most thought-provoking was an incident that occurred one day during a lunch break in the desert. As was my custom, I sat on the shady side of the vehicles with the guards and gulped down my food. The men would usually show me something that they had brought from home, or on occasion we would have an impromptu puppet show with our hats or cleverly folded pieces of clothing as we passed our break time. This particular day I was chewing a piece of the local bread, called *aish baladi,* roughly meaning "peasant bread." It is made by threshing wheat on the ground to be turned into flour and then baked into flat, circular pieces. After a few bites, I painfully bit into a stray bit of gravel. I angrily spit out the bread, stood up, and spun the remainder like a Frisbee into the desert. As I sat back down, disgruntled, one of the guards stood up and strolled slowly out into the sand. Retrieving the bread, he walked back toward me and knelt down facing me. He slowly waved the partially eaten bread before me and gently stated, "Bread is a gift of God." He handed the piece of bread to me, and we continued lunch. This poor, humble man provided me with a powerful lesson about wastefulness and how important it is to appreciate one's blessings.

During our expedition the vehicles were a constant source of concern. The trip to and from the desert each day could be relatively pleasant or a bone-rattling torture, depending upon who might be driving. One of our crew was notorious for accidentally hitting every pothole and dune in the relative vicinity. My personal record for consecutive bounces off the ceiling in the back of the jeep was three, and that's not counting the many throws from side to side. Not only could the vehicles beat us up, but the heat and the dubious sanitary conditions took their toll as well. Most of us were sick, sometimes for weeks, and when it was all over, even the skinny people had lost at least twenty pounds.

With each day I became increasingly struck by the marvel

of my surroundings as the arid wilderness seemed ever friendlier and my appreciation for its many subtle wonders grew. A distinct environmental personality became evident, and the desert began to reveal itself gradually as much more beautiful and complex than I initially perceived. The surface, for example, possesses a tremendous amount of diversity, with its subtle variation in sand color and pebbles of different shapes and sizes. The wind also sculpts the sand in a myriad of ways; a few golden waves and ripples in one spot might merge into a smooth trackless arena, or some stubborn sedimentary crusts might suddenly come to dominate the desert floor. And little resilient towers of hardened sediment, called yardangs, occasionally interrupt the undulating white horizon.

The desert certainly seems to have its own agenda and is an environment in constant motion, whether it's due to dunes slowly shifting or flash floods that can violently and instantly alter the landscape. It exercises a relentless power that humans can attempt to control, but time and again the desert will reclaim its own. The ancient Greek town of Dionysias, for example, just adjacent to the Qasr Qarun temple, was excavated by the French and Swiss fifty years ago. When the digging stopped, nature took over, and the town is once again well on its way to obliteration beneath the sands.

From my own frame of reference, I was surprised by how the desert's expansiveness brought constant comparisons in my mind to the challenge of an enormous, forbidding mountain. The snow and ice of glaciers on a mountain can also be expansive and lonely like the desert, and at times I pondered how many of my beloved mountains could fit into this great space. But on the flip side, the oppressive summer heat, too, brought thoughts of the mountains as I longed for the icy coldness of an alpine morning.

However, the lake near our dig provided a lovely distraction from the heat and sand. At the beginning of the project, most of our group would head down in the early evening for a nice swim, but after a few weeks the numbers dwindled so that I was often the only regular visitor, and I enjoyed the solitude of the mile-long stroll down the dirt road to the shore. Each night the fellahin, those who work the land, would be returning home from the fields, and a wonderful circuslike parade of men and creatures would pass me in the opposite direction: camels burdened high with fodder and resembling walking haystacks; the heavy man astride his small donkey, which managed to maintain a brisk gait despite the weight; and lumbering water buffalo and men with their tools slung over their shoulders. I would see the same faces daily, most smiling and appearing content with a simple life that few of us spoiled outsiders would have the strength or patience to endure.

When I would occasionally jog to the lake, the sight of a foreigner running by in a colorful outfit never failed to cause astonishment. Invariably, the spectators would turn to see who was chasing me. Sometimes a boy on a donkey would challenge me to race his braying steed, the donkey often winning through sheer endurance and the noisy encouragement of his jockey. Down at the lake, I would wade neck-deep in its waters to witness the sunset, the cliffs in the distance evolving through a chameleon transformation from yellow to orange to purple, then gray and ultimately black. The emerging lustrous orb of the moon, the chirping of birds at dusk, and the silhouettes of palms all marked the end of another beautiful Egyptian day.

APART FROM BEING my introduction to Egypt, the Fayyum project provided my first real lessons in excavation. "From the known to the unknown. That's what it's all about," explained my vastly more experienced fellow graduate student Paul Buck as his trowel scraped across a blackened layer of earth to reveal more of the same as the sun's heat screamed down upon us in an unequal contest of wills. "Marshalltown. That's the brand you need, the archaeologist's best friend." Paul continued to scrape away at the ancient, fire-cracked encirclement of stone. Soon several fish bones were revealed, the remains of someone's millennia-old prehistoric dinner. From the known to the unknown—it could serves as the credo for any explorer or a metaphor for archaeology in general.

I learned a lot about digging from Paul in the Fayyum, and in later years I would meet Doug Esse, a master of the trowel, a young man eulogized as the best of his generation and whose impact on Near Eastern archaeology was blooming when he passed away while reaching what would have been a truly stellar prime. "A sensitive touch is necessary," claimed Doug, so sensitive that sight is not necessarily a requirement. Under his skillful handling, a bewilderingly complex record of the past would be revealed, which would require an equally complex mind to interpret. Doug's trowel was refined, its edges sharp, and its surface area reduced through twenty years of use. The handle fit his hand like a custom glove, and the tool was constant and at the ready. "It's my magic trowel!" Doug would pronounce, grinning, as he repeatedly denied my many requests to give it a try during the first summer we worked together. "Nobody uses my magic trowel!" It did what it needed to do and had the amazing capacity to find what needed to be found.

During an apparent moment of weakness the following year and after days of annoying begging on my part, Doug amazingly consented, "but only for a few minutes." The trowel gleamed when I gripped its handle. Its special qualities were soon confirmed as it cut through the earth like a knife through warm butter. The sharpened edges easily found the borders of ancient mud bricks virtually invisible in the glaring sun; the subtle change of texture that indicated the mortar was readily detectable through minor vibrations in the handle. A few minutes of supervision with this magical instrument were all I was allowed. "Time's up! Gotta go!" announced Doug as he retrieved his companion. Subsequent pleading was fruitless. I understand that he was ceremoniously buried with his trowel, a tool that merely assisted his extraordinary intellect in revealing the ages.

THE FAYYUM ARCHAEOLOGICAL PROJECT wasn't all work. Friday is the Islamic sacred day, and on Thursday afternoons we loaded ourselves into vehicles and made the tedious journey to Cairo for some relaxation before returning on Friday evening to resume work the next day. I usually checked in to Garden City House, while others sometimes opted for the luxury of the Hilton or other nicer hotels to indulge themselves, if just for a day. The contrast between Cairo and the Fayyum was drastic. Cairo provided lots of activities and a wide array of food. I chose to spend most of my free day exploring the ancient sites, including several more trips to Giza along with the pyramids and tombs of Sakkara just south of the city, and I spent numerous hours in the astounding Egyptian Museum off Cairo's central square.

At one point we were allowed an extended break and headed down south to Luxor to see as many of the ancient sites as we could possibly cram into a few short days. It was at that time that I made my first visit to the Valley of the Kings, and the impression would be profound and lasting.

After three hot summer months, it was time to go home. I left Egypt with a wealth of experience and, equally important, enough enthusiasm and ideas to motivate me for years.

FOUR

EGYPT ON MY MIND

WHEN I RETURNED to the rainy Pacific Northwest and the Big University, thoughts of my experiences in Egypt and the Fayyum were unshakable. I had to return. It wasn't a mere desire, it was a *necessity*. I didn't know how or under what circumstances I could return, but I knew I hadn't seen nearly enough. I also knew that although I'd received an excellent education at the Big University, we were a bad match in several ways. On top of that, my adviser, Dr. W, was leaving for a couple of years to serve as director of a research center in Cairo.

In December 1982 I turned in the final requirements for my master's degree and was off to Egypt again, this time on my own. With little money to finance my excursion, I had secured airline reservations as inexpensively as possible on a red-eye flight on an obscure African airline, which brought me to Cairo. Stepping off the plane at 1:30 A.M., I was greeted with a cold blast of January air. Having only experienced the sizzling summer, I was dressed in light clothing and was completely unprepared for winter conditions. Freed from the constraints of a formal expedition, I had no particular agenda, and with only two hundred dollars in my pocket, I would stay for about two months.

I met a young Scotsman on the plane, Iain Bamforth, who had never been to Egypt before. I knew the procedure for getting into downtown Cairo, and Iain had a list of the cheapest accommodations in the city. He, too, was on a limited budget, and even the modest Garden City House was too rich for us. After we'd done quite a bit of walking downtown, a hotel sign hanging over the empty sidewalk indicated a potential temporary home. We had arrived at the Golden Hotel, the legendary ultra-budget, hippie-backpacker flophouse. It consisted of a nondescript lobby and a couple of tawdry rooms, the latter crowded with packs and clothing strewn everywhere. We were informed that we could find a place on the floor or on a mattress for 1.50 Egyptians pounds per night. The hotel hosted an ever-changing international cast of migratory characters, and one never knew with whom or how many one would be sharing his room on any given night. It would serve as a tolerable base camp from which we would explore Egypt at our leisure.

The hotel was owned by an elderly man in his eighties by the name of Mr. Faris. Faris was educated at Oxford during the 1920s and spoke impeccable British English. He was quite wealthy and maintained the hotel as a service to the budget traveler. He also had great compassion for young people, and each afternoon he held court in the lobby, providing assistance to all who asked. Mr. Faris was a wonderful encyclopedia of local knowledge, including the best and cheapest places to eat, bus schedules, obscure places worth visiting, cautionary advice, and consolation for the distraught. "And how was your adventure today?" he would sincerely inquire of every returning traveler as each one entered his hotel. A kind word and plenty of sympathy or congratulations was always offered by the gentleman in the black suit. I would like to assume that he was naïve to the questionable behavior of some of his residents; he generously ascribed it to the follies of youth and looked the other way.

Iain, the Scotsman, became a fast friend. We would travel together through Egypt for about a month. Another fellow denizen of the Golden Hotel was a young woman from New Zealand named Maria. Maria, whom we somehow assigned the nickname "Madame Nadia," had traveled the distance from South Africa to Cairo over the previous year, temporarily residing here and there in places she found appealing. Egypt was the last stop on her African journey before Europe, where she hoped to find employment and fund her journey home.

Being the resident "expert," I accompanied Iain and Maria out to the pyramids and other sites near Cairo, and at one point I invited them to join me for an excursion out to the Fayyum, where we visited some of the local friends I had made during the 1981 project. My reunions with old friends were delightful, and we were treated with overwhelming hospitality, as if we were long-lost relatives.

After returning to Cairo, Iain, Maria, and I decided to travel by train up to Alexandria for a few days to examine the old city on the Mediterranean coast. It had been established by Alexander the Great in the fourth century B.C. and became one of the most cosmopolitan cities of the ancient world. Two of the most spectacular monuments of antiquity had once stood there: a giant lighthouse that made it onto the list of the Seven Wonders of the Ancient World and a library that contained the accumulated knowledge of the Western world in its day. Sadly, neither survived, the latter perishing in a fire that produced an immeasurable loss. It wasn't a particularly good trip; it rained furiously for days and literally dampened our enthusiasm before we returned to Cairo.

After several weeks as vagabonds in the name of Egyptian antiquities, we bade adieu to Maria. All of us had quickly learned the art of living on the cheap in Egypt. I could eat three acceptable, and usually tasty, meals a day for about a dollar. Sandwiches made of beans and falafel were a staple, as was koshari, a filling dish of pasta, lentils, and tomato sauce, purchased and consumed on the street. Occasionally I'd eat some shawarma—little meat sandwiches carved from a vertical spit—or some freshly squeezed guava juice, but if I wanted to splurge, I'd venture to Felfela's, an inexpensive restaurant serving Egyptian comfort food in downtown Cairo. Despite my budget accommodations and spartan existence, life wasn't bad at all.

With Maria gone, Iain and I excitedly agreed that the mountains of Sinai would be our next travel destination. It had been just a few months since the Israelis had officially vacated the peninsula after about fifteen years of occupation after the 1967 Six-Day War. United Nations troops were now in place, and the Sinai was once again accessible to tourists from Egypt. Before leaving I consulted Dr. W about my latest plans, and he offered a few words of caution: After so many years of conflict, many of the beaches were mined, and several people had been blown up while traveling through remote desert valleys. Be careful, he warned.

We bought seats on a small airplane that traversed the eastern desert, soared over the Suez Canal, and deposited us on a small airstrip beneath craggy Sinai mountains near the village of St. Catherine. The area is most noted for its ancient, fortresslike monastery built at the foot of a mountain, Gebel Musa, which has been traditionally identified as Mount Sinai and the location where God presented the Ten Commandments to Moses. Dedicated monks have lived here since the monastery was established by the Roman emperor Justinian in the sixth century A.D.

I badly wanted to climb to Sinai's summit, so Iain and I hiked up a rocky valley past the monastery to pitch a tent among huge boulders. The ascent the next morning was cold but not particularly difficult, and the summit, topped with both a small mosque and a Christian chapel, offered splendid views of the surrounding snowcapped mountains. Snow? In one of the world's great desert wildernesses? To our great surprise, we returned from a trip into the village for supplies to find our tent collapsing under heavy new snow later that day. News of the weather in various parts of the country was a regular topic of discussion by the steady stream of drifters passing through the Golden Hotel with their reports. "Intense cold and windy on the northern Red Sea coast! Head south!" and many did. When the Cairo winter is chilly and dreary, the southernmost Egyptian city of Aswan can be a pleasant seventy degrees so it seemed perfect for our next destination.

In keeping with the general penurious theme of our visit to Egypt, Iain and I purchased tickets on the most inexpensive form of transportation we could find, the third-class train. These trains are usually occupied by the poorer folk of Egypt, like the hard-laboring occupants of rural villages. Passengers are seated on uncomfortable wooden benches next to windows that are often broken or completely missing as the train crawls across the landscape, stopping at nearly every little town on the banks of the Nile. Despite its simplicity, traveling in such a way allowed us to enjoy remarkable views of the lovely Egyptian countryside and to meet lots of interesting people.

While seated in the dark third-class compartment, I noticed

something falling on me from above. Looking up, I saw an Egyptian soldier in the luggage rack directly above me snugly tucked away, peeling and eating an onion. At first we were merely amused by the spectacle, but after a short while it became clear that the luggage rack was the best seat in the house. Thus inspired, Iain and I each picked out a nice section of rack upon which we laid our sleeping bags. Inside the bags we stayed warm and relatively comfortable, and by grasping or tying ourselves down to the slats that made up the racks, we could spend a comfortable night, lulled to sleep by the continuous rocking of the train.

After about eighteen hours, we arrived in Aswan to find a quiet, wonderfully warm, pleasant little city. The ambience there was completely different from most places I had been in Egypt. Perhaps it is the low-key Nubian people or the small-town atmosphere. Even the Nile here seemed different, broken up as it is by large rock islands. Though brutally hot during the summer, Aswan is probably the nicest part of Egypt to visit during the coldest times of the year in the north.

Iain and I made our way to another classic cheap accommodation, which made the Golden Hotel look like the Hilton. The Continental Hotel was aptly named, filled with the typical budget travelers, except with private rooms instead of a dormitory floor. The price was right, about a dollar a day, and establishments of this sort are always excellent places to meet all kinds of characters. Many sat in front of the hotel whiling the days away, sipping drinks or playing backgammon, joined by locals who might bring along a pet monkey or a water pipe. Aswan was indeed pleasant. We hired a sailboat to visit tombs on the western side of the river and to explore the many antiquities of Elephantine Island. We even took a stark look at the present and future by hiking across the top of the giant and controversial Aswan Dam.

Among the principal attractions of Aswan that interested me were the granite quarries that provided Egypt's pharaohs with some of their most desirable stone. The reddish Aswan granite can be found as far north as Giza, where it lined Cheops's burial chamber, or it can be seen in profusion at such places as the temples of Karnak at Luxor. Huge blocks of stone, including towering obelisks, were cracked out of the rock and loaded onto sturdy river barges to be shipped sometimes hundreds of miles.

One does not need to look far to find granite in Aswan; it is everywhere—in the quarries on the banks of the Nile and the rock islands in the river that once defined ancient Egypt's natural southern borders. As a climber, I kept a lookout for appealing ascent possibilities, and during our wanderings I found a natural fissure splitting a granite bluff above the river for several dozen feet. With rock shoes tightened, I jammed my hands and feet into the crack and began to walk my way up the vertical stone. A number of feet off the ground, I passed the name of Rameses II well incised in hieroglyphs on the wall to my right, an experience one could have only in Egypt.

In due course it was time for Iain to return to Scotland. He was a fine friend, and here and there I met others whose paths I would cross occasionally. I traveled again to Luxor to see more of its innumerable attractions and revisited the Valley of the Kings, a site I found increasingly intriguing. Eventually it was time for me, too, to go home. I returned with a hefty load of stories, a wealth of travel experience, and ever more fascinated with Egypt.

SOKNOPAIOU NESOS IS the desolate shell of a once-thriving town. There are no tourists here. My friend from the Fayyum prehistoric project, Paul Buck, seemed to enjoy the sound of that name, and occasionally I would hear him muttering those words to himself as we drove across the desert. Sometimes he would break out in a loud spontaneous outburst. "Soknopaiou Nesos!" It was the Greek name for the remote ruins of an ancient city abandoned on the desolate plateau of the north Fayyum. Translated, it means "Island of Sobek," Sobek being the ancient Egyptian crocodile god associated with the Fayyum. The name is almost preposterous, because the nearest water is the Birket Qarun lake situated far below the plateau upon which the city sits, as it was in ancient times. And crocodiles? Luckily, they were the least of my worries in this sandy wasteland. The site is perhaps better known by a more recent name, Dimai, which somehow defies translation.

Dimai remained as an ancient mud-brick edifice on the horizon, an eerie sentinel serving as a geographical landmark for modern explorers. Startling from a distance even on a clear day, its ghostlike image initially appears as a mirage when blowing dust obscures the view. Its high walls still stand resilient, almost defiant against the forces that continue to whittle away at its structural integrity over the past two thousand years.

It was 1984, a year after the end of my low-budget adventure, and once again I found myself in the Egyptian desert. This time I wasn't a mere footloose traveler but had a mission. I was in Egypt to study certain aspects of ancient technology, and along with that, Dr. W had facilitated my participation with Paul's efforts to explore prehistory in the north Fayyum.

We were heading for a site just a few miles from Dimai in the real wilderness. Everything we might need for survival, including water, food, and fuel, had to be carried. It was March, and it was cold, with a continuous brisk wind unsuccessfully tempting us to quit. Paul was particularly interested in geoarchaeology— the application of geological knowledge to learn about ancient environments—and he pointed out the places worthy of surveying. We mapped some sites, and when we had our day's fill, we'd retreat to the Pink Palace, a tiny brick hut in which we prepared hot food and drinks. Strangely, even in this isolated place we weren't completely alone. In some curious way, word of our presence would imperceptibly carry across the sands, and the few guards from the widely spaced sites of antiquity in this area would appear, grinning in hopes of a hot bowl of chili or some of Paul's specialty, "Seven Treasures Rice."

While the days in the desert are rather tranquil, the night comes alive: The distant yips and howls of roving desert canines in search of prey, the continual slap of wind meeting tent, and the gnawing feelings of apprehension increase as one's imagination is tempered by loneliness and the resonance of the desert night. The discovery of multiple snake tracks around one's tent in the morning is no consolation, but another day is met and the exploration continues.

The desert, with all its hardship and occasional anxiety, was often preferable to the noisy chaos of Cairo. When I arrived in Egypt, I had established myself once again at the Golden Hotel. The hotel had recently shut down, but old Faris was still holding court in his lobby, seemingly unaware that it was no longer in business and the young tourists were no longer passing by. Regardless, for the bargain rate of thirty dollars a month, I leased a room and Faris handed me some keys to a room I could share with another tenant, a homesick businessman from Sri Lanka.

Much of my time, though, was spent outside the apartment and ideally outside Cairo. I made trips to Sakkara and Luxor to photograph tomb scenes, and I spent a good bit of time in between in specialized Egyptological libraries and museums. It was great to be living for a while in Egypt with a relatively flexible schedule of archaeological pursuits accompanied by the occasional surprise. One day, for example, while collecting my mail at the research center, I read a posted advertisement in which a cruise line was soliciting junior lecturers to give educational chats in exchange for a deluxe ten-day voyage on the Red Sea. A big-league scholar would be brought in for each cruise, and those of smaller credentials such as myself were asked to give talks on the occasional bus trips and to entertain the passengers during dinners and tours. I signed up immediately.

I traveled to the Cairo airport to meet the arriving passengers, and to my amazement the featured scholar was none other than T. G. H. "Harry" James, the Keeper of Egyptian Antiquities at the British Museum. Less than two months prior, I had appeared in London at his venerable department, a letter of introduction in hand from a mutual friend. Harry had graciously come out to meet me and wished me the best of luck with my studies. I left the museum in total awe and grateful for my brief audience with him. The prospect of spending more time with him was thrilling.

In his characteristic sense of wry humor, Harry greeted the cruise passengers as they boarded a bus, soliciting suitcases as he pretended to be the baggage handler. When his bluff was called, he finally announced, "I am Harry James!" Then, pointing to me, "And this is my acolyte." I didn't mind at all. I was able to spend ten days with this marvelous gentleman, quizzing him for a wealth of insights on Egyptological matters and visiting such wonderful places as the Wadi Rum and Petra in Jordan and sites in the eastern desert of Egypt. Many of the passengers, too, were quite fascinating, including Countess Tauni de Lesseps, the granddaughter of the man who built the Suez Canal, and I would have readily signed up for more, but it was time to move on. I was once again pleased to return home and find Sherry relieved that I'd been off on an archaeological adventure rather than something more precarious in the mountains.

DESPITE MY ENTHUSIASM and growing experience, I wasn't qualified to direct my own archaeological expedition in Egypt at this stage in my career. A Ph.D. and a formal affiliation with an appropriate institution such as a museum or university are among the criteria, and I had a good ways to go before I would achieve either. Apart from continuing my graduate-school education, which I wasn't interested in pursuing for a while, there were other things I could do to keep myself well involved in archaeology, including fieldwork and the constant study of subjects that somehow piqued my interest or just came my way.

ONE DAY WHILE READING the newspaper in Tacoma, Washington, I learned that there was a mummy being examined with modern medical technology by a local physician named Ray Lyle. I immediately called Ray to see if I could get a piece of the action. I was welcomed aboard Lyle's team as a "consultant," since I was one of only a few in the Pacific Northwest with a background in ancient Egypt, and it was a fascinating experience. The mummy and its accompanying coffins were examined every which way. While physicians scrutinized his physical characteristics, I helped organize and investigate some of the contextual information regarding his identity and place in time.

The mummy was acquired in Egypt in 1891 by a Tacoma businessman named Allen Mason. Although it might seem strange today, back in the nineteenth century, tourists could buy mummies and coffins, or the two together, and bring them home as exotic souvenirs. Antiquities dealing was big business, and there was a seemingly endless supply of dead ancient Egyptians to satisfy the customers. As a result there are mummies and pieces thereof—hands, heads, et cetera—to be found in museums, in antiques and curio shops, and even in private homes all over Europe and North America. When you consider that mummification in Egypt was practiced for perhaps three millennia, there were plenty of dead folk whose bodies were embalmed, wrapped, coffined, and interred.

The ancient Egyptians were interested in preserving the actual body because it served as a physical home for a manifestation of the soul known as the *ka*. Not everyone, though, got the same treatment. The average Egyptian laborer was probably wrapped in a mat with a few personal items for the afterlife and buried in a pit. But those who could afford it could have their body prepared by experts to survive the ages in a state that more or less resembled them in life. There are very few Egyptian texts that describe the process of mummification, but the Greek historian Herodotus provides a few insights, indicating that there were three different methods of preparation. His description of the deluxe procedure is morbidly fascinating:

> They take first a crooked piece of iron, and with it draw
> out the brain through the nostrils, thus getting rid of a
> portion, while the skull is cleared of the rest by rinsing
> with drugs; next they make a cut along the flank with a
> sharp Ethiopian stone, and take out the whole contents
> of the abdomen, which they then cleanse, washing it
> thoroughly with palm wine, and again frequently with
> an infusion of pounded aromatics. After this they fill
> the cavity with the purest bruised myrrh, with cassia,

and every other sort of spicery except frankincense, and
sew up the opening. Then the body is placed in natron
for seventy days, and covered entirely over. After the
expiration of that space of time, which must not be
exceeded, the body is washed, and wrapped round, from
head to foot, with bandages of fine linen cloth, smeared
over with gum, which is used generally by the Egyptians
in the place of glue, and in this state it is given back to
the relations, who enclose it in a wooden case which they
have had made for the purpose.

Natron is a kind of salt found naturally in the desert and
was used even in the cheapest methods to essentially dry out the
body, leaving flesh and bones intact. The difference in quality is
easily noted. Some of the more economical treatments resemble
bones covered with beef jerky, while some of the royal mummies
are astoundingly well preserved. The face of the New Kingdom
pharaoh, Seti I, for example, resembles a peacefully sleeping man,
even though he's been "napping" for over three thousand years now.
His son, the great warrior pharaoh Rameses II, also retains a regal
composure—and a head of curly reddish hair.

Apart from humans, the Egyptians also mummified millions
of animals considered sacred due to their associations with deities,
including crocodiles, certain species of fish and birds, baboons,
and the ever-popular cat. Beneath the ancient cemetery of Sakkara,
there are mazes of catacombs containing many thousands of mummified ibis birds, each housed in its own ceramic container. At the
same site, there are huge subterranean tunnels (resembling subway
tunnels) containing numerous mammoth stone sarcophagi that
once held the preserved bodies of sacred bulls.

There were plenty of mummies to go around. Mark Twain,

who visited in Egypt in 1867, noted in *The Innocents Abroad,* in his own humorous way, that they were indeed prolific:

> I shall not speak of the railway, for it is like any other railway—I shall only say that the fuel they use for the locomotive is composed of mummies three thousand years old, purchased by the ton or by the graveyard for that purpose, and that sometimes one hears the profane engineer call out pettishly, "D——n these plebeians, they don't burn worth a cent—pass out a King;"*
>
> *[Stated to me for a fact. I only tell it as I got it. I am willing to believe it. I can believe any thing.]

Public or private unwrappings of exported mummies became a popular form of entertainment in the nineteenth century. Wrappings were cut and a body was exposed for the awe and wonderment of the audience. But it wasn't all spectacle. The dissections were often conducted by physicians or those with an interest in anatomy and the phenomenon of mummification. With the advent of modern technology, especially CT scanning, mummies can be examined in great detail without disturbing their often intricate wrappings.

The study of mummies has become a passion for a number of scholars, especially during the last few decades. In 1994 a couple of researchers, Egyptologist Dr. Bob Brier along with a medical colleague Dr. Ron Wade, conducted what was likely the first authentic Egyptian mummification in two millennia. With the procedures outlined by Herodotus and other details derived from the study of ancient specimens, a body "donated to science" was prepared in the traditional fashion and then covered in natron.

The experiment provided a lot of insight and, when periodically checked, the corpse's long-term preservation appears likely.

I recall the first time I ever saw a mummy. It was on display in a small glass case in the Natural History Museum of Los Angeles County. I was there to see the dinosaurs, but what young boy couldn't resist taking a look at such a spooky side attraction? His name was Pu, and he lived during the time the Greeks ruled Egypt, about two thousand years ago. He, too, had been purchased in Egypt many decades ago and brought to America.

Pu's face and toes were exposed, and he wasn't a particularly pretty sight. In fact, his face looked more like a skull than a preserved visage, and it gave me plenty to talk about. My other youthful encounters with the Egyptian dead were from the black-and-white images on the television screen, such as Boris Karloff as the infamous Imhotep returned to life to claim his ancient love in the classic Universal Pictures horror film *The Mummy*. It both frightened and intrigued me. The rational side of me knew it could never happen, but the notion of reanimated mummies was enough to make me want to sleep with the lights on.

The Tacoma mummy was a surprise to me. I would never have guessed that such an interesting thing was lying about just a few miles from where I lived. What's more, buying a mummy in nineteenth-century Egypt was one thing, but what do you do with it once you return home? Allen Mason kept it at home for a while, then moved it to his downtown office, and finally, after nearly twenty years, donated it to what is now the Washington State Historical Society, a strange item indeed to be found among all manner of items relating to that state's history, including old wagons and political posters. Despite its irrelevance, this white elephant, so to speak, remained a popular attraction at the society's museum. In 1959 it was lent to the University of

Puget Sound, where it served as a kind of curious teaching and research novelty. In 1983 it was returned to the historical society's museum, where it was placed in storage. When Dr. Lyle, a local amateur Egyptologist, learned of the mummy, he put his skills as an orthopedic surgeon to work. The mummy was taken to a local hospital, X-rayed, and run through a CT scanner. Historically speaking, this was one of the earliest mummy CT scans performed in the United States, a procedure that has become increasingly common in such studies.

After joining Lyle's team, I visited the museum to get my first look. The mummy lay in one of his two coffins, still partially wrapped with his head and forearms exposed. His skin was thin and black, and his eye sockets were sunken. I had seen worse. I had once been taken to an abandoned tomb in Egypt where the local villagers disposed of the mummies they would occasionally find. This tomb had a low chamber whose walls were lined with limbless torsos with the heads still attached; another room was filled with a random assortment of arms, legs, and other body parts. It was a horrific sight that was both repulsive and riveting. I didn't stay long, but the memory has certainly persisted.

Back in Tacoma, Ray Lyle's examination revealed some basic facts. The mummy was definitely an adult male who'd died between the ages of twenty-five and forty. In life he stood about five feet three inches tall, and his feet were remarkably small. He'd probably wear a size four or five in a modern man's shoe size. Cause of death? Undetermined.

The body itself lay within a coffin more or less in the shape of a human body, which in turn fit inside another of rectangular shape in the form of a shrine. A botanist friend of mine took some tiny samples from these items and determined that their material of manufacture was primarily wood from the acacia tree. Texts on the coffins indicated that the mummy's name was Ankhwennefer and came from the town of Ipu, which is known today as Akhmim. Ipu was a major center for the worship of a fertility god named Min. Ankhwennefer appears to have served as "second prophet," a very high-ranking priest in Min's temple. He lived around the time of the Twenty-fifth Dynasty, approximately 700 B.C. according to the radio-carbon date of his wrappings. Egypt was in something of a decline at the time, being ruled by Nubians, longtime rivals of the Egyptians who exploited political disunity by sending forces in from the south.

Ankhwennefer is currently being reexamined by a project study-ing as many of the mummies from Akhmim as can be located (the Akhmim Mummy Studies Consortium). Not surprisingly, given the comings and goings of those nineteenth-century tourists who bought them, they're scattered far and wide. Despite logistical difficulties, studying mummies originating from a single ancient location can provide some interesting comparative information regarding medi-cal practices and religious ideology of the time. Furthermore, the CT-scanning technology is vastly more sophisticated than during our 1985 inspection, and it will likely reveal far more than the basic facts that we were able to determine around twenty-five years ago.

If Ankhwennefer could awake from his extended slumber, he'd have one heck of a surprise. He has gone from once serving the temple of Min and being afforded a proper burial to having his cof-fin unearthed and his body sold as a tourist commodity, only to be relocated to a history museum's storeroom in a cool, forested part of the world he never knew existed. What a long, strange trip it was for him, and what an interesting learning experience for me.

ANOTHER DEVELOPING INTEREST of mine was the documenta-tion of ancient sites. In the case of Egypt, the detailed survey and description of ancient monuments remains an important priority, as many are suffering rapid decay due to a variety of factors, both human and natural. Tourism, agricultural and residential expansion, and natural erosion all take their toll, and the need to document, if not preserve, these precious remnants of the past is vital. Ideally, there will at least be as detailed a record as possible of what once existed, whether the actual monuments withstand the abuses of time or not.

Enter the epigraphers. Epigraphy is the study of inscriptions and the art of recording them. There are several methods. At its simplest, a skillful artist sketches an inscription or copies a painted wall with pencil, ink, or watercolors. Howard Carter began his Egyptological career doing just that, first coming to Egypt at age seventeen to document ancient inscriptions and paintings, and his work was some of the best of this sort ever produced. Other epigraphic techniques include physically tracing inscriptions or paintings onto thin paper or clear plastic sheets. While typically involving direct contact with a decorated wall, these are much less intrusive than some of the older methods, which involved making molds with plaster or wet paper.

Within a few years of the invention of photography, Egypt became a popular focus for the new technology. Its ancient and contemporary cultures provide plenty of alluring images, but photography could also be applied to epigraphy. Both recording by hand and photography, though, have their drawbacks. While sketching and painting can be compromised by the subjectivity of the artist, the so-called objective details of a photograph can be subdued by such factors as shadows and the inclusion of irrelevant features. The most effective approach is to use both.

The University of Chicago is at the cutting edge of documentation, and its Epigraphic Survey has been busy in Egypt for many decades. With money contributed by John D. Rockefeller, the facility in Luxor known as Chicago House was established in 1924 and remains active during the six cooler months of the year. Its stated goal is "to produce photographs and precise line drawings of the inscriptions and relief scenes on major temples and tombs at Luxor for publication."

During my first trip to Egypt, I met a scholar who once worked at Chicago House and was willing to explain their method of documentation. A large-format black-and-white photograph is taken of, say, an inscribed temple wall. The image is developed into a print, and an artist then traces with ink over the salient hieroglyphs or other decoration displayed in the photograph. It is taken back to the wall and any missing or unclear details are filled in and refined. Eventually the photographic image is bleached out, leaving only a line image that is then corrected, then corrected again if necessary, until a consensus of accuracy is reached by the Egyptologists. This sometimes involves standing on very tall ladders perched against gigantic stone columns and plenty of time in the heat. Precise artistic rules are used, and the end result is an incredibly accurate facsimile that becomes part of a published volume that will serve as a permanent record, even if, sadly, the original monument should crumble to dust. It is a long, exacting, and expensive procedure. People sometimes joke that the process of documentation has taken much longer than it took the Egyptians themselves to actually build and decorate some of these temples. The careful work nonetheless is certainly worth the effort.

Although I wasn't particularly in a position to work within the lofty world of Chicago House, my interest in epigraphy brought me to a place relatively closer and actually much more familiar to me: Hawaii. My parents first took me there when I was nine years old, and I loved everything about it. We were frequent visitors, and while it wasn't exactly Egypt, I found its culture, environment, and archaeology likewise captivating, and I was actually able to apply some of my interests in epigraphy to ancient sites found on these beautiful tropical islands.

When Captain Cook encountered the Hawaiian Islands in 1778, the native population had no writing system. They were certainly sophisticated in numerous ways and maintained a wealth of oral traditions that had been memorized and recited for generations, but there was no Hawaiian script until after the first American missionaries arrived in 1820. However, there are many ways to communicate, including artistic expression, and what really interested me were petroglyphs: symbols and other drawings scratched, incised, or pecked into stone surfaces and often found in very remote or abandoned places. In the Hawaiian language, they are known as *ki'i pohaku*—"images in stone"—and in many ways they are a mystery that is difficult to decipher.

Being exposed to the elements in a hot, rainy climate, the petroglyphs, like the monuments of Egypt, are subject to natural deterioration. Worse yet, nonnative species such as kiawe, a tree related to mesquite, have taken root in many coastal areas and thrive like weeds, their strong-growing trunks and roots shattering the lava with the potential of decimating irreplaceable ancient records. In addition, the wild descendants of animals such as goats and donkeys that are not native to the islands roam the lava beds consuming the tasty leaves and sweet seed pods of the kiawe only to disperse and deposit seeds in tiny cracks with their dung and further the destruction.

Modern development, too, has had its effect, and once-desolate areas have become resorts and expensive communities, putting people, some with vandalistic tendencies, in close proximity to these precious images from the past. Indeed, Polynesian petroglyphs are very worthy of epigraphic attention, and in between my journeys to Egypt in the early 1980s, and several times thereafter, I went to Hawaii to record and preserve what I could.

On the western coast of the "Big Island" of Hawaii, one can find a region called Kona. It's on the dry side of the island, and a significant portion of its landscape is miles upon miles of black lava descending to the sea from a large, hulking volcano named Hualalai. Kona had been a home base for the great warrior-chief Kamehameha, who unified the islands into a kingdom, and it was here that the first missionaries came with their goal of Christianizing Hawaiian society. Today the town of Kailua-Kona is a delightful population hub and tourist destination.

About a dozen miles north of the town is an ancient region called Ka'upulehu. The name itself means "roasted breadfruit" and derives from an ancient legend in which the volcano goddess, Pele, visits two sisters in the area. (Legend has it that one sister shared her breadfruit with the incognito goddess, and her home was spared during a volcanic eruption.) Up until about the 1960s, the coast here was accessible only by boat or by hiking for miles on old trails. Around that time a man named Johnno Jackson came up along the coast and laid the foundation for what would become the Kona Village Resort, a quiet complex of Polynesian-style huts that continues to attract those seeking a simple yet luxurious hideaway. And it just so happened that in the lava field right behind the resort lay one of the most impressive collections of petroglyphs to be found in the Hawaiian Islands, if not in all of Polynesia.

Old Ka'upulehu had once supported a village on a beautiful bay, but by the mid-twentieth century there were just a few inhabitants at best. Most everyone had moved to towns with modern conveniences. When an archaeological survey came through in the early 1960s, the researchers found mere remnants of civilization: some stone platforms that served as the floors of grass houses, shelter caves littered with seashells from ancient meals, some well-hidden burial caves, and the petroglyphs. Unlike others found in the Islands, the petroglyphs at Kaʻupulehu are distinctly different. At other sites one tends to find simple carvings of sticklike figures and a lot of circles and dots. At Kaʻupulehu the style and motifs are remarkably unique, some appearing dynamic and almost animated rather than static. There are many dozens of depictions of what appear to be canoe sails, some showing ripples in their fabric as if being blown by the wind. There's a figure of a man fishing with a long line outfitted with huge hooks, a group that appears to depict two men carrying a body on a pole, and there are several examples of men wearing headdresses as if chiefs. There are also numerous examples of what in Hawaiian are called *papamu,* rectangular patterns of dots pecked into the rock, which some locals will interpret as venues for the playing of *konane,* a checkerslike game involving black and white stones.

It has been proposed that the profusion of sail motifs suggests that Kaʻupulehu might have once served as the site of a kind of sailing school for canoe voyaging, and perhaps the *papamu* are actually a teaching tool in which white stones could be placed in various holes to duplicate the patterns in the sky used in celestial navigation. As opposed to the typical static norm, the petroglyphs at Kaʻupulehu were excitingly dynamic.

Sadly, several of the most intriguing examples had suffered rudely from attempts to bring their mystery elsewhere. Some had been excessively rubbed, their edges degraded from repeated copying by paper and crayons. Worse yet is an example in which latex was poured directly into a petroglyph in an attempt to make a cast. The damaging result was scarring with latex embedded in the porous surface of the lava. Likewise, an ill-considered attempt to use resin for the same purpose left a disastrous result.

Motivated by a desire to preserve these precious items, accompanied by what I had learned about the scholars at Chicago House and their epigraphic methods, I asked the manager of Kona Village if I might attempt to document the petroglyphs on that property. Being fascinated with Hawaiian history and culture himself, he enthusiastically agreed. I set out for Hawaii alone, old survey reports and maps in hand, and headed for the Kona lava fields.

An example of Hawaiian petroglyphs studied by the author.
Are they fighting or dancing?

The first step was to locate as many of the petroglyphs behind the village as I could. It was an incredibly daunting task as the area was thickly infested with the nasty kiawe trees, whose thorns tore at my skin and clothing and whose leafy debris covered much of the lava surface. Scattered jagged chunks of black rock surrounding the

trunks of the kiawe were a constant reminder of the destruction taking place in the midst of this amazing site. How many petroglyphs
were being literally exploded apart by these botanical outsiders? And
it was genuinely hot. Not the dry heat of the Egyptian desert but the
humid heat of a tropical island, accelerated by the black surface of
the lava rock, which in places became too hot to touch.

As I crawled across the lava with brooms of various sizes, the
task of locating all the petroglyphs, let alone effectively documenting them, was quickly turning from my imagined jolly concept of
easy, fun Hawaiian epigraphy to something bordering on the truly
arduous and impractical. The amount of plant debris to sweep
away so that I could confidently declare that all petroglyphs had
been revealed was immense. Also, the solo surveying technique I
had contrived was nearly impossible to implement, as the kiawe
interfered with my line of sight. Lighting, too, was an issue, and
some petroglyphs visible in the early-morning or late-afternoon
light were barely discernible for much of the day. It was terribly
frustrating.

However, I had more success in another area. About half a mile
away, across the lava desert, are scattered groups of petroglyphs in
an area that the kiawe have yet to conquer, some of which are truly
exceptional and vibrant. In one such example there is a dramatic
figure that seems to be wearing a tall, elaborate headdress—and
two men dancing or fighting with paddles over their heads. Even
farther along the harsh landscape is another site where stone shelter walls still stand in isolation within just a few yards of a lava
flow that cut across the landscape in 1801. The lava devastated
everything in its path and filled in a good part of the nearby bay,
and one wonders what might have lain beneath. Nearby are more
papamu, sails, and a curious, deeply carved petroglyph depicting a
six-toed foot.

The author mapping petroglyphs solo in the lava fields at
Ka'upulehu, Hawaii. The intrusive kiawe trees in the background
spread quickly, crack the lava, and can damage petroglyphs.

Using a compass along with a protractor affixed to a flat lava
surface and also some long measuring tapes, I was able to map parts
of the open area and at least inventory the petroglyphs in the vicinity. I enjoyed the solitude, and I was often reminded of Egypt by
the wide expanses of dry wilderness, the heat, the fresh air, and the
open sky. After a couple of weeks of work, I issued a report to the
resort with recommendations for conservation. The experience left
me ever more interested in documentation of ancient sites and the
preservation of such things as petroglyphs.

The interpretation of ancient rock art raises persistent questions. Do petroglyphs depict real things and events accompanied,
perhaps, by a symbolic or ritualistic meaning? Do we, or can we,
understand their meaning, or are we merely engaging in our own
brand of storytelling, with a kind of Rorschach test in stone? Could

some examples be mere graffiti, spontaneous creations inspired by the existence of other petroglyphs in the vicinity? Rock art is notoriously difficult to date, too. One might, for example, be able to geologically determine the age of the lava flow in which the petroglyphs were carved, but if the lava flow is five thousand years old and human colonization of the islands took place only about fifteen hundred years ago, then we could surmise that they were carved sometime between then and their encounter with an archaeologist.

Occasionally there are clues to age in the themes. The depiction of a horse or a goat indicates that the petroglyph is more recent. It was only after the arrival of the Europeans that such animals were introduced to the islands. At Ka'upulehu, there is a large inscription that reads "1820," but even then one can't assume it's the date in which the petroglyph was carved. It could be someone's year of birth or any other significant event.

Wonderful things have happened at Ka'upulehu after my own simple efforts. Most of the kiawe were removed from the primary petroglyph field, and a well-crafted boardwalk was installed, with explanatory signs that allow visitors to enjoy the rock art without trampling on it. And a project led by archaeologist Georgia Lee did a very credible job of documenting many of the petroglyphs in a precise, epigraphic fashion.

A number of years later, I returned to Ka'upulehu with a small volunteer team of friends. We called our effort the Experimental Epigraphy Expedition, and our goal was to experiment with methods of documenting such things as petroglyphs using the benefits of modern technology. We brought laptop computers, digital cameras, and other equipment and got to work. In one experiment we attempted to duplicate a kind of Chicago House method out in the lava. Using a digital camera, we photographed a sample of a petroglyph and then immediately downloaded the image into the laptop, where we brought it onto the screen using the Adobe Photoshop program. From there we traced over the image using a digital pen, and with a portable battery-powered printer we were able to immediately produce a hard copy, compare it to the original, make further corrections on the image, and voilà— a quick, inexpensive, and accurate rendition of a petroglyph. Would this work in Egypt? Could similar techniques eventually replace that of the traditional Chicago House method? Perhaps, but it's one thing to document relatively simple subjects such as Polynesian petroglyphs and another to address the superb detail preserved in many pharaonic inscriptions. I'm sure that Chicago House will continue its superb work with the finest means possible.

I was interested, too, in the possibilities of photographing as much as possible of the entire site using high-resolution photographs for the purpose of documentation but also as a tool for studying the relationship between the various petroglyphs as groups. Kite aerial photography seemed like it might have the potential to do the job, and with the generous assistance of the Drachen Foundation— a foundation dedicated to all things kite-related—we recruited an expert who brought a special kite to Kona with a camera rig attached to its line that could take pictures remotely. Kites, of course, are wind-dependent, and there would be some waiting around until conditions were just right. Eventually we got some great pictures from high in the air, but unfortunately it was hard to control the kite with the precision we preferred.

Operating in the jagged lava also provided hazards for both the operators and the kite, especially when landing. We endured some nasty scrapes and cuts, and at one point there was a structural malfunction on the kite and a camera fell from the sky, smashing into the rocks below. Overall the results were mixed, but certainly not discouraging.

On our last day, we improvised one final experiment. At a local store, we bought several party kits that included dozens of colorful balloons and a tank of helium. After inflating a substantial bouquet, we proceeded out to the petroglyph fields, dodging palms and the stray kiawe, which threatened to literally deflate our efforts. Unlike a kite, the balloons required absolutely no wind whatsoever to be effective, and we again waited for just the right conditions. Using lines for control, we were able to float an attached camera over groups of petroglyphs to get some reasonable images from a desired height. With lessons learned and plenty of new insights, we'll probably come back someday and try it again—but next time with more sophisticated gear.

FIVE

UNTYING THE MUNDANE

To a mountain climber, a rope is a valued companion. It has the potential to save one from a fatal fall down a sheer cliff or a plunge into the depths of a crevasse. It can provide a sense of security that inspires confidence in ascending and traversing dangerous terrain, and it can facilitate one's descent to terra firma. As a climber, therefore, I have an intrinsic interest in this technology, it often being tied, literally, to my very survival.

Modern mountaineering ropes are made of artificial materials and are composed of continuous bundles of nylon strands protected by a woven outer sheath. Their thickness, in terms of diameter, is an important factor in their strength, while their length affects their utility. A standard useful rope length today is 60 meters with a diameter of 10.5 millimeters, and ropes are available in a variety of colors and patterns. They are flexible enough to be tied and knotted into one's harness or affixed to anchors and can be coiled for transport or storage. Climbing ropes can be "dynamic," that is, with a bit of stretch to cushion a fall, or "static," with little give in order to facilitate very specific uses, such as long vertical entries and exits into caves.

While my own interests in rope might seem a bit esoteric, its versatility, even in this arguably fringe activity, is dramatic. What we call rope, and things of similar utility, can be grouped under the general term "cordage." Theoretically at least, cordage can be defined as an assemblage of fibers, combined by twisting or braiding into a flexible line capable of bearing weight and being tied. It can take many functional forms, whether it's fine silk thread used to sew a delicate Chinese garment, twine or string used to tie up a package, or big cables made of grass spanning ravines in the Peruvian highlands. If you look around, you'll find lots of examples of cordage in different sizes and materials. And it was even more prominent before the age of duct tape.

The ancient Egyptians certainly made good use of cordage. As masters of simple technology, they put it to use in dozens of necessary, creative ways. Scenes of daily life depicted on tomb walls show elaborate rigging aboard their ships, and one of the most dramatic discoveries ever from ancient Egypt, a well-preserved forty-six-hundred-year-old wooden funerary boat, was literally held together by rope. Uncovered in 1954, in a pit sealed under stone slabs at the foot of the Great Pyramid, the boat was constructed from cedar planks of various sizes, lashed together with rope, which were also found well preserved among the jigsaw puzzle of dismantled pieces.

Scholars and tourists alike marvel at the pyramids and the colossal statues of the pharaohs, but when you think about it, the simple, mundane technology of rope was an essential part of the process. These heavy objects were pulled, lifted, and tied down, and cordage was there as the unsung but vital technology of the ancient world. Simple and taken for granted, it is easy to ignore.

As a climber with an appreciation for rope well-established, I found it an easy decision when Dr. W asked me if I'd like to try to make sense of a sundry collection of cordage fragments recovered from his excavation at a site in Middle Egypt called El-Hibeh. There were about eighty pieces in several sizes, mostly dirty and dating back two thousand to three thousand years. Old Egyptian rope! Where to start? I turned to a likely source, a reference book entitled *Ancient Egyptian Materials and Industries* by Alfred Lucas and J. R. Harris. It's an amazing piece of scholarship covering all kinds of topics from bricks and beads to pottery and wood. Fortunately, there was a little article dealing with cordage that got me started with some general information. Not surprisingly, I learned that there was not very much available on the subject.

I did find some insights, however, outside the realm of Egyptology, in the archaeological literature of North America. In fact, there were some wonderful studies done on the subject based on many surviving ancient examples, especially from the dry regions of the Southwest. There I found strategies and techniques for analysis that could be directly applied to the Egyptian materials I was dealing with. The American examples brought home a reality that holds true with other examples: Egyptologists are spoiled. Their embarrassment of riches in the form of dramatic monuments, good preservation, tomb art, and, most important, the crutch of texts, shaped the development of Egyptology in such a way that there are few specialists who deal with the relatively "common" artifacts. Lacking inscriptions, a well-established framework of history, and, frankly, the alluring glory of the pharaohs, the archaeology of North America developed in a much different way, with an emphasis on scrutinizing every bit of evidence, no matter how minute or seemingly inconsequential. There are specialists who deal with such subjects as stone tools, tiny grains of pollen, pottery, animal bones, and even dung. American archaeology, then, would give me a grasp on how to deal with several dozen pieces of old rope from a land rich in artifacts but weak in the understanding of those bits and pieces that aren't particularly pretty.

Three factors help determine a cord's function: how it's made, its material of manufacture, and its size or diameter. Archaeologists classify the construction of cords by the number of strands and the direction in which they are twisted. Strands can be described as either S-twisted (to the left) or Z-twisted (to the right). The tension between such opposite-twisted strands holds the rope together. Typically, three S-twisted strands are combined to form a single Z-twisted cord. The analyst can effectively record this construction with a simple formula such as $Z = s/s/s$. And cords like this can be combined to make even bigger and stronger rope.

The samples from el-Hibeh varied from what one might call "string" to much larger pieces, some of them appearing as if manufactured just days earlier, while others crumbled into loose fibers at the touch. Even so, it was fun to work with this stuff, sitting in a cramped laboratory surrounded by little boxes and bags full of truly old items handmade by ancient Egyptians. I created a standardized form for recording the data, on which I wrote whatever information I could glean. The construction formula was easily discerned, and determining the diameters of the strands was simply a matter of measuring them with calipers. Actually, most of the time spent with this small project was spent just finding out *how* to study the materials.

There wasn't much to conclude from all this other than adding to the sparse descriptive data on the subject. It would have been nice if it were possible to assign how each piece was specifically used, but there really wasn't much to go on, unless you wanted to speculate based on size or perhaps a knot or two. There was one aspect of the study, though, that did border on interpretation. The samples of cordage were derived from two excavations at different parts of the site of El-Hibeh, and the kinds retrieved from each were quite different. One might suggest, therefore, perhaps with other supporting data, that these two areas varied in function, based on surviving cordage and other objects. At El-Hibeh the evidence seemed to suggest that this was the case, one excavation revealing domestic or home sites and the other associated with some sort of public architecture. But regardless of what little I could add to the history of ancient Egypt by this study, I at least added to my own knowledge and experience, and my interest was piqued.

During my fortuitous encounter with Harry James on that Red Sea cruise, I asked if the British Museum's Egyptian collection possessed any cordage. "Bits of string!" replied Harry. "Yes, in fact, we do." In my own enthusiastic way, I tried to impress upon him how important cordage was to the ancient Egyptians. The man in charge of galleries of superb sculptures, mummies, and priceless works of art was indeed well aware that everything, no matter how mundane, had the potential of contributing a little something to our knowledge. "Come on by the department on your way through London, and we'll have a look!" I arrived a few weeks later, and, as promised, there were pieces of ancient rope to examine, each well preserved and well cared for.

It was a wonderful collection of ropes from different eras and places in Egypt, which together formed a nice, varied sample. There was a huge fragment almost the diameter of my wrist and another that was lengthy and gathered into a coil. Yet another huge piece was composed mostly of a single very large knot. Harry provided whatever data the museum possessed in its records, and I selected seventeen specimens for detailed analysis based on the extent of surviving information on each item. Most of the samples were collected around or prior to the turn of the century when interest in these sorts of artifacts was not a priority to archaeologists working in Egypt. Thankfully, a number of specimens had made their way to the museum with notes recording such data as their place of discovery and the overall context in which they were found.

From my study of the El-Hibeh material, I had a good idea about how to document this stuff. This time, though, I was intent on pursuing the one vital variable I didn't have the skills to deal with before: material. What were these artifacts made of? Determining material of manufacture of artifacts made from ancient plants certainly must fall within the realm of botany, and soon after I returned home, I went to the biology department at Pacific Lutheran University looking for a willing consultant. Professor David Hansen must have thought it a strange proposition when approached by an animated ancient rope enthusiast, but I somehow convinced him that the project was sufficiently interesting to give it a deeper look. His lack of background in Egyptian archaeology wasn't detrimental— I'd cover that—but his botanical knowledge was essential.

After delving into what limited literature we could find on the subject, Dave had a good idea of what would be required. Fiber samples extracted from the ancient ropes could be cut into very thin slices and mounted on slides. As each plant species is anatomically distinct in microscopic cross section, we should be able, in theory at least, to compare the ancient samples with slides made in a similar way from modern reference specimens of plants known to be used in ancient Egypt. So back to London I would need to go, in order to retrieve the necessary fiber samples.

The opportunity came that fall, actually twice, while I was traveling to and from a stint as a tutor aboard an oilman's private yacht in the Aegean, a curious story in its own right that would only distract from my exciting unfolding tale of ancient rope. Needless to say, it was delightful to spend time in the British Museum. I looked forward each day to showing up at the Egyptian department's "students' room," accessed by a nondescript door between statues of the lion-headed goddess Sekhmet, situated on one of the museum's grand staircases. Pushing a button would bring a greeter, and soon I would be going about my work, facilitated by a helpful and hospitable staff. It took several days to examine and document the ropes as I conducted my usual descriptive analysis. With permission, of course, I was able to take samples from each artifact, placing a few fibers in small coin envelopes to be brought home with me to PLU.

Back at Dave's lab, we found that many of the samples were brittle, and the first task was to soften them a bit, which Dave did in an appropriate chemical solution. Afterward individual fibers were embedded into small paraffin blocks before meeting their fate in the microtome. The microtome is a little machine that wields a dangerously sharp blade, capable of slicing samples of many things, from diseased human tissue to ancient cordage fibers, to a thickness of only microns. "It will cut you if you just look at it!" I joked, and I let Dave do the serious stuff. By turning a small crank, like a butcher cutting pastrami in a deli, he guided the microtome to slice each fiber into thin ribbons, which were then mounted on slides and stained to bring out their features.

Under the microscope one could certainly see an array of anatomical features resembling pockets and strands that varied between some specimens but were clearly identical in others. To identify the actual materials, though, a series of reliable reference specimens were needed to compare with our ancient samples. For starters I was able to obtain fibers from date palms growing at the family homestead in Southern California. We would, however, need quite a number of other species, and it was clear that a collecting trip to the place where they grew naturally, Egypt, would be required.

With a list of species in hand, Dave and I ventured off to the Land of the Pharaohs. Unfortunately for my friend, the airline had lost virtually all of his luggage, and Dave was left with just the clothes on his back and a plant press. It's a device consisting of layers of thick paper and cardboard pressed between two wooden frames by tightening straps. Also unfortunate was that the other necessary tools, including our "floras"—reference books for identifying plant species—were also lost in the luggage, as were some devices for retrieving samples. We suspect that one such device used for coring trees, and somewhat resembling a metal pipe, might have been the culprit that invited airport suspicion and thus caused the vital suitcase to be held. (As an aside, Dave's suitcase, mostly intact, arrived on his doorstep in Olympia, Washington, without explanation about three months later.) After waiting a few days for the lost bag, we decided to proceed, and I lent Dave some of my clothes, which looked quite comical on him as I was several sizes larger. Nonetheless, we pressed on.

One of our plants of interest was papyrus, a plant almost synonymous with ancient Egypt, where it served as a source material for making paper. The Egyptians had ample use for the product, and during the Greek and Roman dominations of Egypt it was exported all over the Mediterranean. The Egyptians themselves also used the plant for a variety of other things, including the making of naturally buoyant boats, sandals, and yes, ropes. A couple of ancient Greek visitors to Egypt even noted that the plant could be used as food, prompting a colleague of mine—the late, great Donald Farmer—to coin the word "papriphagic."*

Curiously, the papyrus plant went virtually extinct in Egypt after the ancient civilization declined. It made a comeback, however, about fifty years ago thanks to a man named Hassan Ragab. He was a fascinating individual, having among other things served as an Egyptian military general, as Egypt's ambassador to Italy and Yugoslavia, and as the country's first ambassador to the People's Republic of China. Ragab was intrigued with papyrus, and after having successfully transplanted the plant back to Egypt, he discovered a way of replicating paper. Although it can't be definitively determined that his method is exactly what was used in ancient times, it creates some fine, durable, and usable sheets.

A clever man, he founded "Dr. Ragab's Papyrus Institute," in which he sold sheets of papyrus paper hand-decorated with everything from pharaonic tomb scenes to verses from the Koran. In doing so he unintentionally introduced an industry that continues to thrive today, and dozens of papyrus factories can be found selling these very popular souvenirs in the major Egyptian tourist areas. Unfortunately, some are made of bogus products such as banana leaves, and though the end product is visually similar, the counterfeits will fall apart shortly after the tourist returns home.

At face value one might assume that Ragab's Papyrus Institute was simply a moneymaking venture operating under an educational moniker. I had often heard Egyptologists scoff at the Papyrus Institute, making comments about tacky exploitation of pharaonic heritage or other flippant, skeptical remarks, yet few admitted to having actually been there. They were wrong. The institute actually

---

* As an aside, we actually once conducted a nutritional analysis of the plant and found it comparable to celery with a slightly sweet, strawlike flavor.

did have an educational component. From a riverside street, visitors would descend a set of steps to a pleasant garden, where a young employee would provide an explanation and a demonstration of the paper-making process. Fresh green stalks of papyrus would be trimmed to reveal their pithy white interiors, which were then cut into thin strips, laid at right angles, and pressed, the natural sugars within the plant creating a bonding agent. Eventually, a lovely sheet of sturdy paper would be displayed. From there one was escorted into a houseboat moored on the Nile to peruse a showroom of painted papyrus for sale, along with paper-making kits and books, free of sales pressure.

I met Hassan Ragab more than once and found the elderly man charming and positively interested in the subject of ancient Egyptian technology. His brother, Mohammed, who ran the daily operations of the business, was likewise extremely knowledgeable of things ancient and botanical. Arriving in Egypt without our reference materials, I had no doubt that the Ragab brothers could save us. Once we had explained our dilemma to Mohammed, he led us to a narrow room on the premises of the institute, where we found a wonderful library of all things botanical and agricultural relating to Egypt, including all the essential books that had been lost in the luggage fiasco. We were free to consult and photocopy whatever we liked. Furthermore, many of the plants we sought were currently being grown in a garden upstream at a new commercial educational venture under development, called the Pharaonic Village. And on top of that, a driver was put at our disposal to take us to the garden, where we could sample what we wished.

With our laundry list in hand, Dave and I intended to collect plants known to have been utilized not only in ancient ropes but also in other fibers objects, including baskets, mats, and such, along with woods that could be used to identify coffin and other artifact materials. The trip to the Ragab plantation allowed us to obtain much of what we were looking for in one place in a matter of hours. There was a collection of trees, for example, all scientifically labeled and easily confirmed by Dave. It doesn't get much simpler than that. Did the Ragab brothers operate a genuine "papyrus institute"? Absolutely, and their expertise and resources were always available to anyone with a real interest, even skeptical Egyptologists and foreign botanists lacking luggage.

Botanist Dr. David Hansen wrestles the wild *Juncus acutus* while retrieving specimens to be used in identifying ancient artifact materials.

There were several common wild species, though, that required us to make field trips into the countryside to obtain. Halfa grass, for example, had been reported as a common source of ancient fibers, and we found that there were two grasses of similar appearance that bore the same Arabic name. We would need to collect them both, so I hired a driver who promised that he could take us anywhere. As we rode, Dave would lean slightly out the window of the moving vehicle, his eyes trained off to the side of the road. With each sighting of a likely species, we pulled over, consulted the reference books, and if we had a match, a sample was taken and placed into the ever-thickening plant press. It was a good deal of fun, like a strange kind of safari where instead of hunting for wild game we were in search of leaves from the likes of *Juncus acutus,* fibers from dom palm, and stalks of reeds.

At one point during our plant hunt, we made an effort to visit a village to see if rope was still being manufactured. After asking around, we were taken to an open area in a palm grove, where an elderly man sat amid a pile of brown fibers pulled from the trees. What we witnessed was utterly stunning. With an expertise likely honed over a lifetime of repetition, he clutched lengths of fibers between his toes, skillfully twisting and rolling his palms as lengths of good-quality cordage emerged from his hands. This fellow, with his dark, wizened face, was a veritable human cordage factory and seemed unaffected by the two foreigners gawking in amazement. Unfortunately, our Arabic at the time was insufficient to interview him, as we'd have had many questions. How long had he practiced this profession? Was it difficult to learn? Did he make other things? How did he go about choosing his materials? We did manage to learn that fibers from the date palm were the usual material of choice, but he also pointed to a patch of halfa grass as a second source.

Observing a contemporary rope maker was impressive and edifying, but what of the ancient Egyptians themselves? Fortunately, their propensity for carving and painting scenes of daily life on the tomb walls of the elite served us well. There are a number of such scenes to be found that provide an artistic snapshot of this dynamic process, and it was essential in our research to study as many of these as we could locate. In the Old Kingdom tomb of Ptahhotep at Sakkara, for example, one can see an ancient scene of rope makers at work in association with the making of small papyrus boats. It's convenient that some such scenes often provided hieroglyphic captions, making it clear what task is being performed. Likewise, the New Kingdom tomb of Khaemwaset found in the necropolis of Thebes contains a painted scene of three men manufacturing rope in the midst of a papyrus swamp, complete with materials, tools, and coils of the finished product on display.

Ptahhotep's tomb has long been open to the public, so it was just a matter of visiting the vast cemetery of Sakkara to take a look. The tomb is huge, its walls covered with a myriad of fascinating scenes that proved a wonderful distraction while I searched for the one little section of particular interest. Khaemwaset's modest tomb was a different matter altogether. It was rarely visited, and special permission was required to visit and a map to locate it. Accompanied by an Egyptian antiquities inspector, we managed to find the tomb's small doorway, which was closed with an iron gate fronted by a mud-brick wall. I paid a local man to assist in the opening, and as sunlight streamed into the tomb, for perhaps the first time in decades, I was amazed at the small size of the painting and impressed by its detail and the vibrancy of the colors. Although the scene was technically static, there were enough clues and details to really bring it to life. A few notes and photographs, and the tomb was once again closed to await other future scholars on a curious mission of their own.

With a wonderful collection of fiber and wood samples and a bulging plant press, Dave Hansen and I returned to PLU to take the next step. The newly acquired reference specimens needed to be processed, and once again we hauled out the microtome and made slides. Now we could finally address the business of identifying the ancient materials. Even to this nonbotanist, it soon became easy to discern the differences between various species, both ancient and modern, based on their anatomical characteristics. Much to our surprise, we found that many of the museum specimens had been misidentified. Many were labeled as palm when in fact they were made of halfa grass.

I gave this problem some thought and concluded that most of these erroneous identifications were based on the assumptions of the original collectors of the ancient rope. During the nineteenth century or so, when many of the artifacts were collected, date palm was a major source of cordage fibers as manufactured in the villages and sold in marketplaces. This, though, was not the case in ancient times, as our old specimens seem to indicate. Back then halfa grass appears to have been the material of preference. There was also a sample labeled as hemp—a common material used in ship's rigging during the British Empire—that was actually a Southeast Asian plant apparently unknown to the ancient Egyptians. Our conclusions? A lot of dirty old ropes look the same, and the early excavators were probably basing their observations on recent practices along with the assumption that something as basic as rope making would remain essentially unchanged.

It seems true that there is nothing specific that distinguishes rope making in ancient Egypt from that in any other part of the modern rural world. The end result is basically the same, whether it's made from coconut fibers in Polynesia or cedar root in the Pacific Northwest. It's one of those fundamental technologies whose obvious utility is universally recognized, and perhaps it was independently invented dozens of times. Preference of materials, though, varies with geography and might change in availability due to climate change or other factors. Papyrus, for example, a popular material for ancient ropes, went extinct in Egypt, and the widespread cultivation of the date palm is a relatively recent phenomenon. The best way to confidently identify artifact materials is to do it as we did, by ignoring external appearances and looking at their inner characteristics. These observations formed the basis of my first scientific publication.

So, you might ask, we now know that ancient Egyptian rope was made from halfa grass, papyrus, and occasionally a few other things and otherwise has nothing particularly distinct about it. Who cares? In reality, some really do have some fascinating stories to tell!

One of the rope artifacts I examined in the British Museum, for example, was a wonderfully preserved large fragment discovered with six others in the limestone quarries at Tura southeast of Cairo in May 1942. The thick diameters of these ropes and their discovery within a source of stone used for, among other things, the Giza pyramids, led to some excitement regarding their possible role in the quarrying of the blocks used to build those massive monuments. Our analysis determined that the specimen, which had a diameter of approximately 7.6 centimeters (3 inches), its structure being Z = s/s/s (that is, three left-twisted strands combined to form a right-twisted rope), was made from *Cyperus papyrus*. Radiocarbon dating has proved, however, a much younger date than anticipated, about two thousand years old, from the Greco-Roman period in Egypt. Although not Old Kingdom pyramid-building rope, its place of finding and sturdy size, material, and construction suggest that it very well might have been used in stonework, or in the conveyance of quarried blocks used to produce wonderful things in its day.

Another British Museum rope specimen is one of the most interesting Egyptian artifacts I have ever had the pleasure of examining. This rope was originally retrieved by the famous Italian adventurer Giovanni Belzoni in 1817, during his discovery of the tomb of the pharaoh Seti I in the Valley of the Kings. Upon entering the tomb, Belzoni passed through three decorated corridors before being stopped by a deep vertical shaft, the "well" feature found in a number of New Kingdom royal tombs. In Belzoni's words:

> On the opposite side of the pit facing the entrance I
> perceived a small aperture two feet wide and two feet six
> inches high, and at the bottom of the well a quantity of
> rubbish. A rope fastened to a piece of wood, that was laid
> across the passage against the projections which form a
> kind of door, appears to have been used by the ancients
> for descending into the pit; and from the small aperture
> on the opposite side hung another, which reached the
> bottom, no doubt for the purpose of ascending.

The first rope and the wood to which it was attached "crumbled to dust on [my] touching them," noted Belzoni, while the rope on the opposite side of the well "remained pretty strong." It is this second rope that is housed today at the British Museum; it was originally displayed at an Egyptian exhibition in London put together by Belzoni and eventually was auctioned off with the rest of his collection.

Belzoni's rope is presently 6.2 meters long (about 20 feet), including two knots, and is in seven sections. With a finished diameter of about 2 centimeters (.75 inch), it has a Z = s/s structure, or two left-twisted strands combined to form a right-twisted rope. It was manufactured from *Desmostachya bipinnata,* or halfa grass.

The in situ discovery of Belzoni's rope offers provocative scenarios for its use in antiquity. King Seti's tomb had been robbed late in the Twentieth Dynasty, and his mummy was later removed and placed along with the bodies of other royalty in a hidden cache. The priests who rescued Seti's mummy and the others and rewrapped their battered remains left notes indicating that his tomb, according to Egyptologists, had been robbed initially around 1074 B.C. and afterward served as a temporary repository for the mummies of his father and son, Rameses I and Rameses II, which had been recovered from their own plundered tombs. The three were then transferred to the secret cache around 968 B.C. It's thus easy to wonder whether Belzoni's rope was employed by the original robbers of Seti I's tomb to negotiate the obstacle of a great pit or by the necropolis priests who were shifting the royal mummies about.

Fragments of a rope recovered by Giovanni Belzoni from the tomb of Seti I in the Valley of the Kings and now residing in the Egyptian collection of the British Museum.

A radiocarbon dating of Belzoni's rope conservatively estimated its age at 950 B.C., plus or minus sixty years. Such a date certainly suggests the rope's involvement in one or more of the various dramatic, ancient events that transpired in the tomb of Seti I, thus possibly tying this "mundane" length of twisted fibers to some real, interesting history.

Dave Hansen and I compiled our data into a report titled "A Study of Ancient Egyptian Cordage in the British Museum," and we were thrilled when the museum published the little monograph in their Occasional Papers series. I still announce occasionally that it continues to sell vigorously . . . as a cure for insomnia, but actually we are delighted to see our work put to use and cited in other publications. I also presented the story of Belzoni's rope in Munich at the International Congress of Egyptologists, and it was published in the conference proceedings.

Dave and I went on and analyzed some other specimens, including some samples of ancient wood, and our collection of modern plants and reference slides is housed in Pacific Lutheran University's herbarium, where it remains a resource for those with similar interests.

Who cares about old rope? Compared to the Great Pyramid and the tombs of the Valley of the Kings, perhaps cordage is a ridiculous bore, but only in the sense that it is common rather than unique. But common doesn't mean unnecessary. In fact, it is so necessary that it is common, necessary enough—or should I say crucial?—to be vital in building pyramids, hobbling donkeys, rigging boats, and lowering huge stone sarcophagi down sloping corridors.

In the big picture, the study of ancient Egypt is like a vast jigsaw puzzle with a myriad of pieces both large and small, known and unknown, obvious and subtle. It's not all golden mummies, stone statues, and hieroglyphs. Though at first glance something as seemingly obscure as cordage appears trivial, a closer examination reveals that such humdrum technologies are essential, if uncelebrated, components of the ancient Egyptian cultural fabric. And many of these bits of string have wonderful tales to tell.

Who cares about old rope? Call me a nerd, but I do.

FRISKING THE DEAD

Serendipity can be defined as "the discovery of one thing while in the process of searching for another." It happens a lot in science, often for the better, and the new findings sometimes take on a priority all their own. For example, while I was conducting my study of ancient Egyptian cordage in the British Museum, one of the specimens caught my attention in a special way. It bore the museum registration number EA 45189, was constructed from three strands of twisted papyrus fibers, and was about half a meter in length. Most interesting was its source—it was noted as having come from the excavations of David Hogarth at a site called Asyut. Even with my interest in the history of Egyptian archaeology, I had heard neither of Hogarth nor of any such excavation. When questioned, Harry James had at least a partial answer. Hogarth was a scholar commissioned in 1906 to conduct excavations on behalf of the British Museum, and since he was neither an Egyptologist nor did he publish the results of his work, his actual efforts were essentially unknown. He did, however, return from Egypt with hundreds of objects that are a valuable addition to the museum's collections.

Harry led me to a cabinet in the Egyptian department's archives, where I was shown two old notebooks from Hogarth's excavation, one containing descriptions of several dozen tombs and the other a hand-drawn catalog of artifacts. The notebooks were certainly intriguing, and I asked if I might examine them in depth. "Why not?" replied the Keeper, and I was provided with copies of both, along with additional related material from the museum's records. It turned into a major research project. Through a variety of documents, I was able to reconstruct and vicariously relive a "lost" excavation from an earlier time, when archaeology was practiced much differently from the way it is today.

My unearthing of Hogarth's work involved neither shovels nor trowels nor any physical hardship. Modern London base camps such as the British Museum, the spectacular Reading Room of the British Library, and other sophisticated venues provided a comfortable atmosphere for exploration. The only sweat I experienced was that on the pint glass of Guinness in the Museum Tavern across the street after work each day. Organizing and making sense of Hogarth's notes was a pleasant challenge, especially when it came to reading his handwriting, which at first glance is nearly illegible. Eventually I learned to read his script, including its shorthand ligatures, with relative ease, which greatly facilitated the pace of my work. For a while at least, my life and Hogarth's were tied together, ostensibly by an ancient piece of rope. The story revealed was fascinating, with a cast of intriguing characters, a splendid yet unappreciated archaeological site, and a personal glance at Egyptian archaeology at a time when professional standards were still in development.

In 1894, Ernest Alfred Wallis Budge was appointed Keeper of the Department of Egyptian and Assyrian Antiquities at the British Museum. Academically diverse, energetic, and unswervingly loyal to the museum, Budge worked very hard to enhance his department's collections during the thirty years he occupied that position. And, as a result, he has quite an interesting place in the history of Egyptology. For one thing, he was a prolific academic writer—perhaps too prolific—with over 130 books to his credit. But he also had a notorious reputation for his ability to locate, and often shrewdly acquire, choice items of antiquity for export to Britain from foreign lands. Working through networks of dealers, Budge came home from such places as Egypt and Mesopotamia with amazing artifacts, including Egyptian papyri and clay cuneiform tablets for the museum.

The other strategy for museums to augment their collections at the turn of the twentieth century was through excavation. With a regulatory antiquities bureau in place in Egypt directed by Europeans (the Service des Antiquités de l'Égypte), foreign museums and some individuals could apply for permission to excavate at one site or another. If the application was successful, a concession was granted, essentially a piece of archaeological turf to explore that ideally would be free of competition from other excavators. When the work was completed on these projects, the artifacts recovered were divided between the antiquities authorities and the sponsoring institutions. Therefore there was a good incentive for a museum to sponsor such work—a split of the findings.

In March 1906, Budge journeyed to Egypt with the purpose of meeting with the head of antiquities, a prominent French Egyptologist named Gaston Maspero, to discuss the possibilities of obtaining a concession for excavation. The goal of such a project, explained Budge, was "to obtain objects necessary to fill up the gaps in our collection." He also noted that the British Museum "could not afford to issue large publications or plans of sites on a large scale," which explains why the new project would become essentially "lost," or unknown to scholars for decades. Maspero offered him a cemetery at a place called Khawaled near Asyut, which was said to contain "many tombs of the XVIIIth Dynasty and tombs of a far earlier period, containing wooden statues, etc." Part of the site had already been conceded to an Italian, Ernesto Schiaparelli, but an adjacent area was available. Budge indicated that the British Museum was willing pay a thousand pounds "for a few years provided the results were satisfactory."

When Budge returned to England, the museum's trustees considered his report and directed him to apply for the recommended site, but while his letter of application was in transit, he received word from Maspero that the concession at Khawaled had been granted to another Englishman, the prominent archaeologist W. M. Flinders Petrie. As consolation Maspero offered two other sites: Abydos and Asyut, "the latter containing tombs of the X–XIIth dynasties." Weighing the merits of each, Budge selected Asyut, and the director of the British Museum telegraphed this intention to Maspero. Budge's preference for the site was given as follows:

"Of the history of that period [Tenth to Twelfth Dynasties] very little is known and it may reasonably be expected that successful excavations on the site will materially advance the knowledge of the history of that time."

Asyut is located on the west bank of the Nile, about 250 miles upstream from Cairo and in ancient times was situated between two power centers, Memphis and Thebes. This geographical position made the region of the town a frontier between north and south in times of political disunity. The town sits in a fertile plain beneath the backdrop of a large limestone mountain, running generally west to east, honeycombed with tombs.

Ancient Asyut is known to Egyptologists for several things, including its role in the tumultuous events of a time period referred to as the First Intermediate Period, c. 2160–2055 B.C., which was essentially a civil war. At the end of the Old Kingdom, the central authority of the pharaoh was weakened and the fight for control of Egypt devolved into a three-way power struggle among Memphis, Thebes, and Herakleopolis, a regional capital in Middle Egypt. The reasons for the conflict are still debatable, but when it was resolved, Egypt was again unified, stable, and prosperous during the subsequent Middle Kingdom. Unfortunately, the governors of Asyut backed the wrong side, but the city continued on.

Asyut is also notable as the cult center for a god in the form of a canine named Wepwawet, such that the ancient Greeks renamed the city Lycopolis, "city of wolves." For those inclined to ancient texts, five inscribed tombs of provincial governors of the First Intermediate Period and the Middle Kingdom can still be found there, bearing important historical, biographical, and funerary texts. Likewise the city's vast necropolis has a reputation as a source from which many wooden funerary figures and decorated coffins have been recovered.

A number of Western antiquarians visited Asyut during the late eighteenth and early nineteenth centuries, several copying the texts found in the inscribed tombs. At the same time, local exploitation of the Asyut cemetery for the purpose of obtaining salable antiquities was no doubt extensive. In 1893, for example, a native digger by the name of Faraq "excavated" a large uninscribed tomb of a Middle Kingdom high official named Mesehti. The tomb contained, among other things, Mesehti's coffins, bearing funerary texts, and, most notably, two amazing groups of wooden model soldiers, each standing over a foot tall and well armed with miniature weapons. The latter are currently displayed in the Egyptian Museum in Cairo, where they are a unique and popular attraction.

The first official foreign excavation in the ancient cemetery of Asyut was conducted in 1903 by the Frenchmen Émile Chassinat and Charles Palanque. Their excavations uncovered twenty-six small and undecorated tombs, only five of which had been robbed. Of the sixty-one coffins recovered from these tombs, thirty-four were inscribed with texts that provide a wealth of biographical, funerary, and religious data.

The Italian Egyptologist Ernesto Schiaparelli excavated at Asyut beginning in 1905. His concession contained most of the large inscribed tombs and the area extending eastward. He worked at Asyut through 1913, and his labors were apparently productive. Although Schiaparelli published nothing on the subject, objects from his excavation can be found today in the Museo Egizio in Turin, Italy. In short, the British Museum would be working at a potentially very exciting and productive site, even though bits of it had already been picked over, legally and illegally.

David Hogarth was recommended to direct the museum's project as one "whose skill and experience are well known." I looked up his name in an essential reference book for anyone doing such historical research, *Who Was Who in Egyptology,* and there was no entry for him at the time. My investigation was now taking a turn toward the biographical, as I hunted for whatever information I could find about the man.

Born in England in 1862, David George Hogarth studied classics at Oxford, with an expertise in the language and culture of ancient Greece. Upon graduation he began a somewhat vague introduction to archaeological exploration by assisting with the copying of inscriptions in Asia Minor and participating in an excavation on

Cyprus. Given such a tenuous background, Hogarth would seem to be an odd choice to be sent on a special mission to work in Egypt, but that is exactly what happened.

From 1893 through 1895, Swiss Egyptologist Édouard Naville conducted consecutive seasons of excavations on behalf of the Egypt Exploration Fund at the magnificent mortuary temple of Hatshepsut on the west bank at Luxor. The fund, which was established in 1882 for the exploration and publishing of such sites, was footing the bill. The immense temple was considered an exceedingly worthwhile and an especially demanding project. All, however, were not pleased with the choice of Naville as the temple's excavator. W. M. Flinders Petrie for one was particularly disturbed to hear of the plan, as Naville seemed to be most interested in finding large artistic objects at the expense of small finds and exercising good archaeological technique.

Attempts to remove Naville from the project failed, but supporters of Petrie finally managed to have the fund send a young archaeologist to join the excavation with the aim of observing, assisting, and improving the work. Thus in 1894 Hogarth ventured to Egypt for the first time. Of this opportunity he wrote, "I ought not to have agreed, but, having so agreed, because the call of the East compelled me, I should have begun humbly at the bottom of the long ladder of Egyptology." Surprisingly, Hogarth's report vindicated the Swiss scholar, on the grounds that many of his alleged excesses were justifiable, given the nature of the site.

The next couple of years found Hogarth exploring a few other sites in Egypt, with his distinct preference for Greek remains. During the winter of 1895–96, he participated in the exploration of some Greek town sites in Egypt with the goal of recovering papyrus documents from their ancient garbage heaps. He was joined by two other young Oxonians, Bernard P. Grenfell and Arthur S.

Hunt, who would achieve fame for their persistent and successful efforts in this activity and their subsequent translation of many of the papyri.

Curiously, after three years working along the Nile, Hogarth developed a distinct disdain for ancient Egypt, which he expressed quite blatantly in his 1896 book *A Wandering Scholar in the Levant.* Though he admitted a certain appreciation for the Egyptian landscape, he found the art and architecture of the ancient Egyptians unexciting and rigid, in contrast to that of the Greeks:

> I know nothing more saddening than to pass from a
> study of Greek art to a study of art so-called in Egypt.
> Where is that pursuit of the ideal, that artistic conscience
> which inspires every work of the Hellene? Look up and
> down the Nile valley; look at the structures of Upper
> Egypt, the most part well seeming on the outside, but
> rubble and rottenness within, continuously jointed and
> casually patched, able to endure only in a land where
> frost and rain are not: look at the *gesso* laid over the
> walls to cover a multitude of sins: look at the back or
> any obscurer part of a statue, and you will perceive that
> the "artist" was influenced as little by any pride in his
> work for its own sake, as by a belief in the omnivision
> of his gods. Everywhere one sees temples incomplete,
> tombs half decorated, reliefs left in outline, inscriptions
> pirated and served up in hideous half-obliteration. The
> artists are no better than artizans, modelling and limning
> unconsciously century after century gods and kings and
> soldiers and slaves, according to impersonal conventions:
> twenty generations serve to produce a modification of
> but a single detail. The personality of the creator is never

once obviously instinct in the creation, and there is hardly a statue in Egypt that suggests for a moment individual inspiration.

Nor was Hogarth overly impressed with Egyptologists. In the same book, he wrote:

> It must be for want of comparison also that Egyptology is spoken of so habitually by its votaries as if there were no other archaeology, and that discoveries in Egypt are qualified by absolute superlatives. In the Nilotic mist Mycenae, Nineveh, and Pompeii are forgotten, and Hawara or Dahshur [two Egyptian pyramid and cemetery sites] extolled as the spots where explorers' eyes have seen the most wonderful resurrections of a bygone age; . . . To a greater extent than perhaps any other archaeology the study of ancient Egypt has fallen within the province of the curious amateur or the narrow specialist, little acquainted with any other scholarly study; and only of late has it seemed to be understood that some link with the modern world must be found, or Egypt will remain ever barren, a Memnon, as Hegel so finely put it, ever waiting for the day.

Though Hogarth decidedly did not acquire a taste for pharaonic art, it was nevertheless in Egypt that he learned some of the higher archaeological standards of his time, developed by Petrie. In a book describing a number of his archaeological adventures, he admitted:

> If, however, I had done little for them [the Egypt Exploration Fund], I had done much for myself. In those

three seasons, largely through becoming known to Petrie,
and living with men who had served apprenticeship with
him, I had learned to dig. When I set foot first in Egypt,
I had no method in such search, nor any understanding
that the common labourer's eyes and hand and purpose
must be extensions of one's own. . . .
Moreover, in handling remains of imperishable antiquity
in the Nile land, I learned to observe as an antiquary
must. And some of his spirit was breathed into me.
. . . But I was not to be won to Egyptian studies at the
eleventh hour.

It was also in Egypt that he had the opportunity to develop
skills with Arabic, which would serve him especially well later on
in his career. During the next several years, Hogarth maintained
a busy and varied career serving as a war correspondent for the
London Times, directing the British School of Archaeology in Ath-
ens, and excavating in Greece, Crete, Turkey, and at Naukratis, an
ancient Greek town site in the Egyptian delta. With a little background knowledge about Hogarth, I was now ready to review the
excavation itself through any sources I could locate, including his
notebooks and correspondence with Budge.

Back to the story of the dig. Now that permission was obtained
and an archaeologist recruited, it was time for action. Budge suggested that Hogarth be paid three pounds per day, round-trip fare
from England, and other travel expenses. It was anticipated that the
season's work would be completed in three or four months, and a
sum for all expenses was suggested at fifteen hundred pounds. The
trustees approved.

Hogarth's book *Accidents of an Antiquary's Life,* source of the
passages quoted last above, devotes much of a chapter titled "Dig-

ging" to the poetic description of his work at Asyut. In the context of a dinner conversation with a sophisticated young lady, he charmingly describes his trials and travails in a way that might impress, yet at the same time dissuade, his conversational companion:

> I was bidden to search the tombs in part of the hill
> behind Siut, whose soft calcareous cliffs are honeycombed
> with graves of every age. This vast cemetery, lying near
> a large town, has been ransacked over and over again,
> chiefly for wooden statuettes and models, which seem
> to have been carved at the Wolf Town more often and
> more cleverly than anywhere else in old Egypt; and I was
> warned I must hope for no untouched burial, but content
> myself with raking over the leavings of hastier robbers.

Furthermore, his mission was poetically characterized by him as "that body-snatching sort, which science approves and will doubtless justify to the Angel of Resurrection by pleading a statute of limitations. To rob a tomb appears, in fact, to be held dastardly or laudable according as the tenancy of the corpse has been long or short."

On Hogarth's arrival in Egypt, the limits of the concession were clearly defined in the immense tomb-pocketed mountain directly behind the town of Asyut, and a magnetically oriented boundary line was established from the mountain's base beginning slightly to the east of one of the decorated tombs. The British Museum was free to explore the mountainside to the west and fifteen kilometers north; the eastern side of the line was the domain of Schiaparelli. Unfortunately, Hogarth's hand-drawn map illustrating both the boundary of the concession and the tombs he was to discover was nowhere to be found among his papers. A letter sent to Budge, though, gave me clues that eventually enabled me to find it, improbably bound up in a book of official museum correspondence.

Hogarth apparently started his excavation on December 15, 1906, but before work began, French Egyptologist Gustave Lefebvre, the local antiquities inspector, pointed out where robbers in the last year had discovered an inscribed tomb door at the foot of the hill in the courtyard of a large tomb. Hogarth began at this spot and revealed, over the course of the next ten days, a tomb bearing inscriptions on its door lintels and jambs and containing a variety of objects in its fill. The tomb was given the Roman number I, and thus began a tomb-numbering sequence that would end with fifty-seven tombs "cleared with good result" by the end of his nearly three-month project. Tomb I was mapped, and others in the immediate vicinity were investigated as the general boundaries of the concession were explored.

Many excavations were made in the search for relatively unravaged tombs. In one account Hogarth estimated that "for every profitable tomb, at least twenty profitless had to be opened and, moreover, examined scrupulously. . . . " In a letter by Hogarth from Asyut on January 1, 1907, he wrote, "Meanwhile I began tombs high up the mountain . . . but, although again and again tombs were found which had not been robbed in modern times, they were never intact. The tombs lie in terraces, and it was not till we had worked systematically down to the third terrace from our starting point that we hit a virgin grave."

It was fun to examine the expedition's surviving salary ledgers, which provided insights and details. The size of the expedition's labor force increased greatly during the first three weeks. On December 15 there were thirteen employees; by December 18 there were twenty-seven; on December 19, forty; and by December 24 fifty-four locals were on the payroll. Overall there were at least sixty-three Egyptians employed over the duration of the excavation, a few dropping out and some working part-time. The average wage was five piasters per day, though one fellow, Omar Hussein, received six per day (probably as headman), and Gabr Seidan (perhaps a child) received three and a half per day. Achmet Hussein was paid ten piasters per day for his services and those of his donkey.

Bonuses were occasionally paid, presumably for exemplary service, for hardship, or as baksheesh. ("Baksheesh" means "tip" or, more cynically, "payoff," and some archaeologists in Egypt would reward their workers by offering a competitive price for objects discovered.) At best the baksheesh system was productive and effective, but it could also promote "salting," the surreptitious addition of objects found elsewhere. On December 24, for example, twenty-one piasters were paid out for the discovery of the missing fragments of a statue found in Tomb I. Petrie, the role model for archaeologists in his day, was a proponent of the baksheesh system and argued that it encouraged careful digging for the discovery of unbroken objects and for those that were especially small. Weekly bonuses could exceed twenty additional piasters. Faraq Ali Ali and Mussi Hassan were two of the most successful diggers for Hogarth, receiving an additional twenty-three and a half and twenty-four piasters respectively during the week of December 31, 1906, to January 5, 1907, which makes one wonder if perhaps they were involved in the discovery of the intact tomb found on January 1.

Early on, Hogarth expressed certain doubts of success in his concession. His area appeared to be exceedingly plundered and quarried and lacked the big tombs found in Schiaparelli's neighboring concession to the west and Petrie's to the south. In a letter to Budge, Hogarth wrote:

The facts militate against success here. The Copts in
the early centuries of the Christian era evidently used
this cemetery as a dwelling place, turned tombs into
homes and systematically robbed grave pits, etc; and in
very recent times—especially since Faraq's discovery of
the soldiers [in 1893]—there has been most thorough
plundering. I often find a dozen tombs communicating
by holes and passages made by these robbers who
worked constantly underground. But the most serious
consideration is the absence of the larger type of tomb
in our part of the cemetery—if one may judge by such
tombs as have long been opened. The central and
southern parts, conceded to MM. Schiaparelli and Petrie
respectively, seem to contain the larger graves. I have little
doubt that I can find small graves here and there intact
and of good period; but about large and well furnished
graves I feel much doubt unless M. Schiaparelli's
concession is ceded to me.

It is clear that Hogarth's ultimate ambition was to find intact
burials in large tombs, not at all an unusual goal in the Egyptian
archaeology of his day. This can explain the extraordinary effort
and stamina expended in the excavation of two large collapsed
tombs, Numbers XXVII and XLII. Tomb XXVII occupied his
serious attention from January 14 through February 1, as he dyna-
mited fallen blocks of stone. Teased by what appeared to be a shaft
sealed with palm logs, wherein "the dust from the [ancient workmen's] chisels still clung to the walls and floor," Hogarth persisted
and found the shaft essentially empty and unused.

Tomb XLII was addressed from January 22 through February 16, producing very little for the effort. Near the end of the

season, Hogarth wrote, "What has never been forthcoming during the season has been one fairly large virgin Middle Kingdom tomb, wherein both upper and lower chambers were well furnished. I have found virgin upper chambers and virgin pits, but never the two together . . ."

Such comments can be flabbergasting to the modern archaeologist, who would be more than delighted to have investigated Hogarth's many disappointments. He even comes off as impatient, if not a bit spoiled, but one must not forget that this is archaeology in a different era, with different methods and expectations.

Schiaparelli's concession expired on December 31, 1906, and Hogarth wrote to Maspero regarding this, presumably to request that the British Museum be ceded that territory. By the end of the excavation, word had been heard that Schiaparelli would be back, and Hogarth responded as follows: "He [Schiaparelli] would probably not exhaust it [the concession], if the results of his excavations elsewhere afford any guide, but he would, in any case, make it more difficult for anyone else to succeed by disturbing the superficial indications. On the other hand he may only do a little work, sufficient to retain his claim, and once more renew his concession at the end of the year, as he did on the last occasion."

Hogarth doubted that Maspero would react against such concession-maintenance games.

Despite his dismay, by the end of January, Hogarth had achieved a certain level of success in finding several intact tombs and others still containing a variety of objects. The unviolated tombs were often very small, with their doors blocked by tightly wedged stones, and tended to be "hidden away in odd corners of the cemetery, or cut in promontories of rock, which have, by their position, escaped the methodical subterranean progress of the native plunderers." Other similarly closed doors and chambers were discovered, but when opened they revealed that the tombs had been robbed from above, below, or from the sides, sometimes producing vast networks of communicating chambers.

Surprisingly, some of the larger plundered tombs contained more and higher-quality objects than did the intact tombs, which had the tendency to be quite small and sparse or common in their artifact content. Bemoaning the paucity of objects in the intact tombs, Hogarth wrote, "One [intact tomb], for example, opened yesterday, contained no less than ten coffins, all plain, but of the Middle Kingdom, apparently, and nothing else but rough pottery. On the other hand, two large tombs plundered in antiquity, and recleared by me in the last two days, have yielded three [model] boats with rowers, etc.; several wooden figures, and other objects of value."

Around the second month of excavation, Hogarth transferred the focus of his operations to the vicinity of Schiaparelli's concession boundary in hopes of making higher-quality discoveries.

Hogarth was very worried about thieves in the area, and he made note of several objects having been stolen. From Tomb LV, for example: "I hear that, in spite of my 'bakshish' system, there was some leakage to the dealers from this tomb. Two wooden statuettes are reported stolen, besides some small objects e.g. scarabs. Lying as this cemetery does just above Assiout it is as favorable a spot for intrigue between dealers and workmen as any in Egypt."

In *Accidents of an Antiquary's Life,* Hogarth elaborates:

Had I been an annual digger in Egypt, able to call a trained and trusted crew to Siut, and had the scene not lain so near a large town notorious for its illicit traffic in antiquities, that penance might have been avoided. And even in performing it one was robbed. Dealers waited for my men at sunset below the hill and beset them all

the way to town, and one digger, a youth of brighter wit
and face than most—he was half a Bedawi—gained so
much in the few weeks before I turned him off that he
bought him a camel, a donkey and a wife. The order of
his purchases was always stated thus.

Like a variety of other things done by many of the official diggers of his day, the competitive tactics Hogarth employed against
thieves cause the modern archaeologist to cringe. Describing Tomb
XXXIX, for example, he notes: "got into tomb at 3:30 p.m.—only
1/2 hour to get 8 coffins out."

There are several references in Hogarth's field notes to a certain
"R.N.," especially in regard to the documentation of tombs. For
example, in the comments concerning Tomb XXVI, a note reads,
"Plan in R.N.'s book." The sketch plan of that tomb had been cut
from elsewhere and added to the adjacent blank page. In all the
materials I scrutinized relating to the excavation, I found no clues
to the identity of this "R.N."

Quite recently, though, with the help of computer search
engines such as Google, I was able to finally solve the mystery.
"R.N." was an American named Richard Norton who served as
director of the American School of Classical Studies in Rome. How
he was recruited by Hogarth is unknown, but he must have played
a significant role in the project, despite never being mentioned in
the correspondence with Budge.

Reading through Hogarth's material regarding this excavation,
one feels his growing sense of frustration, the hit-or-miss process of
sorting through many hundreds of plundered tombs in hopes of
finding something large and unplundered but at best recovering a
few relatively intact yet pathetically furnished burials. There were
thieves in their midst and a seemingly better yet unexploited con-

cession next door. Hogarth's sincere desire to provide his employers with quality objects, too, likely contributed to his anxiety.

On February 3 he wrote:

> In the course of the month I have opened some twenty virgin tombs, mostly, to judge by the style of the coffins, burial, and pottery of the Middle Kingdom. From these I have taken out nearly fifty coffins, of which about fifteen are painted. As a whole, however, these virgin tombs with doors intact are small and contain little beside coffins (generally plain) and rough pottery. Bows and arrows and in a few cases wooden *ushabtis* and other statuettes, have been the only companions of the dead. . . . It is hardly worthwhile to find any more of the small types. . . . I shall bring home a considerable mass of antiquities from which you will be able to judge whether further search is desirable. . . . One can go on finding tombs every day and all day. The question for you to decide is whether the ten percent of these tombs which are rich, make it worthwhile to find the ninety percent which are comparatively poor, or have been completely robbed.*

Living conditions on the Asyut excavation weren't particularly luxurious, but not uncommon for turn-of-the-century excavators. Hogarth evidently resided in the decorated tomb of an ancient official named Khety, although it lay within the boundaries of Schiaparelli's concession. As he described, his evenings were spent in this

---

*Ushabti*s are figurines placed in the tomb to do the bidding of the deceased as symbolic servants in the afterlife.

huge grotto with storied walls, because the lower Nile
Valley is a thoroughfare of furious winds all winter long,
and tent life, a constant misery in Egypt, would have
been most miserable on the face of the Siut bluff, which
stands out into the wind's track, and is buffeted by all
their storms. Not that our wide-mouthed grotto, however,
proved much better than a tent. The north wind struck
its farther wall, and was sucked around the other two in
an unceasing, unsparing draught which dropped dust by
the way on everything we ate or drank or kept. Warmth
after the day's toil we never felt December to February,
even when sitting closest to the fire which we kindled
nightly with unpainted slats of ancient coffins on a hearth
of Old Empire bricks. The dead wood, seasoned by four
thousand years of drought, threw off an ancient and
corpse-like smell, which left its faint savour on the toast
which we scorched at the embers; and a clear smokeless
light fell fitfully on serried coffins, each hiding a gaunt
tenant swathed and bound, to whose quiet presence
we grew so little sensitive that we ranged our stores
and bottles, our pans and our spare garments on his
convenient lid.

It's fair to say that most archaeologists of today would consider
the burning of ancient coffin planks to be outrageous, but there was
certainly precedent for such behavior in Hogarth's day. In a letter
home written from Kafr Ammar, Egypt, in the year 1912, a young
archaeologist named T. E. Lawrence wrote, "Even our very fire-
wood comes from 24th dynasty coffins, and our charcoal brazier
first performed that office in the days of the fall of Carchemish." At

the time Lawrence was writing from the camp of one of Hogarth's mentors, none other than Petrie himself.

Hogarth's diary certainly verifies the fact that it was often cold and windy, noting both the state of the weather and his own health. And there were dangers, too. The threats of landslides and cave-ins occasionally presented themselves: "Success seemed to flee before us, and to pursue it was dangerous, where rock was rotten and screes of loose chips, thrown out from plundered tombs above, might slip at any moment over the only channel of air and escape, and condemn us to the death of trapped rats in a most unworthy cause and most unpleasant company."

One workman was half buried when a threateningly large bank of earth finally slipped while he was excavating Tomb XXXIII. While some large stone blocks in Tomb XXVII were being blasted away, cracks developed along the cliff, and what remained of the original roof collapsed.

Hogarth dramatically mentioned other unpleasantries, such as "the dim light of smoky candles in the choking dust-laden air of a narrow cell, which reeked of mummy clothes and the foul rags of fellahin," and further elaborated in a—probably exaggerated—gothic description of his enterprise:

> Crawling on all fours in the dark, one often found the
> passage barred by a heap of dim swaddled mummies
> turned out of their coffins by some earlier snatcher
> of bodies; and over these one had to go, feeling their
> breast-bones crack under one's knees and their swathed
> heads shift horribly this way or that under one's hands.
> And having found nothing to loot in a thrice plundered
> charnel-house, one crawled back by the same grisly path

to the sunlight, choked with mummy dust and redolent
of more rotten grave-clothes than the balms of Arabia
could sweeten.

Hogarth nonetheless persisted, and by the end of February he
had explored the whole of the "Middle Kingdom" cemetery within
the British Museum's concession. The lower part of the concession
had been tested and found to contain Ptolemaic and Roman graves
carved into poor rock.

The last field notebook entry, dated February 27, 1907, said
the expedition's final efforts were proving fruitless. The border area
and the lower section revealed only more late plundered tombs.
Addressing the director of the British Museum, Hogarth wrote, "In
my opinion, there is nothing whatsoever to be done further in your
present concession, which would be in the least worthwhile. . . ." To
Budge, "I would not advise anyone, unless he wants things Ptolemaic
and Roman, to put a spade into your part of the site again."

"A good representative selection" of the objects was packed,
and others, including unpainted coffins, "hundreds of common
vases, and other things not worth sending," were left in the tomb
of Khety II. By March 7, Hogarth had packed and sent off thirty-
seven crates of objects from the excavation to the museum in Cairo
for the expected division of artifacts with Maspero. Nineteen of the
thirty-seven cases were left at the Cairo museum, and apparently
Norton got a small share, too, which he donated to his school in
Rome. Maspero evidently was not interested in examining the contents of all the crates, and Hogarth urged Budge to consider making a claim for additional objects during some future trip to Egypt.
The eighteen remaining cases were repacked into twenty-seven and
shipped to England.

The cases reached Britain, where the objects were cataloged in the British Museum beginning on May 11, 1907. Altogether, about seven hundred objects were registered. Several of the wooden figures, models, and some of the coffins have been displayed over the years to an appreciative international audience of millions. However, there are still some gaps in the record. Despite several attempts to locate them, Hogarth's many excavation photographs have been lost. They would provide a wonderful addition to our information about his important project. Two images, though, survived by being published in his *Accidents of an Antiquary's Life* and provide tantalizing glimpses of a tomb's sealed door and the in situ contents of a burial chamber.

After Asyut, Hogarth would never again dig in Egypt, and his career as an excavator would continue for only a few more years. In 1908, he engaged in a reconnaissance of the ancient Hittite site of Carchemish in northern Syria, where he would initiate the first season of excavations there under the auspices of the British Museum in 1911. He seems to have had an interesting hidden agenda. The site was strategically located so that observations could be made and data collected in anticipation of a future war involving Britain and Germany with their Turkish allies.

Hogarth returned to Oxford in 1909, to become the Keeper of the Ashmolean Museum. Ironically, though much of his adult life was dedicated to archaeological pursuits, Hogarth is best remembered as a spymaster and as the mentor of T. E. Lawrence, the famed "Lawrence of Arabia." A student of his at Oxford and his apprentice at Carchemish, Lawrence served under Hogarth during the First World War. With the outbreak of hostilities, Hogarth offered his services to Britain in 1915 and was appointed director of the Arab Bureau in Cairo, the bureau playing a vital role in the gathering of regional intelligence and British diplomacy.

Then, following the war, he participated in the Versailles Peace

Conference as the British commissioner for the Middle East. Upon his return to Oxford, Hogarth's career continued with distinction, his leadership ability being actively applied to the university until he passed away in 1927.

Although it is true that Hogarth was not personally enamored with pharaonic Egypt, his sporadic involvement in its study left its own very special mark. And given the unheralded significance of much of his efforts, our appreciation is well overdue. Blowing up stones, engaging in a furious hunt for intact tombs to enhance a museum's collection, working fast and furiously, and seemingly frisking the dead, Hogarth finds a solid place in the history of Egyptian archaeology as a man of his times. The smug judgment of modern archaeology aside, he wasn't all that atypical of some of the better practitioners of his day. With Petrie as a teacher, he did a decent job given the standards of his time, an issue we will deal with again when we consider the cases of Giovanni Belzoni and Howard Carter in future chapters. Are Hogarth's notes an anomaly? Not at all, I would venture to say. There are no doubt many "lost" or unpublished excavations in museums and archives awaiting rediscovery and explication, with the potential of filling in yet more blank spaces in the vast quilt of archaeological inquiry.

And then there is the phenomenon known as serendipity. In this case a dirty piece of ancient cordage took me to intriguing places I never expected to go, and surprises of this sort are what keep scholarship fun and exciting. An old excavation at Asyut was a wonderful adventure for me. After all is said and done, both David G. Hogarth and the British Museum provided me with an enlightening scholarly journey.

THE CURSE OF
THE QUEEN

Archaeology is a wonderful way to learn about past times, whether it's done by getting dirty out "in the field," scrutinizing objects in a museum collection, or studying antiquity in libraries and archives. There are numerous ways to approach the subject, and it seems to have something interesting for everyone. I enjoy talking about it, and most people seem to enjoy hearing about it. Unfortunately, there aren't that many jobs to be had. I certainly didn't have one initially, but between mountain-climbing instructing and assorted other related employment I remained actively occupied in archaeology. There were, for example, the trips to Egypt, the cordage study, and the petroglyph survey, along with involvement in several excavations and research projects in museums.

I also taught a few classes and did some tutoring while I myself was being tutored through Sir Alan Gardiner's mighty *Egyptian Grammar*. In the latter I was nicely assisted by an Egyptologist living in Seattle, Emily Teeter, who was working on her Ph.D.

dissertation for the University of Chicago. Emily was absolutely passionate about the subject and agreed to help me work through the intimidating chapters of Gardiner's masterpiece, which I had begun on my own without checks or supervision. The book quickly displayed its reputation, and in the process of struggling through it I learned about paying attention to obscure details and the importance of reading the fine print. Emily knew the *Grammar* chapter and verse, literally, and as we worked through the increasingly difficult exercises, the occasional glint in her eye revealed that she, like many before her, had been tricked from time to time by the subtleties in the hieroglyphic text.

I really enjoyed all this, but at one point I was offered some sage advice. If I wanted to continue seriously in archaeology, I would need to return to school and earn a doctorate, the so-called union card of the professional scholar. The thought was unappealing. I had no interest in repeating anything like the Big University experience, but my counseling was correct: If I had ambitions of teaching and conducting my own excavations, a master's degree was insufficient. I looked long and hard and eventually found a school with a program that seemed better matched to my personality and that could accommodate my specific interests.

The "Union," as it was referred to by its faculty, was a radically different approach to a doctoral program. It had its origins as a 1960s educational experiment within the bounds of a major state university system and eventually took on a life of its own. The school looked at itself as "progressive," with the aim of improving and restructuring what it considered to be the many inadequacies of traditional Ph.D. programs. The Union was strident in maintaining its approach, refusing to bend its agenda even at the cost of being marginalized. Eventually the school did modify its ways, but just enough to achieve formal accreditation, which is the stamp of legitimacy for any college or university.

What the Union offered was a flexible model for a doctoral program that retained most of the components of a traditional structure with several innovative changes. The school also had its own additional requirements, including an internship and demonstrations of personal and professional development. The approach was highly interdisciplinary and cleverly demanded the recruiting of two outside scholars not affiliated with the Union to participate in one's program. As an archaeologist "cross-training" in Egyptology, I found two such committee members: Dr. Mark Papworth, an archaeologist who taught at The Evergreen State College, a radical school not unlike the Union, and Dr. David Lorton, a brilliant but somewhat reclusive Egyptologist. They, with the rest of my committee, were overwhelmingly supportive and encouraging, and although I certainly wouldn't recommend the Union for everyone, it was well suited for me, and it demanded excellence.

I eventually accomplished my many requirements, and, with degree in hand, it was time to initiate my own project, the theme of which was described in the first chapter of this book: an exploration of undecorated tombs in Egypt's Valley of the Kings. Pacific Lutheran University served as my institutional base camp, and I put together a formal proposal for consideration by the Egyptian Antiquities Organization. The paperwork was facilitated in Cairo by the American Research Center in Egypt, an organization that promotes and facilitates scholarship in that country.

For my first field season in the valley, I put together a small and diverse team. Apart from myself, there was Mark Papworth from my Ph.D. committee and Paul Buck, my buddy from my first fieldwork in the Fayyum. He, too, had recently finished his doctoral program. And then there was Dr. Garth Alford, a scholar of the ancient Near East with a vast knowledge of ancient languages and art, who had been teaching at Pacific Lutheran. It was a small and competent team with a wide range of interests and skills, but it would get even smaller.

When it was time to leave for the excavation, the team had been reduced to only two: myself and Papworth. Paul had been offered a high-paying summer job surveying petroleum-stained beaches on the Alaskan coast in the aftermath of the famous *Exxon Valdez* oil spill. Garth? He just couldn't make it. So it was just me and Papworth, and it actually worked out quite well.

Papworth had long been something of a renegade. In graduate school at the University of Michigan, he and fellow archaeologist Lewis Binford turned archaeology upside down by instigating a theoretical revolution that became known as the "New Archaeology." Confronting the long-term inadequacies of American archaeology, their anthropological approach emphasized explaining the past rather than merely describing it, and the discipline has never been the same. It was Binford, however, who published profusely and remains one of the best-known theorists among archaeologists today. In a book entitled *An Archaeological Perspective*, Binford credits Papworth as the cofounder of this revolution, but Mark was rarely remembered as having even been involved, except by those who recall his role as noted in the book.

Papworth eventually felt that the New Archaeology had been taken too far, misapplying many concepts in its overembrace of anthropology. The change from the somewhat sterile earlier approaches was certainly refreshing, but the New Archaeology swung like a pendulum, slowly working its way back toward the center as archaeologists begin to critique and reassess. Ultimately Binford became very famous in the archaeological world and made a career of developing the New Archaeology while Papworth drifted into relative obscurity.

Papworth landed a job at Oberlin College in Ohio and later became one of the early faculty members at The Evergreen State College in Washington State, a freethinking experiment in higher education, where he fit right in and from where he eventually retired after teaching there for well over two decades. Apart from teaching, Papworth was heavily involved in the world of forensic anthropology. With a background that included anatomy, he routinely worked as a deputy coroner on horrific crime cases in which he applied his expertise to the examination of human remains, including the infamous Green River serial murders in the 1980s and '90s. Mark treated crime scenes as archaeological sites of relatively recent age and occasionally trained investigators with associated skills in order to extract as many clues as possible. He got a lot of satisfaction when his efforts resulted in social justice, but at the same time the disturbing nature of this sideline was cumulative and sometimes wore on him heavily.

Before we ever met, Papworth was described to me as a colorful, super-smart, fun, eccentric character, all of which proved true. On our first meeting, he struck me as a lunatic-fringe genius, spilling over with advice and enthusiasm and easily dropping quotes from early archaeological explorers and theorists. With a knack for theatrics and good-natured hyperbole, Papworth could be both brilliant and wildly entertaining. He was reluctant to talk about his past, but every so often, during some random moment, he would claim that he'd worked as a young sailor on a barge in the Great Lakes or that he'd served as "a towel boy in Maisey's House of Delights," an establishment about whose services one could only guess. Much to my amusement, at a moment's notice he could transform himself into any number of improvised characters. Once

I suggested that he fold his hat up on each side in the manner of a cowboy. He gave it a try and immediately became a satirical version of a North American archaeological professional. "I'm gonna spend the summer up at Mesa Verd', yup!" he carried on in his best turnip-truck-driver accent, referring to the famous Anasazi ruins in the Southwest. "I'm gonna be a site supervisor—it's my fifteenth year!" And then immediately, with a straight face, he would express his disdain for the monotony of uncovering yet another Hopi dwelling or ancient fire pit No. 123564. "The ideal archaeologist," he explained indignantly, "wears size-fifty-four overalls and a size-three hat!"

Most of Papworth's fieldwork had taken place in North America, but he was no stranger to Egypt. In the early 1960s, he participated in the great international rescue operation to save the ancient remains of Nubia in the far south of Egypt, doomed to be submerged beneath the waters rising behind the newly built Aswan Dam. The Egyptians were faced with a difficult choice, providing for the needs of the future with electricity and flood control versus saving the incredible record of the past that would be destroyed in the process. Modernity won out, but salvage operations did their best in recovering what they could, including the dismantling and relocation of several temples and the documentation of a tremendous number of ancient burials and settlements.

When I mentioned to Papworth that I was interested in working in the Valley of the Kings, he was immediately enthralled and offered his expertise to the project. Grateful for his quarter century of archaeological experience beyond mine and respecting him as a friend, I welcomed Mark aboard. Among other positive traits, he had a special way with the Egyptian workmen, of whom he was very fond. They in turn adored him, bestowing upon him the name "Abu Rumaadi," meaning "father of the gray," referring to his white hair. When he was unable to return for our third field season, there were visible tears in the eyes of our workmen.

Archaeological work can be quite expensive. In the case of Egypt, foreign archaeologists are expected to pay all their own expenses from beginning to end. There are plane tickets to buy, equipment to purchase, workmen to hire, vehicles to rent, plus room and board. I was very fortunate to have private funding from a wonderful couple in Los Angeles who gave generously to several major schools with programs in history and Near Eastern archaeology. A few years before, I had sent them a copy of my master's project on cordage and thanked them for sponsoring Dr. W's first work in Egypt, which at least indirectly benefited me. They invited me to meet them and took a kind interest in my research and career, then very generously funded many of my projects, including my first field season in the Valley of the Kings, for which I will always be grateful.

With funding secured, there were numerous preparations to be made. As part of the planning, I consulted with Kent Weeks, an American Egyptologist living in Cairo who was directing a very important and ambitious project to create maps noting all the tombs in the Theban cemeteries. The Valley of the Kings, of course, was a real focus, and already Kent and his Theban Mapping Project team had effectively documented all the accessible tombs there. As a first-time director, I needed every bit of advice I could get and Kent shared many useful tips from his wealth of experience.

On June 18, 1989, the momentous day arrived when I would finally be traveling to Egypt to direct my first big project in one of the world's most spectacular archaeological sites. Sherry and Papworth's wife, Linda, wished us luck at the airport as we left Seattle for London, and I recalled the words of Howard Carter: "The Valley of the Tombs of the Kings—the very name is full of romance, and of all of Egypt's wonders there is none, I suppose, that makes a more instant appeal to the imagination." What a great adventure.

Arriving in Cairo, we checked in with the research center and proceeded to the antiquities offices to receive our papers. All foreign expeditions are required to sign a contract that acknowledges the permitted goals and activities of their project and "spells out the rules." The offices of the antiquities bureau were located in a tall building in a part of Cairo known as Abbasia. Navigating its unbelievably busy floors was a challenging experience in and of itself, but we emerged successful and made our way by train to Luxor, where there were other offices to visit.

An American Egyptologist named Otto Schaden had recommended to us a small hotel called the Windsor on the east bank of the Nile just a block or so away from the river. The rooms were plain, and the price was right. A simple breakfast was served each morning, and the kitchen provided adequate lunches and dinners on request. We were also joined by Egyptian archaeologist Hisham Hegazy. He was perpetually enthusiastic and we were delighted that he could work with us for a week or two. We went shopping, bought some tools—including a broom—and, as described earlier, managed to quickly rediscover the lost Tomb 60 on our first day in the valley.

As thrilling as opening an ancient tomb might be, it signals the beginning of the real work. The initial excitement turns to the chore of routine archaeological documentation as it becomes time to carefully go through this tortured mess of a burial and try to make sense of its pieces. It can't be done hastily. The archaeologist has but one chance to do it right. Once the objects are removed from their position of discovery, the record is permanently disturbed. In the case of Tomb 60, we were confronted with a curious situation in which there was no guarantee that anything we found was in its original ancient context. We faced questions at every turn. That pile of little wrapped bundles, for example—was it a collection gathered from here and there in the tomb by Howard Carter in 1903? Or did those pieces remain in their original place, unmolested for over three thousand years?

One of the first things we needed to do before we could properly document Tomb 60 was clear the large rocks that choked the bottom steps and blocked the lower section of the doorway. Some of these rocks weighed hundreds of pounds, and we puzzled over the best way to remove them from their confined position without causing any damage to the tomb's steps. Our various "sophisticated" schemes all lacked some sort of practicality but were put to rest when the local village engineer, Reis Ibrahim, appeared with a wooden beam, a pulley, some rope, and a young assistant. Ibrahim never gave it a second look, descending into the pit and cleverly fastening ropes around the stones while the beam was adjusted to lean diagonally on a rock wall above. Within minutes the hefty boulders were gently rising out of the shaft, then swung out to the side to be unloaded. Papworth and I were extremely impressed, and it reinforced our belief in the secret of the ancient Egyptians' ability to accomplish the incredible achievements they had. They were masters of simple technology, and guys like Reis Ibrahim had inherited this ability to do a lot with little.

We also needed a protective door to fit over the top of the tomb. Ibrahim made a few quick measurements and assured me that a custom-fitted hinged steel gate would arrive and be installed soon. It did, rather quickly, and was mounted horizontally and flush against the sloping entranceway leading to Tomb 19. Entering the tomb required lifting the door up as if one were going into an old-fashioned cellar, and a lock provided security.

With the tomb now secure, we could begin the documentation process. Starting with the entrance, we divided the extending corridor into one-meter sections along its length and began photographing and collecting everything that might be found in the litter on the floor. Then we documented the little room off to the side, with the cow's leg and the pile of wrappings. The burial chamber was amazing, with the provocative mummy ever apparent. She was the last "item" to be removed when the rest of the tomb was finally cleared, and she was then installed in her new simple wooden coffin.

Curiously for an explorer, Papworth suffered severely from claustrophobia. On one occasion we visited the giant pyramid of Chephren on the Giza Plateau, whose entrance was discovered in 1818 by the Italian adventurer Giovanni Belzoni. In an effort to claim recognition for his efforts, Belzoni painted a huge inscription on the wall of the pyramid's burial chamber. I suggested to Papworth that this was something historical and worth seeing, and he reluctantly agreed to descend the long, stooped passageway that penetrated deep into the monument's interior. Mark made it perhaps fifty feet before I heard his rapidly retreating footsteps. I continued to the burial chamber, and when I eventually emerged into the fresh air, he was nowhere to be seen. A guard had last spotted him running across the desert in an easterly direction. I eventually found him on the other side of the plateau, calm and seemingly unaware that I was looking for him.

Working underground in tombs in the valley, though, didn't seem to bother him much. Perhaps they felt less confining for some reason, or maybe his fascination with them neutralized his fear. In Tomb 60 he spent many hours over many days, often on his hands and knees, patiently documenting and collecting the artifacts strewn throughout, while singing or talking to himself. He was especially fond of improvising episodes from *Treasure Island*, using the scrappy voice of Long John Silver to address me as "Young Jim" while adapting the story to two archaeologists excavating an Egyptian tomb. One needed only yell "Arghhh, Cap'n!" to resume the narrative. On one occasion I yelled a pirate phrase into the tomb as I retrieved something from its entrance, returning an hour later to find the newly instigated monologue still in progress.

It was not too long after we opened KV 60 that the rumors started. The rediscovery of the tomb had been a surprising event, and even the oldest local experts seemed to have had no idea that it was there. From those looking on, it seemed that a new, unknown archaeologist had strolled into the valley and found the tomb right away. There were stories, as one can imagine, about lots of gold and perhaps another Tutankhamun-like treasure. In reality, the only gold we found were a few tiny flakes the robbers had missed. If there'd been any treasure, it was long gone. Perhaps the most curious of the stories being passed around was that while our inspector, Mohammed el-Bialy, and I were first entering the tomb, two falcons circled above, suggesting an ancient omen.

Horus was a sun god often depicted in the form of a falcon, and the ruling pharaoh was considered his living embodiment. I, of course, never witnessed the event, as I was inside the tomb at the time, but it was reported to me quite seriously by the workmen. This disturbing sense of abnormality was further enhanced when just a few days later I had to be removed from the valley when I suddenly collapsed from severe pain, writhing on the ground and holding my hands to the sides of my head. Kent Weeks kindly loaned his driver to evacuate me from the valley to Luxor, where I was treated by a physician. Curses were suggested, especially when I didn't reappear during the next few days. Ryan had opened a new tomb, the tale went, and was getting what was coming to him. The truth was, I had a severe ear infection, probably contracted at a late-night going-away party for Hisham at a Luxor hotel. Being tired and nearly falling asleep, I had spontaneously jumped into the hotel pool in an effort to wake myself up. It had the proper effect, but several days later I suffered immensely from it. I returned to work, and the curse stories dissipated for a while.

There are very few examples of what might be called a genuine tomb curse from ancient Egypt. There is one inscription from an Old Kingdom tomb that threatens desecrators with being "strangled like a goose," but not many more. The Valley of the Kings is very well known, of course, for an alleged curse associated with the tomb of Tutankhamun. Much of it was fueled by the untimely death of Lord Carnarvon, who was Howard Carter's sponsor in the hunt for the tomb. Carnarvon was one of the first to enter the tomb, and he died in Cairo just a few months later, the result of a chain of events that began with a mosquito bite and ended with blood poisoning and pneumonia. There were many stories circulating, including that of an inscribed tablet bearing words that threatened the lives of those who disturbed the pharaoh. Several individuals who visited the tomb died not long after, and the legend continues still.

In reality there was no such tablet found. With King Tut's tomb as a new attraction, there were many thousands of visitors coming to the Valley of the Kings, and some of them would no doubt die sooner or later, whereupon the curse story could be dredged up as an exotic but misguided link to cause and effect. It was good fodder, too, for bored journalists looking for an unusual story.

The greatest evidence against the curse rumor is Howard Carter himself. Not only did he discover the tomb in 1922, but he worked within it for years, even removing the golden mask, a wealth of jewelry, and other precious items from the mummy itself. Carter not only survived the experience but did so until 1939, when he died of Hodgkin's disease. There were lots of others involved with the tomb who likewise did not succumb, some surviving for several decades after Carter. The stories are still repeated, and sometimes believed, leaving me amazed that a curse said to bring death has taken on a life of its own.

If there is any real ongoing "curse" in the Valley of the Kings, it's the unbelievable heat in the summer. We started our workdays at four-thirty in the morning, walking down the darkened Luxor corniche to the local ferry boat that crossed the river. It was usually quite pleasant when we began our work, but as the morning progressed and the shade began to vanish from our part of the valley, the heat would increase almost ten degrees per hour. At nine o'clock it would be 90, at ten it could reach 100, and by the time we left around noon, 120 degrees Fahrenheit wasn't unusual. Papworth regularly took note of the temperature, and at one point he was amused to see that a large thermometer posted in the valley had gone off the dial after 125! The limestone walls of the valley seemed to act as reflector ovens, baking everything within, both living and inanimate.

The sun will suck the water right out of you. You can live for weeks without food, but only days without water. Add the intense Saharan sun and your chances diminish significantly. As a moisture-rich grape is transformed into a raisin, the same happens to your body. Skin dries and wrinkles, and one becomes a human prune in the process of turning into a mummy. The earliest mummified bodies from Egypt, in fact, involved no special preparation at all other than being deposited in the hot, drying sands. Skin adhering to bone is what you find, occasionally with a healthy head of hair still attached to an arid skull.

The locals know better than to linger in the heat. They've known for millennia how to survive beneath the sun's inferno and dress up (rather than down) accordingly, to avoid dehydration and to seek relief within the coolness of their mud-brick dwellings, or at least under the shade of a tree or a tarp. In the insightful words of Noël Coward, "Mad dogs and Englishmen go out in the midday sun."

Dehydration is an ugly thing. Alone in the desert, miles from the nearest outpost, I have myself felt the effects. The body initially sweats to start cooling, and, failing that, the skin begins to turn dry. The heart beats alarmingly fast, and a sickening feeling churns the stomach. Physical activity diminishes dramatically, and the mind becomes blurred. A torturous parched mouth and an angry sore throat go without saying. Without rest, shade, and ultimately water, it's all over, sometimes within hours. The heat can sneak up on you, and we tried to be wary. Actually, Papworth and I didn't complain about it all that much, as we were just happy to be working in the Valley of the Kings.

While we're on the subject of curses, it's possible that I was indeed hit by another kind of curse related to an actual mummy: the woman in KV 60 herself! It wasn't the kind that attacks and leaves you for dead—it was another variety, that attacks and can possibly kill your career. Here's the story, for whatever it's worth.

Papworth and I finished up our work in the valley in early August, tired yet exuberant. On my way home through Cairo, I turned in a mandatory summary report to the antiquities authorities, including an album of photos of what we had found. There wasn't much publicity about the project, and my first major public description came out in 1990. At an Egyptology conference, an accomplished writer and editor named Dennis Forbes approached me with the news that he was starting up a new magazine dedicated to all things ancient Egyptian. It would be called *KMT* (the ancient name for Egypt, which can be pronounced "Kemet"). The previous year Forbes had heard me present an entertaining lecture on the life and times of the British Egyptologist

Wallis Budge and wondered if I might be interested in writing it up for his new endeavor. "I've got something much better than that!" I replied, and explained some of the details of our first field season.

My article—titled "Who Was Buried in KV 60?"—appeared in the very first issue of *KMT,* describing our work with some detail and best summarizes my position. When it came to the matter of the female mummy, I mentioned a very provocative idea originally proposed by Elizabeth Thomas in her *Royal Necropoleis of Thebes:* If KV 60 were ever to be rediscovered, perhaps the long-lost mummy of Hatshepsut would be found cached within.

Hatshepsut! She was one of the most interesting and unique individuals known from all of ancient history. When her husband, the pharaoh Tuthmose II died, the heir to the throne, her stepson, Tuthmose III, was much too young to take on the serious duties of the ruler of Egypt. Hatshepsut stepped in and assumed what was traditionally an exclusively male role. Her reign was quite successful and is noted for impressive building projects and expeditions to exotic lands. After her death, Tuthmose III eventually carried out a campaign to erase her memory by removing her name from her monuments and destroying many of her statues. His motives are debatable. It could have been personal or he might have desired to eradicate the precedence of female kingship. He even built a new tomb in the valley for his grandfather, Tuthmose I, and removed him from KV 20. In the words of Elizabeth Thomas, "It is merely possible to ask a question with utmost temerity: Did Thutmose III inter Hatshepsut intrusively in this simple tomb below her own?"

My conclusion to that question was stated as follows:

> Let it be clear that I am not advocating that the mummy in KV 60 is, indeed, that of Hatshepsut. Such an

unequivocal position would be foolishly premature. The Hatshepsut hypothesis is just one of several propositions for consideration, in this case, based on a cautiously posed question by Valley of the Kings scholar Elizabeth Thomas. Perhaps the mummy is that of another Eighteenth Dynasty nurse, or some other royal female of the period. There is an excellent chance that we may never know for certain. And if that is our fate, or rather that of the KV 60 lady, as scholars we have no option but to accept it.

That had always been our conclusion. There was nothing in the tomb to tie the mummy to any particular individual. Perhaps we might eventually come up with some other clues as our work progressed during future field seasons.

That was that, or so I thought. That same year I was pursued by a writer from one of the better British newspapers. It was amazing how he could locate and phone me when I least expected it. He wanted to do a story on our work and the mummy. I finally agreed, *if* he promised to mention that we were working under the kind permission of the Egyptian antiquities authorities and that we had no firm conclusions about the identity of the mummy. We had an interview, and I provided him with a picture of the KV 60 lady.

The story soon appeared, under the headline ANCIENT EGYPT'S LOST QUEEN FOUND IN HUMBLE TOMB. The article was accompanied by the photo I'd provided and included a picture of Howard Carter in relation to the history of the tomb. *I was appalled*. For one thing, it misrepresented my work. Worse yet, the writer had put me in a situation where the Egyptian authorities would be first informed about such a great "discovery" from the pages of a foreign newspaper. The fallout was almost predictable.

The story was repeated in other papers and eventually became the subject of a major article in an Egyptian newspaper, in which several archaeology professors questioned my legitimacy as a scholar. I was even working in Luxor at the time when the paper came out, yet no one had bothered to contact me to ask my actual opinion on the subject.

The paper included both of the pictures from the original British article, but under the photo of Howard Carter there was a caption in Arabic that read, "Donald Ryan: 'I am sure.'" In retrospect, perhaps I should have been flattered by the unintended comparison, but this was serious business. There was a chance that there could be major repercussions. So I went up to Cairo to do some damage control and out to Abbasia to speak to some of the authorities in person. One high official asked me about "all of this Hatshepsut business" and inquired as to the whereabouts of my original report from the last field season. It could have been used to straighten things out when they were approached by the press, he explained. The report, unfortunately, had been lost in one office or another and had as a result been unavailable.

My next stop was London, where I confronted the author of the original article. In an incredible blanket of bluff, his response was that the headline about "ancient Egypt's lost queen being found" could be construed in any number of different ways other than how I had chosen to interpret it. It soon became apparent that I would only be wasting my time waiting for any sort of retraction or apology.

I worried for months that I wouldn't be allowed to work in Egypt again, but, happily, all was well. And I would return again to the valley more than once. As for the mysterious woman resting in a pine box in Tomb 60, her "curse" was short-lived, and it would be more than another decade before much of her story would be credibly sorted out.

EIGHT

IN THE FOOTSTEPS
OF THE GIANT

A S IMPROBABLE AS IT MIGHT SEEM, one of the great pioneers of Egyptology, if not archaeology in general, was a carnival performer, essentially a circus strongman who through unusual circumstances arrived in Egypt in 1815 and after four years of incredible adventures left his mark. His name was Giovanni Battista Belzoni, and our lives would intersect in the Valley of the Kings, where his presence is still felt. He was the first Westerner to excavate there, discovering several tombs, including a certain KV 21, a large undecorated tomb containing the mummies of two women.

The story of Belzoni is curious indeed. Born in Padua, Italy, in 1778, the son of a barber, Belzoni grew up to be extraordinarily large—some say as tall as seven feet, but more likely six foot seven or so—and of considerable bulk and possessing amazing strength. An encounter with such a veritable giant in his day was no doubt notable, whether in the streets of Venice, or London, or Cairo.

Detailed knowledge of Belzoni's early life and education are a bit sketchy, but we know that around 1803 he left Italy with his brother, Francesco, to seek his fortune elsewhere than in the midst of the havoc of the Napoleonic Wars. England, isolated as it was from the European mainland, appeared to offer a safe respite, and Belzoni quickly gained employment at a theater in London, playing extra-large characters and eventually perfecting the strongman act that would keep him traveling to fairs and other entertainment venues for many years. Billed exotically as "the Patagonian Sampson," Belzoni, dressed in feathers and a tunic, or tights, could dazzle a crowd. A highlight of his act was placing a frame on his sturdy shoulders upon which up to eleven members of the audience were invited to climb aboard. The weight seemed to leave the giant sufficiently unencumbered for him to amble about the stage, nonchalantly waving flags in each hand. His wife, Sarah, and his assistant, James, facilitated the act and might have assured that only smaller and lighter participants made it to the stage for lifting.

Along with his feats of strength, Belzoni also distinguished himself as a well-rounded entertainer, adept at playing the musical water glasses, performing dramatic magic tricks, and orchestrating colorful fountain displays. One can imagine this gentle giant striking the little glasses with spoons while sprays of water erupted in time to a melody.

It was actually Belzoni's interest in hydraulics that brought him to Egypt. While traveling with his act away from his adopted home of England, he encountered an agent representing Muhammad Ali, the pasha of Egypt, who was seeking technology and innovations to modernize his country. Convinced that he had the design for a new kind of waterwheel that would revolutionize irrigation, Belzoni took a chance and set out for Egypt in 1815, with Sarah and James in tow.

The Egypt that met the threesome was an unfamiliar world,

and although Belzoni's invention was apparently effective, it was ultimately rejected, leaving the strongman from Padua stranded and unemployed in a very strange land. While in Cairo, Belzoni met one of the great explorers of the Middle East, Johann Ludwig Burckhardt. Hailing from Switzerland, Burckhardt had distinguished himself by traveling far and wide in the Islamic world, where few Europeans of his day dared tread. Adept in Arabic language and customs, and traveling in local dress, he even visited the sacred city of Mecca incognito to observe what few outside Islam had seen. Today he is perhaps best remembered as the one who discovered the ancient city of Petra in what is now southern Jordan, immortalized by the poet John Burgon as "the rose-red city, half as old as time."

Burckhardt had recently paid a visit to southern Egypt, and even farther south into Nubia, and Belzoni was dazzled by stories of immense temples buried in sand, colossal statues of ancient kings, and a seemingly endless stream of antiquities, neglected and ripe for exploration, if not for the taking. A friend of Burckhardt's who had a notion for collecting choice antiquities for his homeland, the British consul in Egypt Henry Salt, commissioned Belzoni to travel south up the Nile to the area of ancient Thebes, modern-day Luxor, where in the midst of the ruins of a temple he would find a huge stone head and torso, remnants of the seated statue of a once-great pharaoh. The beautiful quality of workmanship and its benevolent face would make a fine addition to the growing collection of London's British Museum.

With a permit from the pasha to secure the bust, Belzoni enthusiastically set out to retrieve it, a frustrating task that would introduce him to many of the cultural and technical dynamics of working in a place like early-nineteenth-century Egypt. Belzoni found the head as Burckhardt had described it, in a monument we now know as the mortuary temple of Rameses II. It lay faceup and, in Belzoni's own words, "smiling on me, at the thought of being taken to England." With great difficulty, and after weeks of effort, especially in terms of the suspicion and obstinacy he met with on the part of the local officials and workmen, Belzoni was successful in removing the bust from the temple compound and inched it on rollers to the banks of the Nile, where it would be loaded aboard a boat for the trip northward. A number of months later, the statue arrived in England, where ever since it has remained a prized feature of the British Museum's collection of Egyptian stone sculpture.

After this first success in 1816, Belzoni maintained a remarkable career in Egypt over the next three years, as both an explorer and collector of antiquities. He traveled far south into Nubia to investigate the magnificent temples built by Rameses II into mountainsides at Abu Simbel, discovered the entrance of the pyramid of Chephren at Giza, and made major journeys of exploration on the Red Sea coast and into the Fayyum and the Western Desert. In the process he collected an extensive array of antiquities, including a huge obelisk, which like almost everything else was eventually shipped to Britain. Most important for my interests, Belzoni was the first to excavate in the Valley of the Kings.

His initial efforts there resulted in the discovery of the royal tomb of Aye, the successor of Tutankhamun. Later he would return and find five more tombs, including that of Rameses I, Montuhirkhopeshef (whose entranceway was anciently carved over the top of KV 60), and the huge and beautifully decorated tomb of Seti I, the father of Rameses II and an impressive pharaoh himself. The last of these contained a stunning, nearly translucent inscribed sarcophagus of alabaster, and Belzoni and an Italian artist documented much of the tomb in beautiful watercolors.

Belzoni wasn't the only European collecting antiquities for

museums back home. The competition was often fierce and hostile, and there were some who laid claim to his accomplishments, sweeping him aside and taking credit for his ingenuity. Eventually Belzoni grew weary of the increasing threats and antics of his rivals, and he left Egypt for Italy in 1819, then returned to England in 1820. There he wrote a memoir of his travels under the ponderous but descriptive title *Narrative of the Operations and Recent Discoveries Within the Pyramids, Temples, Tombs and Excavations in Egypt and Nubia: And of a Journey to the Coast of the Red Sea, in Search of the Ancient Berenice; and Another to the Oasis of Jupiter Ammon.* The book was a bestseller, and it went through three editions as well as being published in French, German, and Italian. It was also accompanied by a volume of lovely hand-colored plates that beautifully illustrated what Belzoni ably described.

With his acumen as a showman, he opened a popular exhibition of Egyptian antiquities in London in 1821, with all the status of a celebrity. Much to his embarrassment, he would occasionally be recognized as the remarkable "Patagonian Sampson" of not so many years previous, but Belzoni had refashioned his life; he was now Belzoni, the explorer and antiquarian.

Within a few years of urban life, Belzoni's urge/need for exploration and adventure became overwhelming. No doubt inspired by his old friend Johann Burckhardt, Belzoni set out in quest of one of the great goals of early-nineteenth-century exploration: the search for the legendary African city of Timbuktu. In 1823 he first made an unsuccessful attempt by land. His second try was by sea, and he arrived by boat at the mouth of a tributary of the Niger River on the continent's west coast. Belzoni trekked inland and soon became ill. Within two weeks he was dead of dysentery, a common fate for many other would-be explorers in this part of the world.

Belzoni's widow, Sarah, grieved greatly and commissioned an

amazing memorial lithograph of her husband. The drawing features a handsome portrait of Giovanni in European dress at its center, surrounded by many of his greatest Egyptian discoveries, including the bust of Rameses II, an obelisk, the sarcophagus of Seti I, and the Chephren Pyramid. It is a rare and touching tribute, and Belzoni would not be easily forgotten. His exploits became legendary and were repeated in print, including a chapter in *The Book of Gallant Vagabonds* and as the subject of a children's book entitled *Fruits of Enterprise*. Within the pages of the latter, stories of Belzoni are told by a mother to her children, who are duly impressed by the explorer's persistence and strength of character. Even Richard Burton, one of the greatest explorers of the nineteenth century, sought out Belzoni's simple grave when he led his own journey into Benin in 1868.

My first encounter with Belzoni was probably through the pages of *National Geographic* magazine, where his role in the exploration of the temples of Abu Simbel was well noted in an article written about the salvage of those monuments from the rising waters behind the Aswan Dam in the early 1960s. A real interest arose, however, through the unsuspecting pages of a book titled *The Rape of the Nile* by archaeologist Brian Fagan. In this book, which aims to chronicle the abuses of Egypt's past by many of its early visitors, a whole section is dedicated to Belzoni under the title "The Greatest Plunderer of Them All." The book offers very little objective assessment, basically paraphrasing Belzoni's own published work and then passing harsh judgment on the man and his activities from the smug and comfortable armchair of the late twentieth century.

Rather than inspiring a sense of dismay and disgust, Fagan's book had the opposite effect on me. I found Belzoni to be an utterly fascinating character. My own father possessed a love of the circus and the "variety arts," which he passed on to me, and thus I saw Belzoni, at least in his early career, as a kindred spirit. As I read further, it became clear that the reputation of Belzoni as a "rapist of the Nile" was widespread, although with some prominent exceptions. The definitive biography, *The Great Belzoni* by Stanley Mayes, offered a detailed and sympathetic portrait of an amazingly clever, bold, resourceful, and very sensitive man with a genuine sense of showmanship and an authentic spirit of exploration. This is the Belzoni I hoped to find, and my own additional research into the topic verified my suspicion: Not only was Belzoni *not* the grand butcher of Egypt's past, he can be demonstrably shown to have possessed a sophistication well ahead of his time.

Reading Belzoni's own published comments in the only book he wrote, one can be struck by the detail he offers, including the laborious prose enumerating the dimensions of this chamber or that. And then there are the plates accompanying his *Narrative* book, which includes, especially notable for my interests, a topographical map of the Valley of the Kings, showing the valley from above and noting its subterranean features, certainly brilliant for its day. Likewise, his cross-section drawing of Seti's immense tomb, complete with a scale of measurement, surely demonstrates Belzoni's accomplishment of a degree of archaeological documentation that was rare, if not unique, in his day. And this stuff is all published, for those who care to look.

Not only did Belzoni show a precocious interest in archaeological documentation, but he possessed a mature interest in a wider range of antiquities, remarkable for his time. While most of his peers concentrated on the collection of stone statuary and decorated objects like coffins and such, Belzoni had an appreciation for some of the more ordinary remnants of the Egyptian past. A catalog of objects from his exhibition reveals that he retained such objects as that piece of ancient rope found in the tomb of Seti I and an ancient pair of sandals. What they lacked in glory, they made up for by relating the Egyptians of old to the common humanity of daily life.

But, alas, the image of a giant-size carnival performer coming to Egypt and carting away giant-size treasures from Egypt's past is almost too good a symbol to represent the excesses of the nineteenth-century exploitation of pharaonic antiquity. Belzoni became the all-purpose poster boy for everything that was retrospectively shameful and abusive.

Did Belzoni's methods conform to our own? No, nor can we expect them to have. Was he more archaeologically astute when compared to his peers? There is no question that he was. Should we cry over the spilled milk of the early nineteenth century, regretting that we could do so much better today? Cry if you like, but what happened happened, and archaeologists today can only hope that their own work won't be as harshly judged by future scholars wielding ways and means perhaps far more sophisticated than we can yet imagine.

If I harbored any doubts about Belzoni's capabilities in the back of my mind, they were quickly dismissed when I examined some of his materials kept in the archives of the Bristol Museum in England. Among the museum's collections are some of the original paintings of scenes from the tomb of Seti I that Belzoni presented in his exhibitions. Among this material was a watercolor that had never been published nor commented upon. On this sheet of paper is Belzoni's own imaginative drawing of the great temple of Abu Simbel, a cross section through the mountain of the temple and its chambers, complete with scale. It was a clincher for me and a clear demonstration of Belzoni's underappreciated brilliance.

I was once invited to Padua, Italy, to speak to a local group of amateur and professional historians known as the Amici di Belzoni (Friends of Belzoni). Well over two hundred years since his birth in 1778, Belzoni is still considered a proud citizen of the city, and the Amici were eager to hear about their native son as well as my work in the valley. Working through a translator, I presented a lecture that was enthusiastically received, and the hospitality surrounding my visit was impressive. I was taken to the great man's birthplace and shown memorabilia relating to his life and travels. At the end of my talk, I opened the floor to the audience and was asked the awkward question, "So, do Americans love Belzoni, too?" The sincere questioner was no doubt expecting an answer in the positive—after all, who couldn't fail to love Padua's hometown boy made good? I didn't have the heart to say that most Americans had probably never heard of him and that those who had probably looked at him as an infamous looter. All I could mutter was something to the effect of, "Not everybody understands him."

My opinion of Belzoni is not universally appreciated. On more than one occasion, I've experienced incredibly angry reactions at the very mention of his name, although I've noticed a softening of judgment in recent years. Belzoni was certainly a man of his times, but when placed next to a qualitative yardstick against his peers, he stands tall, exercising an astounding degree of archaeological insight in a time when there were no real standards for such.

My own interest in developing a project in the Valley of the Kings was partially inspired by one of Belzoni's discoveries there, a tomb now referred to as KV 21. The tomb was one of those whose entrances were invisible when I did my impromptu survey of the valley in 1983. Consulting his *Narrative,* I found the description of the tomb to be both enchanting and provocative:

On the same day [October 6, 1817] we perceived some
marks of another tomb in an excavation, that had been
begun three days before, precisely in the same direction
as the first tomb, and not a hundred yards from it. . . .
This is more extensive, but entirely new, and without a
single painting in it: it had been searched by the ancients,
as we perceived at the end of the first passage a brick
wall, which stopped the entrance, and had been forced
through. After passing this brick wall you descend a
staircase, and proceed through another corridor, at the
end of which is the entrance to a pretty large chamber,
with a single pillar in the centre, and not plastered in
any part. At one corner of this chamber we found two
mummies on the ground quite naked, without cloth
or case. They were females, and their hair pretty long,
and well preserved, though it was easily separated from
the head by pulling it a little. At one side of this room
is a small door, leading into a small chamber, in which
we found the fragments of several earthen vessels, and
also pieces of vases of alabaster, but so decayed that
we could not join one to another. On the top of the
staircase we found an earthen jar quite perfect, with a
few hieroglyphics on it, and large enough to contain two
buckets of water. This tomb is a hundred feet from the
entrance to the end of the chamber, twenty feet deep,
and twenty-three wide. The smaller chamber is ten
feet square: it faces the east by south, and runs straight
towards west by north.

Belzoni's published plates, too, show an accurate cross section
of the tomb, complete with scale.

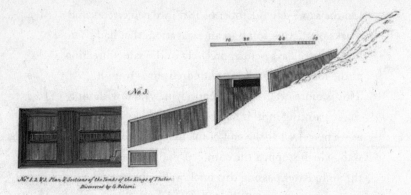

Belzoni's plan of KV 21 (which he here refers to as "Tomb No. 3") is accurate and evidence of his insight and skill as an early archaeologist. The plan was published with his *Narrative* in 1820.

A couple of other early visitors to KV 21 likewise offer interesting tales of mummies and pots. James Burton mapped the tomb in 1825, and provided the following comments: "A clean new tomb, the water not having got into it. Two mummies remaining nearly whole—females—some hair on the heads—distorted hand and foot—mummies in small chamber—vases entrails stopt with earth—large—common red pottery all broken."

The tomb was also visited by Edward Lane (c. 1826), who wrote:

This might easily escape observation being surrounded by rubbish rises higher than the top of the entrance. It is on the same plan as most of the others; but without any sculpture; being unfinished. We first descend[ed] a sloping passage then a flight of steps and next another sloping passage at end of which is a square chamber with square pillar. Upon the ground were lying two female mummies quite naked. On the east of this chamber same

side as the entrance is another chamber, smaller and
containing many broken jars . . .

Of course, these descriptions were all written before John Gardner Wilkinson came about and marked the valley's tombs, thus
initiating the present numbering system. Belzoni merely referred to
his new discovery as Tomb 3, and Lane and Burton used their own
designations: Tomb 5 and Tomb T, respectively.

Elizabeth Thomas's comments about the tomb in her *Royal
Necropoleis of Thebes* likewise encouraged my interest, and in 1983
I began a file housed in a blue folder bearing the title "Tomb 21
Project." I pursued every avenue of inquiry, including the archival
notes of those who visited the tomb in Belzoni's wake and the comments of the Theban Mapping Project. I typed letters to museums
and individual scholars and kept a record of responses, enjoying
every bit of related data, no matter how trivial or ancillary. I envisioned that KV 21 would be the centerpiece of what would someday become the Pacific Lutheran University Valley of the Kings
Project, and if it weren't for the unexpected rediscovery of KV 60,
it might have been.

In 1989, with our hands thoroughly busy with Tomb 60, I
nonetheless decided to at least locate the entrance of KV 21. At best
a small shallow depression less than a meter in diameter could barely
be discerned in the right lighting. In keeping with the unanticipated
theme of that summer of surprises, I was able to locate the long-
buried entrance of KV 21 in about ten minutes with the astute application of my trowel. With the depression serving as a subtle clue, I
approached the edge of the hillside where a tantalizing bit of exposed
bedrock beckoned me to initiate my search. Within a few minutes, I
exposed what appeared to be an artificial right-angle cut and, shortly
thereafter, the ultimate definitive confirmation of hopes: the num-

ber 21, painted in red by none other than Wilkinson himself during his 1827 survey. So there it must be, somewhere beneath my feet.

While the careful work of documenting and clearing KV 60 continued, I set a crew to removing the tons of flood debris that deeply obscured the entrance to Tomb 21. Prevented by tradition (along with practicality) from participating in the physical labor myself, I had to content myself with watching while seated on a wooden chair just meters from the action. My boom box nearby played a mix of Egyptian pop music and Edvard Grieg, the latter's Piano Concerto in A Minor being a favorite, as the sun arose in the valley, the concerto's opening chords embellishing the beauty of the sunlit cliffs. Howard Carter's hill of excavation debris, "the Beach," also proved a wonderful vantage point, especially when one was emerging from the dramatic confines of KV 60.

It took the team of at least ten workmen about a month to reveal the entrance to the tomb. Typically, one or two would wield crude local hoes to pull dirt into rubber baskets clenched between their feet. Once full, the baskets would then be passed to a line of workers stationed a few feet apart, who would in turn pass the burden down the line until it was ultimately sifted and dumped. The empty baskets would then be thrown back into the pit, making a series of steady clunks, their soft sides rarely annoying the diggers who were routinely struck by the flying receptacles.

There were a few false alarms. At one point I was convinced that the tomb's doorway was imminent, as the vertical rock surface we were following began to indent inward. But we were not even close. This feature of natural rock, though, eventually evolved into an artificially planed surface that continued downward. At the same time, we began to reveal steps, steps of which Belzoni himself seemed unaware. Eventually eighteen would be exposed, fourteen of which were carved into the bedrock and an additional four added in the rubble above. As we dug deeper, it became necessary to build support walls on either side of our excavation to protect us from cave-ins. We also began to notice that we seemed to be excavating an earlier trench dug to the tomb's entrance sometime before and whose outline seemed to appear on an old photograph. By chronologically following a deepening debris trail of windborne newspapers and other material that refilled this trench, we were able to date the tomb's last intrusion to around 1895.

As stated, it took about a month to reveal the top of the doorway with the continual efforts of a basket brigade. The tomb's door, surprisingly, was blocked with stones, no doubt the efforts of a post-Belzoni protoconservationist, and there the digging stopped. Mark Papworth and I had a conference. Well occupied and obsessed with KV 60, should we enter KV 21 or wait till the following year to explore its interior? The discussion was very short. Papworth was all for it, and with weak resistance from me, the decision was made: We should take a look inside so we would at least have an idea of what we might need to plan for in the following field season. Only enough stones from the crude stone wall were removed to allow the passage of a single archaeologist, namely me.

Entering KV 21 was indeed a remarkable experience. Here was the tomb that had originally inspired my interest in working in the Valley of the Kings. Here was the tomb that had haunted my sleep, including one memorable dream in which I finally entered the tomb, only to find a cache of Kent Weeks's surveying equipment safely stowed. "Time to take a dive," offered Papworth. "Go get it!" In great anticipation, with Belzoni's description running through my head, I stuck my arms through the small gap between the stones and began to crawl within. Papworth captured the moment on film, with only the heels of my boots visible as I slithered into the tomb's intimidating interior.

Local workmen uncover the ancient steps leading down to the
doorway of KV 21. Note the "21" painted on the wall, the result of
John Gardiner Wilkinson's tomb-numbering system in 1827.

I recall a very odd sensation. Although my flashlight was on
full beam, my surroundings appeared dim and disturbingly gloomy
as I proceeded to crawl forward. I yelled nervously back at Mark
but then discovered the cause: In all my enthusiasm for entering
the tomb, I had neglected to remove my sunglasses. Once I'd done
so, the surroundings became somewhat more inviting and interesting. The first few feet involved crawling over a tapering pile of
flood debris that within several yards allowed me to crouch, stoop,
and eventually stand up. I knew from Belzoni's description what
I should expect ahead, and, just as described, the tomb's walls
showed no sign of decoration. Of course I hoped to reach the burial
chamber and find the mummies he'd described, in place and intact.
Sadly, such was not the case. Before I even reached the end of the

first corridor, I noticed something that almost resembled a coconut in the dusty debris. It was the back of a mummified head attached to a partial torso. This was an initial portent of what I would soon find beyond.

Following the first sloping corridor was a set of stairs, steep and covered with rubble. I carefully descended its right-hand side, clutching the walls while I checked the uncertain footing, my light casting limited, mostly opaque views through the haze of kicked-up fine dust. Splayed out on the steps were more clues to the desecration: a mummified human leg attached to a portion of pelvis. The stairs led to another sloping corridor, whose floor was littered with boulders, a clear sign that Belzoni's clean tomb had suffered significant flooding since 1817, and at the hall's end some crushed mud bricks, indicating that at some distant time the chamber beyond must have been sealed as telltale traces of plaster around the door confirmed.

My first glimpse of the burial chamber confirmed what Belzoni and the early-nineteenth-century visitors had described: a rectangular room dominated by a single pillar. Along two of its walls were long niches resembling shelves, an unusual characteristic in the valley's many tombs. While the room's white limestone walls, speckled with natural flint nodules, were bare and unprepared for decoration, there were swaths of the ceiling bearing the marks of crack repairs, with the handprints of the ancient workmen still visible in the plaster. The floor was a different matter altogether, it being blanketed with the shattered, randomly scattered, decayed remains of burial equipment. The fine silt on the floor and the stain of a "bathtub ring" from flooding several centimeters deep around the chamber's perimeter told the story. Sometime after the time of Belzoni, the tomb had taken on rain- or floodwater, which turned this room into a slowly evaporating lake and woefully damaged whatever might have survived. And as for the two women described by Belzoni, I continued to find their body parts here and there. Most disturbing was a pile of hands and feet, gathered together by whom and for what purpose I did not know.

It was necessary to tread lightly as I explored this depressing room and then made my way over to a large square aperture in one wall: the anticipated side chamber. Peering inside, I was relieved to see that the elevated sill of the entrance had protected the chamber's contents from water damage. Unfortunately, other forces of destruction had been at work. The floor of this little room was covered with the well-preserved remains of a couple dozen large, handsome, ancient white storage jars, all shattered, their contents scattered about the floor. A big, heavy rock found in the midst of the shards told the story. It had been intentionally heaved into the mass of pots, perhaps in a spontaneous act of immature delinquency, accompanied by a rare and short concert of shattering intact Eighteenth Dynasty ceramics. Some graffiti on the chamber's ceiling ambiguously suggested a culprit: Scrawled in black, twice, was ME! accompanied by the date 1826. Whether these letters are the initials of a certain M.E. or merely a childish self-reference remains a mystery. We do know from the notes of Burton and Lane that the tomb was still accessible at that time, and any number of visitors might have made the descent with the possibility of unrestrained pilfering or vandalism. The torn-up mummies, the shattered pots, and the graffiti certainly demonstrated a profound lack of respect, and yet another agent of destruction, bats, had left deposits of their guano here and there as a kind of final, natural insult.

I clambered out of the tomb and described my experience to Papworth, who had been eagerly awaiting my return above. The two of us visited the interior of the tomb again the next day. Papworth was as dismayed as I was at the natural and human degradation of the tomb, and we both agreed that KV 21 would be a handful to clear and document. With a reasonable idea about what we might expect to deal with in the future, we installed a metal door, blocked it with stones, and returned our attention to KV 60

The beautifully decorated Twentieth Dynasty tomb of
Montuhirkhopeshef (KV 19) served as our "office" during
the first two seasons of fieldwork in the Valley of the Kings.

The excitement of that first year in the Valley of the Kings was irrepressible, and I couldn't wait to return yet again, the beastly heat and the array of annoyances forgotten within weeks. Papworth remained excited, and I added others to the team for our second field season, including two students and an art professor from Pacific Lutheran University. The students would be invaluable in piecing together shattered pots and coffin fragments, and the artist, Lawry Gold, would produce exquisite drawings of our rare decorated items. Our small team arrived in Luxor in May 1990 and I once again set up our office and laboratory in KV 19, the nearby beautiful tomb of Montuhirkhopeshef.

With much of the work in KV 60 completed, our efforts that year were concentrated mostly on KV 21. Additional digging was required to clear off and reveal 21's steps, and the members of our workforce, evenly spaced on the steep incline, passed their baskets, often in rhythm to some of their traditional work songs. It soon became clear that the tomb's ancient exterior steps would need to be protected, as they certainly wouldn't be able to stand the wear and tear that would be exacted upon them as we began to excavate its interior.

Papworth, who possessed the building skills I do not, designed a set of wooden stairs that would fit directly over the originals. The local carpenters, operating from what resembled a medieval workshop, skillfully produced the steps, which fit perfectly and were still intact nearly twenty years later. Papworth likewise would soon order up another set for the interior stairs, which not only preserved their friable limestone edges but were an important safety measure for the constant traffic that would soon materialize as we cleared the burial chamber. I was delighted to discover one day that Papworth had installed a sign on top of these steep steps reading SPEED LIMIT, 70 MPH, NO PASSING NEXT 2 MILES.

Another improvement was the installation of electric lighting throughout the tomb. A line of cable was run along the tomb's walls, and, with the help of the resourceful valley electricians, lightbulbs were spliced in at intervals, providing a wonderfully well-lit environment for working. The cable extended for a hundred yards across the landscape, where it was tied into another tomb's electrical system.

As the exterior steps were cleared, the full extent of the doorway, which was mostly blocked with stone, was finally revealed, and we left the lower courses intact to the level of the sloping debris inside. At one point while I sat on the bottommost step examining the lower blockage, half of the remaining wall collapsed, just barely missing me, and, curiously, in its wake were revealed specks of gold flake, which, as in the case of KV 60, were likely residue from the work of ancient robbers.

The first corridor was readily cleared, with only a few objects found within the debris, including a crude servant or *ushabti* figurine characteristic of the time of Rameses VI. Given that everything else about the tomb screamed Eighteenth Dynasty in date, this Twentieth Dynasty intruder must have come in with the exterior debris, a phenomenon not uncommon in the valley.

From an archaeological standpoint, the second staircase and corridor were easy to deal with, the operation being mostly an exercise in removing a lot of stones either in baskets or individually on the shoulders of the sturdy workmen. The burial chamber, though, was another matter altogether. The floor was photographed and sketched and then the larger rocks removed. As in Tomb 60, Papworth measured out a grid of one-meter squares around the room using a spool of string and numbers marked on little slips of paper. Thus prepared, we addressed each square systematically in its turn, often seated in an adjacent, cleared spot or on our knees. With a brush, a dustpan, and a basket, any objects were collected and noted.

It was actually a grueling task. Despite the fact that we were well underground, the temperature was often over ninety degrees Fahrenheit, slowing us down and contributing heavily to lethargy. More serious was the poisonous combination of the fine silt on the floor mixed with the pungent debris of bat guano. Dust masks were not readily available, and even when we had them, they made breathing so uncomfortable that they were often ignored. I preferred a cotton scarf wrapped over my mouth, but even that proved stifling in such conditions. The result was that twice during our clearance of KV 21, I awoke in my room at night with a severe and terrifying respiratory attack, my heart racing and my survival until daylight questionable. Fortunately, a large dose of asthma medication seemed to do the job, and the lesson was learned. All future tomb excavations would thereafter require dust protection.

Safety on our projects is of course always a priority, and although it was easy to talk our team of foreigners into taking various precautions, it was another thing to convince the local workmen. Some refused to wear shoes, even when swinging their heavy hoes precariously close to their bare feet, and the inevitable occurred on occasion. The effects of the substantial heat, too, were always a worry, and many of the workers preferred their heads bare. Part of that problem was solved by the issuing of baseball caps that were gratefully provided by Quaker Oats, then the makers of Gatorade. The previous year I had brought a few packs of powdered Gatorade with me to the valley, and when an Egyptian colleague passed out from the heat, we brought him to a cool place and mixed him up a small batch, which proved very effective in his revival and rehydration. When I returned home, I wrote a small testimonial to the company in hopes of obtaining a few free samples. I didn't hear from them for months, until one day a truck appeared in my driveway and unloaded ten fifty-pound boxes containing large bags of the powdery substance. Five hundred pounds of Gatorade, perhaps enough to flavor a large swimming pool, accompanied by about a dozen hats with the product logo.

Obviously, we wouldn't be able to take the whole lot with us to Egypt, but I did distribute a number of the bags to my digmates to carry and also took the hats, which became a sort of collector's item. One of my workmen, a gentleman from the village who was probably in his mid-sixties, had apparently given or traded away his cap and pleaded for a new one with a ridiculous story that could easily have been concocted by a crafty ten-year-old. A small mouse, he claimed, came into his house at night and carried it away. His tale was so seriously and dramatically presented, complete with hand gestures and expressions of surprise and dismay, that he had me laughing hard. He got a new hat. And the company generously furnished me with more the following year.

The supply of Gatorade would last for years, and the workmen, with their well-developed sweet teeth, would occasionally mix it up in an earthen jar until it resembled a viscous syrup, which they claimed was utterly delicious. Some of my team had a difficult time watching as the green goo oozed out of the jar into clear cups cut from the plastic bottoms of mineral-water bottles. Nonetheless, our more diluted version of the drink served us well, its lemon-lime flavor greatly facilitating our consumption of the large quantity of liquids necessary to survive in such heat.

Despite the hardships, we managed to clear the floor of Tomb 21's burial chamber, which was frustratingly sparse in any artifacts that might shed light on the tomb's occupants or even the nature of their burial provisions. A few painted fragments of wood could be matched together, including some that bore the text of a routine funerary inscription. Par for the course in our experience, the portion of the inscription that would normally contain the name of the deceased was not present. As in the case of KV 60, no artifacts in the tomb would reveal the identities of its owners, except in the broadest of terms.

The little side room was both a treat and a nuisance. Working in its relatively tight confines was a bit of an annoyance, and the reality of the shattered pots all around was dismaying. The pots' contents were strewn about the floor, and, interestingly, much of those contents seemed to be soiled linen rags and little tied-up bags of natron, the white dehydrating agent used in the mummification process, no doubt leftovers from the embalming of the tomb's occupants. Within the mix were several seals bearing the stamp of the royal necropolis: a recumbent jackal poised over nine bound captives, representing the traditional enemies of Egypt. They had once been used to seal some of the large pots, whose style established the date of the tomb's use between the reigns of Hatshepsut and Thutmose IV in the Eighteenth Dynasty.

Mark Papworth had the gruesome task of dealing with what was left of the two women. In a strange procession that included a box of hands and feet, a linear plastic bag containing leg and arm pieces, and two cartons, each containing a torso, the workmen transferred the various bits and pieces from Tomb 21 to a large table set up in KV 19. Papworth was barely fazed. His years of viewing such things as a coroner and crime-scene investigator, though usually with fresher material, of more recent vintage, had prepared him for performing the inevitable sorting of the body parts. Each component was laid out and then matched with other fragments. The end result was unpleasant. One had a tragically damaged face and a bashed-in chest cavity, and the other was missing its head. And all that was left of the long hair Belzoni described were a few curly locks. One of the mummies smelled like dirty socks.

Intriguingly, the left hand of each of the women was clenched in a manner that some would argue is characteristic of a royal female pose of mummification, much like the mummy in KV 60. Papworth was convinced, too, that when the flesh and wrappings of the left arm of one of the mummies was articulated with its fragments, it was bent at the elbow. This is a clue that might address one of the many big questions in Egyptian archaeology: Where were all the burials of the many known women from the Eighteenth Dynasty and other eras of the New Kingdom? Could some of them have been buried right under everyone's noses right there in the Valley of the Kings? The name "Valley of the Kings" is actually a later Arabic appellation and doesn't define its complete history. We already know that a few royal family members and favored friends or officials were also buried there.

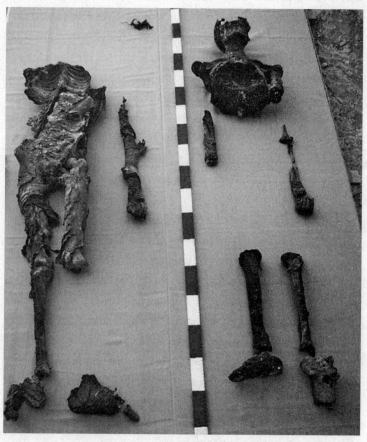

The horribly damaged remains of the two female
mummies recovered from KV 21.

KV 21, too, which in many respects resembles a small royal tomb, might also fit into such a scenario, and I would suggest that the valley does have a broader component of occupants, including royal women—queens and/or princesses—buried in the midst of the pharaohs with whom they were associated.

As he had done with the lady in KV 60, Papworth designed a wooden coffin to accommodate the remains of the KV 21 women. The local carpenters did a nice job, and as the heavy box was carried through the valley on the shoulders of several workmen and maneuvered down the tomb's steps, we couldn't help to think what a rare scene this must be, something not witnessed for thousands of years: someone actually putting burial apparatus into a tomb here rather than taking it out. The nameless mummies were returned to KV 21. One would lie on the box's floor, while the other would reside on a shelf above. "Bunk beds," we joked, but it was actually quite sad when we carefully laid out the pathetic fragments of each in their approximate anatomical order and then closed and locked the lid.

I often imagined Belzoni looking over my shoulder as I investigated KV 21. The valley must have been quite desolate in his time, except for a dozen or so gaping tomb entrances, resembling more a rocky canyon than a royal cemetery. Finding additional tombs in such an environment would require a real sense of the landscape and good archaeological deduction. Belzoni had both and was indeed successful, but after uncovering just five tombs, he offered the following surprising conclusion: "It is my firm opinion, that in the valley . . . there are no more [tombs] than are now known, in consequence of my late discoveries; for previously to my quitting that place, I exerted all my humble abilities in endeavouring to find another tomb, but could not succeed."

History of course would show that Belzoni's personal assessment of the valley was well off the mark, as close to forty more tombs would be discovered in the years ahead. His early documentary efforts are clearly to his credit, and he should rightfully take his place as a genuine pioneer of Egyptology and a protoarchaeologist who stood, both figuratively and literally, above his peers. The carnival's loss was archaeology's gain.

NINE

THE DIGGER'S LIFE

TOMBS 60 AND 21 WERE wonderful to explore and very provocative in their own ways, but there were four other tombs in our project zone that likewise required attention. Tombs 28, 44, and 45 were each known to be tombs of a design and size that were about as simple as it gets in the Valley of the Kings: a vertical shaft leading to a single, simple room. In comparison to what we had previously experienced, they appeared to be relatively easy to clear. They were each, though, in their own way, intriguing if not problematic, and we took all on with great interest. KV 27, with a shaft and four chambers choked by flood debris, would eventually prove to be the most time-consuming and difficult of them all.

The entrance to KV 28 was clearly visible, with a big red number readily noting its presence. Like so many other, similar tombs in the valley, its shaft was clogged with garbage, some of it windblown but much of it obviously deposited by employees of the old rest house on the other side of the hill. (The rest house is now long gone, and under the present conservation plan this kind of convenience dumping is absolutely forbidden and fortunately now rarely occurs.) I first entered the tomb by wading through a mass of cartons, newspapers, bottle caps, and entrance tickets dating back decades. Scorpions and snakes were certainly on my mind as I tumbled into 28's chamber, an almost spacious rectangular room about 9 by 5.5 meters (about 30 by 18 feet) with walls precisely cut into the limestone. Fortunately, no venomous creatures were to be found—that I noticed, at least—and I was amazed that the tomb somehow seemed to have been previously excavated. Its chamber was nearly free of flood debris, but for a layer of boulders and other smaller stones. Shiny black soot on the ceiling indicated that someone had been lighting fires within, perhaps to burn garbage or even to keep warm during a cold winter's night.

In terms of artifacts, there really wasn't much inside—a few pieces of wood, including one with some unreadable, incised hieroglyphs. There were bones, though, constituting the remains of three individuals, along with quite a mess of mummy wrappings. Curiously, we found a funerary cone mixed in the tomb's debris. These cone-shaped ceramic objects are typically found associated with the tombs of bureaucrats in the huge New Kingdom cemetery located on the other side of the cliffs from the valley. Their flat ends would be stamped with hieroglyphic inscriptions bearing the names and titles of the deceased, and their pointed ends were stuck in mortar above the tomb's entrance façade. Most of these exterior structures were made of mud brick and thus have collapsed through time, scattering thousands of cones here and there in the vicinity. They are quite valuable, as their inscriptions give us information about who might be buried in the cemetery, and, intriguingly, there are many cones associated with tombs that have yet to be discovered. They are also very portable and could be carried from place to place to be offered for sale (now illegal) to wandering tourists wherever they may be found among the monuments of Thebes, including the Valley of the Kings.

Tomb 28, then, in modern times had taken on a new role as a little storage depot for the souvenir hawkers of the twentieth, if not the nineteenth, century. Neighboring KV 27 served a similar function. One day I walked by that tomb's entrance and noticed Mark Papworth apparently engaged in a spirited conversation with himself. Such was not the case; he was just having a friendly chat with two local entrepreneurs inside, who had been napping away in the limited space between flood debris and ceiling, escaping the heat between bouts of relentless sales confrontations involving postcards, small stone carvings, and the other usual fare.

When we cleared the debris at the bottom of 28's shaft, we recovered a fragment of a small limestone canopic jar (a vessel for holding the entrails removed during the mummification process) and the shards of a couple of shattered pots. The shaft itself also retained a fascinating feature: Along two of its walls were carved indentations that provided foot- and handholds for the ancient workmen. One day I decided to give it a try myself. The holds, though adequate, were minimal, and the ascent was accomplished with legs widely stretched from one wall to the other. My climbing skills gave me the confidence to climb up and out, but a slip would have surely involved breaking at least one leg. The nimble and practiced ancient tomb carvers could no doubt scramble up and down such shafts with ease and little care.

Apart from its ancient history, there was also the question of the tomb's archaeological history. Who had discovered and apparently "excavated" this simple tomb? A couple of astute contemporary Italian scholars, Patrizia Piacentini and Christian Orsenigo, seem to have found the answer. Just a few years ago, they came to the conclusion that both KV 28 and 27 were discovered and investigated in 1857, by the celebrated French Egyptologist Auguste Mariette. Mariette, who established both the Antiquities Service and the national museum in Egypt, apparently briefly excavated in the valley but left no known surviving record of his work.

Despite the paucity of artifacts, KV 28 possesses its own austere fascination. Its location and architectural style appear to be Eighteenth Dynasty, as confirmed by its pottery. Interestingly, a single surviving fragment of a cartonnage coffin was recovered from the tomb's interior. Cartonnage is a style of coffin made from the application of plaster to linen, which can then be beautifully decorated. Our fragment, bearing the painted image of a lovely lotus flower, is more than just pretty, it's a major historical clue. Cartonnage coffins are characteristic of the post–New Kingdom era, very notably from the Twenty-second Dynasty, and suggest that the tomb had been reused well after the valley was abandoned as a royal cemetery.

We next paid our attention to tombs KV 44 and 45, excavated in 1901 and 1902, respectively, the latter under the auspices of the American millionaire businessman and lawyer, Theodore Davis. Davis was allowed to conduct excavations in the Valley of the Kings between the years 1902 and 1914, and during that time he made some truly remarkable discoveries, including the virtually intact tomb of Yuya and Thuya, the in-laws of one of the great Eighteenth Dynasty pharaohs. Had the tomb been discovered today, it would have been a world sensation, but its undecorated walls and indirect association to a pharaoh made it just another interesting tomb in Egypt at the time. Davis did find some genuine royal tombs—all robbed, of course, but royal nonetheless. It must have been a good life. He spent winters in Egypt living in his own beautiful sailing houseboat on the Nile, where he was joined by his friends, later returning to his spectacular mansion in Newport, Rhode Island.

Davis's most memorable discovery remains a true Egyptological mystery: an undecorated single-chambered tomb with the assigned number 55. Inside were found a curious assemblage of burial materials that seem to be related to the era of Akhenaten, the so-called heretic king whose bizarre religious obsession temporarily upset the ancient status quo. There were pieces of a gilded shrine belonging to his mother, beautiful canopic jars that belonged to one of his secondary wives, and a damaged coffin with the name of its owner chopped out. The bones of the accompanying mummy have been debated as to age, and even gender, and some have argued that it is the body of Akhenaten himself. KV 55 is still controversial, and several books and numerous articles have been dedicated to its discussion.

It was Davis's practice to hire professional archaeologists. Howard Carter worked for him over the course of a few years and, among other projects, supervised the excavation of three tombs in our concession, KV 44, 45, and 60. Of the former two, we started our investigation first with KV 45. Carter's published description in the *Annales du Service des Antiquités de l'Égypte* is as follows:

> It proved to have only a perpendicular shaft of about
> 3 metres deep, with a small chamber on the east side at
> the bottom containing a burial of the XXIInd dynasty
> completely destroyed by rain water. The burial was of a
> man and his wife, each having two coffins, two wooden
> *ushabti* boxes full of rough clay impression from moulds
> of *ushabti* figures and scattered remains of wreaths. The
> coffins had evidently been very fine, but they were so
> much decayed that it was impossible to remove anything
> excepting the face of the man's mummy case. In carefully

searching the debris of the man's mummy, a small black limestone heart-scarab was found, bearing the following name and titles: Merenkhons, Doorkeeper of the House of Amun. On the mummy of the woman nothing was found. This was not the original burial: the chamber was a third full of rubbish and, on our clearing it out, fragments of limestone canopic jars belonging to the former occupant were found, their date being probably middle XVIIIth dynasty, bearing the following name: Userhet, Overseer of the Fields of Amun.

Davis was present at the opening, and a couple of his companions left descriptions of the proceedings. One, Miss Jeanette Buttles, noted the recovery of a brightly painted wooden "mask" from a coffin, with inlaid eyes and eyebrows. Sadly, she notes that the mask soon lost its coloring and disintegrated not long after it was removed from the tomb. One of its inlaid bronze eyebrows fell out and was lost. An accompanying photo depicts Theodore Davis, decked out in a bow tie and walking stick, Miss Buttles in full Victorian dress seated in a chair next to the tomb and holding the described coffin face piece. Three other dapper gentlemen pose nearby. The foreman of the work crew stands tall beyond, a fez on his head and his men standing behind. The notebook entry and picture in many ways capture a prevailing attitude of a day in which a hobbyist could obtain permission to dig at will in a place such as the Valley of the Kings, employ an "excavator," and amuse himself and his friends with the excitement of whatever might turn up.

With this information at hand, we entered KV 45 anxious to see what sorts of leftovers might remain in the wake of Carter's excavation. What we found both surprised and appalled us. The tomb's floor was covered with a thick layer of dirt, and a large pile of debris remained heaped up against the walls. Protruding from this chaotic mess were human bones and lots of wood fragments, some bearing decoration. There was no visible sense of any sort of archaeological care. It was as if the excavation technique employed consisted of digging through the earlier flood debris, clearing half the floor, and then mounding up the dirt before reversing the process with the other half. The wooden pieces were no doubt fragments of the coffins, callously disregarded, as their preservation was in fact quite wretched. The jumble of bones represented the random mixture of the Twenty-second Dynasty man and woman, as well as the folks originally interred in the tomb during the Eighteenth.

Piles of earth filled with human bones and rotted wooden coffin fragments covered the floor of KV 45's only chamber.

The whole scene was dreadful, and we muttered more than a few disparaging comments about Carter's field techniques. True, he was operating in the early twentieth century, but even Belzoni seemed to have taken more care. Twenty years later Carter would find King Tut's tomb, and thankfully his skill level and attention to detail by then had improved remarkably.

We cleared KV 45, sifting every basket of debris passed up the steep ladder extending down the tomb's shaft. Nearly every one contained something or other left over from the burials, including countless fragments of wood, reduced by the rotting effects of the flooding to crumbling bits of charcoal. A few chunks now and again bore traces of colored decoration, some showing smatterings of painted funerary texts. While the face piece from the man's coffin had disintegrated as described by Miss Buttles, we were delighted to find the face from the woman's coffin, decayed as it was but, with a little imagination, still showing signs of its former beauty. And as for the bronze eyebrow that had dropped out and was lost, we found the other one.

Along with the rotted coffin fragments, we recovered over eighty small, crude mud *ushabti* figures pressed out of a mold and perhaps sun-dried rather than fired in an oven. These were the ones Carter mentioned in his report, and he apparently found them sufficiently ugly to abandon in a pile of dirt. I for one had never seen such things before, the majority of such items typically being made of faience (a kind of glazed ceramic), stone, or wood. Many were in fragments, and some seemed to retain a veneer of yellow paint. As servants to assist the dead, they seemed woefully puny and inadequate.

We found the remains of five individuals in KV 45. Two of them, a male and a female, were preserved differently from the other three, so the assumption was that they were the Twenty-second Dynasty coffined occupants, while the others came from the original burial. Theodore Davis kept the three canopic jars of Userhet from the original burials, and their fragments eventually found their way to the Semitic Museum at Harvard University. These jars come in sets of four, so we wondered about the fate of the fourth. We would solve that mystery over a decade later—and in the process leave more questions than answers.

The decayed wooden face from the water-damaged
Twenty-second Dynasty coffin of a woman in KV 45.

Just a few yards away, KV 44 is architecturally similar to KV 45 and was probably constructed around the same time. Like KV 45, the tomb apparently held Eighteenth Dynasty burials and was flooded to the extent that it destroyed these earlier burials. It was then reused during the Twenty-second Dynasty, with the later coffins unashamedly placed directly atop the debris of the earlier entombments. While even the later burials were woefully destroyed by water in KV 45, Carter found some amazingly well-preserved items in Tomb 44. In his own words:

> This Tomb-pit being already known to the reis of
> Western Thebes, I decided to open it, the work taking
> only two days to do. The rubbish being removed to a
> depth of 5 metres 50 cent., the door of the chamber
> was reached, and I entered on the 26th of January 1901,
> finding therein three wooden coffins, placed beside one
> another at one side of the chamber, covered with wreaths
> of flowers. These coffins, though untouched, were not
> the original burial, for there was rubbish in this tomb,
> occupying about one fifth of the space, amongst which
> were remains of earlier mummies without either coffins
> or funeral furniture. The sealing of the door, though
> complete, was very roughly done; and on the ceiling of
> the tomb were numerous bees' nests. Each of these coffins
> contained a complete mummy, and was inscribed with
> the name of the deceased as follows, commencing with
> the coffin nearest the wall:
> No. 1. Heavy wooden coffin, painted black, with rough
> yellow ornamentation, and inscription with red filling,
> containing a well wrapped mummy which had nothing
> upon it. . . .

No. 2. Wooden coffin, painted black, with rough yellow
inscription and ornamentation, the whole of which was
coated with whitish wax, eyes inlaid with glass and
bronze, containing a painted cartonnage covered with a
cloth, both being coated with bitumen. The mummy was
similar to that of No. 1. . . .
No. 3. Rough wooden coffin, containing a beautifully
painted cartonnage, with a flesh coloured ground upon
which was painted in colours the ornamentation and
inscription. . . . The mummy was wrapped in fine
bandages, but nothing was on it, except a pair of bracers
made of red leather, the ends of which are stamped
with an inscription and coloured yellow, bearing the
cartouches of Osorkon I. . . .

The intact coffins were removed from the tomb, and "No. 3"
is on display in the Egyptian Museum in Cairo. Its occupant is
named Tjentkerer, whose visage presents a lovely and poignant portrait of a young Egyptian woman. The whereabouts of the other
two coffins is presently unknown.

The Twenty-second Dynasty coffins may have departed, but
the flood debris containing what was left of the original burial
remained for us to examine. The pile of dirt at first puzzled us; its
surface was covered with what initially appeared to be rows of mud
bricks. They proved in actuality to be the result of symmetrically
cracked mud; the thick, fine silt deposited during flooding followed
by drying was what produced their deceptive appearance. We sifted
every remaining ounce of dirt from the tomb, and it was the extreme
lack of artifacts that was notable. Unlike its neighbor KV 45, this
simple tomb numbers only six items on our register of objects.

What KV 44 lacked in artifacts, it more than made up for in

human remains. What were once several wrapped mummies had through the destructive processes of water and mud become a large collection of bones. Our project's physical anthropologist, my former professor Daris Swindler, made an initial assessment and determined that there were several individuals represented, including teens and some children. Years later, when Jerome Cybulski took a much more detailed look, he came to a startling conclusion: KV 44 contained the remains of thirteen individuals, eight of whom were infants, another being a six- or seven-year-old girl, and the other four being young women in their teens or early twenties. What had happened? Was this a family burial in which individuals were added as they passed away? Or was there some sort of catastrophe, perhaps an epidemic, that tragically took all at once? There is certainly a story there that at present awaits further exploration.

Forensic anthropologist Dr. Jerry Cybulski, assisted by
student Katie Hunt, sorting and analyzing the many human bones
from KV 44 in a lab set up in the burial chamber of KV 21.

The situation inside tomb KV 27 made the other tombs seem almost simple in comparison. Its shaft was mostly encumbered with dirt and garbage, and its four rooms were filled nearly to the ceiling with the debris from numerous episodes of flooding. It was a daunting challenge, and we purposefully left it for last, postponing the inevitable chore. To further discourage us, for a while at least, a vicious, protective mother dog guarded its entrance from intruders, her litter of puppies yipping in a back chamber. As a result it became necessary to make a wide detour around the tomb's entrance, lest the snarling creature emerge and present a genuine threat. We observed that the dog left the tomb at least twice a day to beg scraps of food from tourists near the old rest house, and at one point we decided that we would have to make a move. As Mama jogged away for her lunch, we entered the tomb and collected the puppies. A couple of our younger workmen volunteered to take them home to their village and uncharacteristically raise them as tame pets. Mom of course returned and was sufficiently angry and aggressive for a few days. But another litter was no doubt soon on the way, and she finally left, perhaps finding a home in yet another abandoned grotto.

We dug test pits in each of KV 27's four rooms to determine the depth of the deposit and to assist in future planning. This also enabled us to make a map of its interior features. One of the pits, in a room we labeled C, produced a sample of pottery that provided at least a tentative date—as expected, in the mid-Eighteenth Dynasty—that generally fits with the other tombs we were studying. But given its complicated nature, clearing KV 27 would eventually involve nearly four field seasons.

In 1993 we decided to dedicate several weeks to exploring conservation issues in the valley. It was a serious topic of general discussion at the time, and we felt we should make a contribution.

Heading up this study survey was John Rutherford, a structural engineer who had worked in the valley in the late 1970s and knew the place quite well. There were numerous tomb-damage variables to consider, and the kind inflicted by flooding certainly stood out as the most threatening. The valley serves as great natural drainage for the surrounding slopes, and a rare cloudburst above the Theban mountains can send fierce, churning torrents of water into the tombs below. With surveying instruments, Rutherford supervised our mapping of the valley's rim, taking note of hydrological patterns to assist in our threat evaluations.

We developed a study matrix in which each tomb could be assessed for a number of potentially destructive natural agents, including flooding. We visited nearly every accessible tomb in the valley, both large and small, and some, including KV 60, seemed relatively immune. Others, though, including KV 7, the tomb of the great pharaoh Rameses II, made the devastation in Tomb 27 look almost negligible. Rameses' tomb is immense, and those who aimed to explore it had to tunnel through corridors and chambers encumbered to the ceiling, the once beautifully decorated walls scoured by flood debris. We could see chunks of painted plaster embedded in the mess and were intimidated by the mere thought of clearing and documenting a tomb of such size and condition. The burial chamber, a large room with a vaulted ceiling and crumbling pillars, presented a sad and haunting, if not scary, appearance. Two of the most stunning surviving tombs in Egypt belong to Rameses' father, Seti I, and Rameses' wife, Nefertari. In its pristine state, KV 7 likely surpassed them both in beauty, but the power of nature easily surpassed that of even Rameses, leaving his tomb in utter ruin. (Fortunately, a dedicated French expedition has since taken on the immense burden of addressing the tomb, documenting and preserving that which can be salvaged.)

There was also concern about cracks appearing here and there in the valley's tombs. In the decorated tombs, cracks can severely damage beautiful paintings and, in the most extreme cases, cause pillars and ceilings to collapse. Water, too, can play a major role in all this, as the valley's limestone bedrock and underlying shale both swell when drenched by rain or flood. The process of soaking and swelling, cracking and drying, can leave a tomb in ruins. For our part we installed "crack monitors" in three of our tombs for long-term observation. The monitors are devices that are glued over a preexisting crack whose crosshairs lined up on a grid will detect any movement in the rock.

In 1994, the very year after our conservation study, a long-feared event occurred when a flood rampaged through the valley. There was damage to be sure (although not to the tombs we investigated), and there were lessons to be learned and a genuine call to action. In its aftermath many tomb entrances have been protected, and an impressive master conservation plan for the Valley of the Kings is well under way. Much of this is owed to the cooperative work of the Theban Mapping Project and the Egyptian antiquities authorities. The former spent years mapping the valley, collecting all known data on the tombs, monitoring their conditions, and facilitating a careful long-term strategy. As a result the valley's still-very-fragile tombs have a much greater chance of survival than ever before.

LEST ONE GET the idea that a digger's life in the Valley of the Kings is all work and heat, there are plenty of things to do in whatever spare time one might have. I personally like to explore the incredible number of ancient monuments in the Luxor area, and I especially enjoy hiking in the desert mountains. My favorite excursion ascends the pyramid-like peak called "the Gurn," which rises high above the Valley of the Kings. The view from its top is stunning: The stark contrast between the cultivated land and the desert, with the Nile separating the urban from the rural. The desolate desert valleys to the west, a Coptic monastery to the south, and the Valley of the Kings to the north. Many of the great West Bank monuments are visible, and across the river one can see the massive temples of Luxor and Karnak.

There are a number of trails in the Theban hills, some of which are quite popular with trains of tourists astride donkeys. On one occasion I thought it would be fun to own and raise my own donkey. I found an endearing little fellow on sale for about twenty-five dollars and kept him in a village at the home of two young brothers who worked with me. I named him Monkeyshines, and he was rather cute, as most baby animals are. He was much too small to ride, so, unlike many of his hardworking comrades who bore passengers or pulled carts, he had it easy. A maiden voyage across to the Valley of the Kings was a must, but the distance from the village to the trailhead was a bit far for the four-legged beginner. My driver, Shattah, rebelled when I suggested that we give Monkeyshines a lift for a few miles in the back of his new van. "He'll make a mess!" he complained, but finally agreed. Within minutes Shattah's prediction came true.

Monkeyshines was a good sport and seemed to enjoy the mountain hiking. When we reached the valley, Shattah hid his van off the road in fear that potential passengers might see us reloading the donkey into the vehicle.

At the end of the field season, I bade what I thought was a temporary adieu to my little buddy, but when I returned the following year, he was gone. "We ate him!" claimed his young keepers with a smirk. I didn't believe them. I've never heard of anyone eating donkey meat in Egypt. I suspect they sold or traded him for one necessity or another.

And if trails, donkeys, tombs, and temples aren't enough, there is the city of Luxor itself, a world of its own, with its busy urban streets and many luxury hotels. From the city's location on the east bank of the Nile, one can comfortably gaze west across the river to a radically different land of villages, fields, and ancient cemeteries. A huge number of cruise ships can be found moored along the riverside avenue or "corniche," sometimes four abreast, while buses loaded with tourists disgorge their passengers or move them on.

Luxor seems to have two faces, one that caters to tourists and another that maintains itself as a typical, large Egyptian town. In the former capacity, it can be as obnoxious as the Giza Plateau once was, with aggressive taxi and carriage drivers, souvenir sellers, restaurateurs, shoeshine boys, peanut salesmen, and boatmen all vying for one's attention. Some will relentlessly follow and harangue anyone who appears to be a foreigner—it must be a technique that works, otherwise such tactics would probably go extinct. As annoying as some may find them, most of these folks are just trying to make a living, and with full knowledge that the average tourist is only in town for a few days at most, they see it as their one chance to make a sale. And besides, some of the souvenirs are very nice, there are numerous places to eat with wonderful food, and a good cleaning of one's shoes after a day exploring ancient monuments can be therapeutic. In fact, many of these street rascals are quite nice once you get to know them.

As for the tourists themselves, they range from the respectful to the crass. Some make a genuine attempt to engage with the local culture, striving to garner as much as possible from their Egypt visit. Others seem to treat the whole thing as some sort of pharaonic theme-park vacation, where attractions are superficially viewed and dismissed for the next sight to check off on the list. Some rarely leave their hotel and instead spend their time baking at the hotel pool. Sure, you could do that at thousands of locations worldwide, but right outside the door are unique and amazing things to see and experience, like nowhere else you'll ever be.

My dig team and I enjoy renting a felucca—a traditional wooden sailboat—once in a while just about an hour before sunset. If the winds are adequate, a great triangular sail is hoisted, often assisted by a young boy scampering up the mast as the captain takes the rudder. Crossing to the west side of the river, one can quietly glide along its green banks while admiring the rich local population of birds performing their early-evening activities. The sunsets are spectacular. Even after a difficult day, all is made well. Conditions aren't always perfect, and sometimes the wind dies and the feluccas drift north with the current, only to be collected by a motorboat that will tow home a string of stranded boats.

There is a felucca captain in Luxor who goes by the nickname "Shakespeare." It's a well-earned name, as English literature is his forte and he can ably recite from the Bard and any number of other prominent authors. He is also a master of accents, from Cockney to cowboy, and if you're in the proper mood, a journey on the Nile can be as entertaining as it is beautiful. You might even end up at Banana Island.

Over the years I had many times been solicited for a boat ride to the legendary Banana Island, which was said to be located on the river just south of Luxor. "What goes on there?" I'd ask, and each time my question was answered evasively, with a smile, a wink, and a nod. Although I'd never met anyone who'd ever been there, the constant implications were that it was some wild place where the normal rules of society didn't apply. "So," I asked many times, "what happens on Banana Island?" "Bananas, my friend, bananas!" Smile, wink, nod.

One day we decided to have a look ourselves and hired a motorboat that took us to its shores, where we were greeted by the "mayor of Banana Island" with his wide, toothless grin and his hand outstretched to receive "entrance fees." We were led to a small, open-walled shack and told to wait. Soon a surly teenage boy emerged from the trees and angrily threw a freshly cut stalk of bananas at our feet, then stomped off. Two dogs came out of nowhere, attacked the stalk, and separated, peeled, and ate bananas while we watched. We joined in—the bananas were delicious. Afterward we took a walk around the island and finally learned the truth: Banana Island was exactly what they said it was—one big banana plantation. But we tend to keep that our secret and let others find out for themselves. "Oh, yes, I've been to Banana Island!" Smile, wink, nod. Yes, the sun sets and rises again, and it's another day in Luxor.

RETURNING HOME FROM WORKING in Egypt can be a startling transition, and sometimes it seems as if the work never ends. There are reports to write, classes to be taught, family matters to attend to, and house repairs to be made. Data from the field season must be analyzed and made accessible, as scholarship in such fields as Egyptology is relatively useless unless the information can be shared. Traditionally, the results of one's research activities will be published in an appropriate journal, a formal report, or some other scientific venue. Before a formal publication is available, the information is often presented at conferences where the various players, contenders, aspirants, and armchair enthusiasts gather to consume the latest revelations. In North America the annual meeting of the American Research Center in Egypt is the primary such assembly attracting several hundred performers and spectators attending three days of talks and lectures.

The presentations, or "papers," are really the core of such gatherings, with a constant stream being presented about every twenty minutes, organized by theme and held concurrently in adjacent lecture rooms. The result is a beehive of activity, with a transient audience rushing to catch the paper of choice, carefully selected from program booklets that they've marked off like a racing form. Decisions need to be made: Should I catch the latest discovery at El-Hibeh or the new perspectives on the god Osiris?

Mark Papworth occasionally railed at the state of scholarship often presented at such meetings. "A celebration of minutiae!" he'd derisively declare. "The exalting of the trivial!" It's often amazing to meet the players in one's field, some of whose papers are brilliant and expertly delivered, while other scholars, for whatever reasons, are completely incapable of giving an effective presentation. Some of the better presentations are animated and border on entertainment, no matter what the academic depth of the topic. I at least attempt to share a sense of fun and wonder in my work, in hopes that people will go away feeling that the twenty minutes spent with me were worthwhile, insightful, and maybe even amusing. Most conference lectures fall under the category of "competent." They state their business well, even if the topic is absolutely obscure. I have, however, seen some real disasters—for example, a graduate student, eager to impress with his first paper only to be shut down by the moderator because his slide illustrations are out of order.

As a moderator myself, I've seen a speaker show up with illustrations for a completely different presentation, which she discovered only after about five minutes into her talk. And then there are those who refuse to stop talking when their time is up, having shown up with an hour-long lecture that they try to compress into fifteen or twenty minutes by speaking as rapidly and incomprehensibly as possible. If the old vaudeville gaffer's hook were available, I could have put it to use several times. And so it goes. I gave my first conference paper on the subject of, you guessed it, rope. I was in the same session with another fellow who was talking about ancient baskets from the Roman era.

The papers are only a part of the conference experience. For all the expense involved in travel and registration fees, social and professional networking opportunities perhaps offer the most value for participation. Advice is sought, inside knowledge is exchanged, and plans are made. For students it's an opportunity to meet the professionals, make a good (or bad) impression, facilitate their own research, and sometimes get invited on digs. Especially fun are the many reunions with friends one might see in person just once a year at such events, and don't forget the formal receptions and impromptu parties in hotel rooms.

I've attended international Egyptology conferences where the host cities sponsored lavish soirees. In Munich there was fresh beer tapped from kegs and large, delicious pretzels in the shape of the ankh, the ancient Egyptian symbol of life. In Cairo many of the foreign archaeological institutions seemed to compete to see who could put on the most impressive party, and the Egyptians themselves likewise organized some splendid events. In 1990 my friend Nick Reeves, then a curator at the British Museum, organized what would be a watershed event in the history of Valley of the Kings scholarship. The event, called After Tutankhamun, was held at Highclere Castle, the ancestral home of Lord Carnarvon, Howard Carter's sponsor when he discovered the boy king's tomb. The castle, with its soaring walls, seemed an appropriate venue, with commodious Victorian salons capable of accommodating a sizable crowd of registered attendees. As one of the invited speakers, I found it a genuine privilege to discuss my work in a program featuring truly great scholars and a serious, attentive audience.

WHAT HAS ALWAYS impressed me about archaeology and Egyptology is the large number of folks outside the vocation who are actively involved, some in an almost obsessive manner. I've met quite a few for whom ancient Egypt is a deep infatuation and has become their principal pastime. Some of them are as informed, if not more so, than the professionals, and others have a very admirable armchair knowledge paired with irrepressible enthusiasm. Maintaining one's interest as a serious hobbyist rather than as a practicing professional has its advantages. For one thing, there really aren't that many jobs to be had in archaeology and in Egyptology; in fact, I'd use the word "scarce" to describe employment opportunities. The competition can be fierce, and years of study are necessary for one to even be a contender. There's instruction in history, art history, religion, archaeology, and lots and lots of languages. The literature of Egyptology is written primarily in French, German, and English, and one must have at least a reading knowledge of each, and a listening and speaking ability certainly helps at international gatherings. In addition, if one actually conducts research in Egypt, some Arabic is useful, if not necessary, to enable one to politely and effectively carry out one's work.

And then there are the ancient languages. The classical Egyptian language from the time of the pharaohs is extinct, but it must be learned in order to take good advantage of the wealth of ancient texts that form the core of much Egyptological research. And as with all languages, Egyptian grammar and vocabulary evolved through time, so there are at least five identifiable stages that many students study. The hieroglyphic script must be mastered, and there are cursive versions as well.

It's a tall order to be an Egyptologist. It can make one a specialist, which can potentially limit one's employment opportunities. I'm an archaeologist first, but an archaeologist also trained in Egyptology. As an archaeologist I possess many of the broad skills needed to conduct work in many parts of the world, assisted by specialists as needed to lend a hand in matters of detail. A good general education can certainly be helpful, as I found out when I went job hunting in the aftermath of graduate school. I literally knocked on doors at small community colleges in search of available classes to teach. Could I teach History of Western Civilization? I was asked. "Of course I can!" I answered, even though my knowledge of the Greeks and Romans was rather sketchy. I sure knew a lot about ancient Mesopotamia and Egypt, and I quickly learned Greek and Roman history and culture, actually finding that I enjoyed these relative latecomers to the ancient world. I rarely turned down a class opportunity and taught courses in archaeology, cultural anthropology, physical anthropology, history of the Middle East, and even "geography for travel agents." At Pacific Lutheran, I taught in several different programs, including interdisciplinary courses on "viewing the past" and critical thinking for college-bound highschoolers.

It's very sad that so many incredibly bright scholars holding advanced degrees in esoteric fields are virtually unemployed in their areas of expertise. One of the sharpest Egyptologists I have ever met now teaches foreign languages at a public junior high school, out of necessity. (But he does a splendid job of it!) Another is quite prominent but steadily unemployed, apart from taking on a variety of little jobs throughout the year to support his archaeological work. In graduate school I met a very competent but frustrated scholar of ancient languages who finally had had enough, sold his books, and was retrained as a machinist, making specialized nuts and bolts. And then there are the academic nomads, who might teach one course at three different colleges in a single day for miserable wages with a lot of driving in between. I know—I've done it.

Those lucky enough to be employed in what they love are lucky indeed. I've managed to cobble together several occupations to make it work for me, including teaching, writing, and consulting, but in the back of every archaeologist's mind probably lurks a simple truth: We're basically overeducated ditchdiggers. Then again, as my friend Rick likes to cynically tease, "It's a great way to get paid to go camping!"

I'm often approached by young people who insist that their life goal is to be an archaeologist or an Egyptologist. For some it's just a phase, but for others it's a driving passion. I give the same advice to all of them: Go in with your eyes wide open, your mind steady, and a good sense of reality. Far be it for me to squelch someone's dreams; they very well might come true. Many of mine have.

TEN

ADVENTURES IN
TELEVISION LAND

THE WONDERFUL STORIES REVEALED by archaeology were first made known to me through the printed page, which I could read, and reread, and return to again to marvel at the fascinating accompanying illustrations. Television, too, brought the world of the past directly into my home, with broadcasts of old films, dramas on ancient themes, and news reports of fresh discoveries. Occasionally there would be a real treat like the *National Geographic* specials, one of the earliest in my memory featuring Louis Leakey excavating ancient stones and bones at Olduvai Gorge. His white hair and his mustache, his jumpsuit and his British accent produced an enduring image of a dedicated and energetic scholar, working in difficult terrain in search of the depths of human antiquity.

The popularity of such programs has greatly increased, and today we can find a plethora of television offerings featuring historical exposés and field exploration ranging from the sensationalist and absurd to the scholarly and finely crafted. In between are a lot of mediocre offerings, many dealing with what appears to be one of the most popular subjects of them all: Egypt. There seems to be an endless appetite for ancient Egypt on television. The most cheaply produced programs will incorporate a selection of still images that the camera can pan across and zoom in on, interspersed by "talking heads": experts, so to speak, who comment on the given topic and are paid little or no money. On the other end of the spectrum are those that are finely produced, with careful research and an eye for aesthetics. I was lucky to begin my television adventures in the latter arena, experiencing some of the quality for which the medium has the potential.

During the 1990 Valley of the Kings conference at Highclere Castle, I was approached by a producer for the BBC about a program that was being discussed for the 1992 commemoration of the seventieth anniversary of the discovery of the tomb of Tutankhamun, and I was invited to participate. The program would consist of five episodes. The first two would examine the life of Howard Carter and the events surrounding the opening of the tomb, asking the questions: Who was this man whose name is perhaps the most famous in archaeology? He was forty-eight years old when he encountered Tut's tomb, but what had he been doing all those years before, and whatever became of him afterward? And there was plenty of drama to share, too, with the politics involving the tomb and Carter's somewhat obstinate personality thrown into the mix. Other episodes would discuss the aftereffects of the tomb's discovery, including its impact on popular culture.

The idea of working on such a program was appealing. It would be a new angle from which to approach archaeology, as a participant in television rather than a viewer. And with the BBC no less, which I considered to be at the pinnacle of quality in broadcasting. There was also another benefit: an opportunity for me to learn more about Howard Carter, whose life had intersected with mine in the Valley of the Kings. I truly had mixed feelings about Carter. On one hand there was the man who'd made what might still be considered one of the greatest, if not *the* greatest, archaeological discoveries of all time. This was the man whose image was well known to me through the countless childhood hours I'd spent poring through his three-volume account of finding the tomb. The glow of the treasures themselves seemed to cast a golden sheen upon Carter, who appeared genuinely heroic. On the other hand, there was the Howard Carter in whose wake I had excavated, who presented an image of haste, carelessness, and perhaps a sense of intellectual shallowness. What I had found in KV 44 and 45 shocked me; it looked as if Carter had recklessly shoveled through the debris in a hunt for anything pretty. In Tomb 60 his brief published reports and archival notes neglected to mention an entire chamber and seemed to reflect a genuine disinterest. He seemed to be infected with the hunt for the grandiose decorated tombs and lacked the subtlety to appreciate the smaller monuments in the royal valley.

Harry James was in the process of writing the authoritative biography of Carter and he kindly provided us with copies of the unpublished manuscript chapters. The book, *Howard Carter: The Path to Tutankhamun,* contained wonderful insights into Carter's fascinating, little-known past and his somewhat perplexing personality. Carter was a bit of a stubborn loner, set in his ways and confident in his own righteousness, a man with a lot of acquaintances but few close friends. He seemed far more comfortable among the poor workmen of the Egyptian villages than around the wealthy and noble on whom he often relied for funding. Harry's book also revealed that Carter was adventurous, dedicated, and persistent. The television program would show all of this and reveal Carter as a man who first came to Egypt at age seventeen as a semieducated artist and spent most of his life there involved with antiquities before hitting the ultimate archaeological "jackpot" several decades later, only to eventually vanish into obscurity.

In the months leading up to the series' production, I served as a consultant, making many suggestions for various sequences and film locations. As such, I had an opportunity to inject a little adventure into an archaeological program, something I noticed to be surprisingly lacking in many documentaries. I had often found myself utterly bored by lackluster presentations of what is intrinsically one of the most fascinating subjects around. In our program there would be actual, potentially dangerous visits to tombs never before seen on television. This, I hoped, would be a program unlike anything presented on Tut or on Egypt before.

The director, Derek Towers, seemed impressed with my suggestions but at one point began to appear concerned. "We have contracted a presenter for the series, Christopher Frayling, and I'm not sure if he's up to many of the things you've proposed." I was quite discouraged with this news. I had never heard of Christopher Frayling, and my response to Towers was to suggest that this fellow get himself into a gym and start training. Frayling, as I learned, was a very distinguished fellow indeed, being professor of cultural history at the Royal College of Art, an expert on film and modern design, and an erudite television host. "We don't want you killing our presenter," Towers warned.

Frayling and I would deal with that later, but first I would travel to Egypt in April 1992 to scout out locations in advance of the BBC film crew, which even then was filming sequences in Cairo. The scenes in the Valley of the Kings wouldn't be too much of a problem, except for a visit to KV 20, the royal tomb of Hatshepsut. The valley I knew well, but of more pressing concern was another tomb of Hatshepsut, situated in a very remote and somewhat perilous location in the southern region of the Theban mountains. The tomb, carved into the middle of an intimidating cliff face, was built for the young princess or queen before she became pharaoh, thereafter being entitled to a tomb in the Valley of the Kings. Its role in the story of Howard Carter, in my opinion, was essential, as it revealed so much of his character.

In 1916, Carter caught wind of the fact that robbers had found a tomb and were actively in the process of clearing it out. Crossing the mountains at night, Carter found the robbers' rope dangling down the side of a cliff. He cut it loose and, substituting his own rope, descended to the entrance of the tomb, where he boldly confronted the thieves. They were ordered to get out and ascend his rope or be left stranded in a hole in the middle of a rock face. They did the prudent thing and departed, and Carter spent the next few weeks emptying the tomb of flood debris and finding an unused stone sarcophagus. He was baffled as to how the ancients had managed to move this incredibly heavy object into the tomb. It is a mystery that remains unsolved. A few years later French Egyptologist Émile Baraize managed to remove the sarcophagus, but not until he'd expanded the tomb's natural entrance and built a road to the base of the cliff.

I had seen the site of the tomb once before, but only from below, while on a hiking trip the previous year with a couple of archaeological colleagues. In preparing for the BBC program, I would need to revisit the site with the aim of discovering all the logistics necessary to film an adventure sequence there. I recruited one of my young workmen from the Valley of the Kings, Tayyib, and hired a car to drive us across the desert to the southern end of the mountains, where we continued on foot. The approach requires a hike up a narrow, sinuous wadi to a rock wall, and there one can spot the hole mid-cliff, frightening yet enticing to any climber such as myself.

I'd brought a standard climbing rope with me and a minimal amount of gear, the idea being to find out if such a rope would be capable of reaching both the tomb and the ground from whatever reasonable spot I could find to anchor it from above. Tayyib and I reached the end of the wadi and then ascended a loose slope, which brought us to a flat shelf above the cliff. A narrow crevice descended steeply to a ledge directly above a long drop to the tomb. We scrambled down the crack, and indeed there was a ledge, but one treacherously covered with loose stones and sloping at an angle toward a precipice. I gingerly clambered out to the edge and looked down. The entrance of the tomb could be seen directly below and well down. The big question was: Would the rope reach at least that far?

A large wedged boulder in the crevice provided an anchor, and I threw the rope over the cliff, its end landing soundly on a shelf at the tomb's entrance. I was overwhelmed with temptation. Although I hadn't brought the usual required equipment, I carried my climber's mental bag of tricks, which allowed me to improvise a means of descent down the vertical cliff. It wasn't the most comfortable setup—basically a nylon sling tied around my waist and a couple of carabiners—but soon I was at the tomb's entrance. I decided then to wait for the filming before examining the tomb's interior.

The next big question was the same as the first: Would the rope reach, this time to the ground? If it didn't, I would again have to improvise in order to ascend the rope up the side of the vertical cliff, perhaps with the aid of my sturdy bootlaces or whatever odds and ends I had in my rucksack. Fortunately, the rope did reach, just barely, and I descended to the cliff base and then returned to the top to retrieve both the rope and a perplexed Tayyib, who had never witnessed such a curious thing. The reconnaissance was a success, and I gained sufficient knowledge to facilitate the retelling of what must have been a truly exciting episode in Carter's life.

Eventually the film crew arrived in Luxor, and Derek Towers was anxious for me to meet Christopher Frayling in hopes that the two of us, a distinguished scholar paired with a rambunctious field archaeologist, could somehow get along. A dinner was arranged for all at the luxurious Winter Palace Hotel, and I eyed Frayling across the table with great suspicion. Nattily dressed and with curly brown hair and a mustache, he spoke with an upper-class British accent well used to throwing out a steady stream of clever quips. He'd last about five minutes in the desert, I concluded. As the odd man out in this group of jovial Brits, I barely got a word in, and I imagined my various adventure sequences being tossed aside for the usual safe fare.

After dinner Derek insisted that Frayling and I go for a walk along the Nile corniche. Wincing at the thought, I went along and quickly found that away from his expected role of formality and academic erudition, Christopher was at heart a fun and funny fellow, game for whatever might come his way, a surprising and encouraging revelation indeed.

Filming began immediately in the Valley of the Kings. I was very impressed by the professionalism of the team. Every shot was carefully constructed, even those that would appear for just a few seconds in the final product. Quality was foremost, and for those appearing on camera the sitting around between setups seemed endless. Frayling, though, was brilliant. With a quick glance at his notes, he could deliver an articulate stream of wonderful commentary, often requiring only one take. Eventually we opened KV 60, and I conducted a short tour of the tomb followed by a journey into KV 43, the tomb of Thutmose IV with its surviving evidence of an ancient tomb robbery. Both were discovered in 1903 by Howard Carter and added much to the telling of his story.

The real drama, though, would begin with our descent into the depths of KV 20, the valley tomb of Hatshepsut, one of the steepest, deepest, longest, most dangerous, and nastiest tombs in all of Egypt. Howard Carter had excavated the tomb beginning in 1903 while working for Theodore Davis. It is very likely the first tomb ever carved in the valley, initiated by the pharaoh Thutmose I and continued by his daughter, Hatshepsut. In many ways the tomb appears experimental, as if its builders really didn't understand the geology of the valley. Its single long corridor snakes down through a thick bed of solid, beautiful limestone before penetrating into the underlying shale, which is exceedingly loose and dangerous. At the point where the two beds intersect, one can actually look up at the ceiling and see the underside of the limestone bedrock.

Clearing KV 20 was an ordeal for Carter and his workmen, its corridor and lower chambers being packed with solidified flood debris. The sheer length and steepness of the tomb made the work extremely grueling, and the air was hot, foul, and imbued with the stench of bat dung. Carter described it as "one of the most irksome projects I have ever undertaken." It is indeed a nasty place, and even now, cleared of most of the debris, it is an arduous and extremely unpleasant tomb to explore. I first visited the tomb in 1984 with two friends. At the time its broken door lay wide open, and we began to descend with increasing trepidation. About two-thirds of the way down, my companions, overwhelmed by the dust and bat stink, had had enough. I proceeded on my own and reached the lower chambers with their crumbling shale walls and hordes of bats quivering from the ceiling. I was satisfied to scan the rooms quickly with the dust-opaqued light of my headlamp and beat a quick retreat, but not before unintentionally arousing the ire of the occupants. Pursued by a veritable flock of bats, I scrambled quickly to join my waiting friends, and we struggled to leave the wretched confines of the tomb as quickly as possible. The bats kept coming, and our heads were filled with thoughts of rabies or other bat-inflicted maladies as we lay prone on the tomb's floor within sight of its entrance above. Looking up at the square light at the end of the dark tunnel, we could see the bats flitting about the entrance like a swarm of angry mosquitoes, their flapping wings translucent from the light of the sun. Eventually they all darted speedily back into the depths of their lair, and we emerged from the tomb, savoring every breath of fresh air.

It was this sort of adventure that I hoped we could replicate in the film. It would give a real sense of the peril that Carter was willing to endure so early in his career, and a real sense of his determination. The plan was that Frayling and I would descend into the tomb just far enough to demonstrate its treacherous nature, and then bats would fly out and terrorize us. The steep and slippery floor of the tomb presented a dangerous filming environment and required great care. A rock accidentally kicked near the entrance could be heard to bounce and bounce and bounce, and we were very aware that the same fate could be awaiting a dropped piece of equipment or perhaps a dropped member of the television crew. In preparation for this sequence, however, I had obtained a sturdy wooden beam cut exactly to fit into ancient notches in the tomb's walls. Similar beams had been used to assist in lowering the heavy stone sarcophagi into the burial chamber, and now they could serve as anchors for men with cameras.

Frayling and I donned dust masks, proceeded into the tomb, and were quickly reminded of its dangers. A slip on my part was not staged, and though slightly unnerved, we continued our descent. We would of course need a few bats for drama, and a sufficient number at that, to compel us to leave the tomb. I sent a cameraman and an Egyptian assistant down to the bottom to scare up a few. Excited by the beams of flashlights, the bats flew ahead of their agitators, and soon a voice from below could be heard announcing their impending arrival. Very soon dozens arrived, more than we expected, and Frayling and I crouched against the wall as they buzzed by, grazing our heads in their passing. We eventually made our way out, and the cameras were able to capture their eerie bat ballet in the hazy light of the entrance.

The sound for the sequence we filmed in KV 20 was difficult to capture. The dust masks obscured our voices, and some of the commentary uttered during the bat attack was probably inappropriate for children. The sound would have to be replicated elsewhere, a practice not at all unusual in the art of filmmaking. We found a suitable acoustic environment in a surprising place: a bathroom in our Luxor hotel, which had acoustics that were amenable to the task. I situated myself in the empty bathtub, and Frayling sat on the closed lid of the porcelain throne while a sound technician extended his microphone boom through the doorway. Covering our mouths with the dust masks, we re-created our tomb adventure—"Here come the bats!" and "Let's get out of here!" and so forth—having a good laugh in the process.

The highlight of this whole enterprise, for me at least, would be the sequence at the remote Hatshepsut cliff tomb outside the valley. The potential hazards were very real. For a variety of reasons, we got a late start on our first day filming, but we eventually arrived at the edge of the desert, where I had arranged for several porters to assist with the gear. Additionally, a number of donkeys would be put to use, and we loaded them into the backs of pickup trucks. Donkeys were a common means of transportation in ancient Egypt and in Howard Carter's day as well. Even today these sturdy creatures are hard at work in nearly every Egyptian village, as they can carry heavy loads and travel sure-footedly in terrain where no vehicle can pass. (As an interesting aside and a look into the social life of Carter,

I once saw a photograph in the personal scrapbook of a famous early-twentieth-century Egyptologist that depicted a herd of donkeys scurrying away with a rider in its midst. The photo's caption read, "Carter and his contemporaries.") Carter was often seen excavating in proper English attire, so we found it only fitting that we should wear some nice coats out into the desert. After a few more delays, our caravan lurched forward toward the Theban mountains.

Our mechanized desert caravan was filmed from close, far, and wide, and eventually we arrived at the end of the desert track. While the porters and their loads were organized, Frayling and I selected the donkeys we would ride. "I like the one with the frilly knickers!" joked Frayling. As if to show who was boss, his lanky steed kicked him off in short order. Mine insisted on rapidly spinning in circles, but I would not be dismayed. I had ridden donkeys on a number of previous occasions and knew that if I hung on, the donkey would eventually get bored and stop.

With the cameras rolling, Frayling and I enjoyed our ride in the manner of Carter. Wired for sound, we engaged in an impromptu conversation regarding whose donkey was more attractive and reliable. Needless to say, our comments did not survive the editing process. Already it was becoming incredibly hot, and we had yet to arrive near the dreaded cliff. As we approached the end of the wadi, one of the porters succumbed to the heat. We immediately took measures to have him returned to a local village for treatment and carried on.

Frayling had been prompted very little about what he was to experience that day, with the idea that the camera could capture his authentic reactions. Nearing the end of the wadi, we dismounted from our noble chargers, and Frayling asked how much farther. The rest of the way would be on foot, and I indicated perhaps twenty minutes to half an hour. "That's your pace!" he replied with a laugh.

"No, that's *your* pace!" I added. We began to ascend the hillside, Christopher flagging just slightly behind and feeling the effects of the heat. Soon we reached a vantage point from which we could gain a good view of the cliff tomb's dark and lofty entrance. I silently chuckled as Frayling declared "It looks lethal!" while resolutely maintaining a respectable British stiff upper lip.

We carried on and eventually reached the top, camera crew in tow. At the cleft I removed my coat, and both Frayling and I put on safety helmets. I coached him down the crevice, an exercise requiring the judicious use of fingers, toes, and utmost caution. With experience as a professional mountain guide, I was well used to delivering inexperienced novices through treacherous terrain, and Christopher soon arrived safely on the sloping ledge, where he found a secure place to sit while I set up the anchors and ropes.

Preparations for this moment had actually begun months before, when I sent an equipment list to the BBC to requisition the mountaineering hardware, including helmets, harnesses, and descending devices for the camera crew. During my earlier reconnaissance, I'd explored the range of potential anchors and designed a system that was essentially "bombproof," to use the mountaineering vernacular. Not only was I responsible for my own safety, but I was supervising the crew as well. Since it would be necessary for me to back over the edge of the cliff several times, I attached an ascending device to my harness that would allow me to climb back up the rope, saving me a long, hot hike back up from the bottom of the wadi after each shot.

The afternoon before, a meeting was held at the hotel pool. There was much planning to do concerning the next day, which would involve significant logistics and great personal perseverance on the part of most of the participants. A subject at issue was whether or not Frayling should descend the cliff with me. Christopher was quite willing and insisted that with a little practice he would be up to the task, and I supported him in this request. It would look too easy, argued Derek Towers, if the inexperienced professor managed to make his way down the cliff, thus detracting from the boldness of Carter and the physical seriousness of the situation. I suggested that I could train Frayling from the roof of the hotel or perhaps from one of the steep rock buttresses across the river. But Derek was the boss, and he made a good point that the sense of real danger would likely be lost. A lack of time to pursue either option, however, decisively ended the question.

How, then, could Frayling decline gracefully during the cliff tomb sequence? It was suggested that he would climb down through the cleft to the sloping ledge, at which point he would indicate his reluctance to proceed, preferring instead to leave the rest to the expert. "Fine," I agreed, "and I'll respond to him by saying, 'I readily agree.'"

"Nobody says that!" vetoed Towers. "That's so archaic and unnatural!"

"There's a good chance that I'm going to say it anyway," I cheekily insisted. "Besides, I heard you use that very phrase during yesterday's meeting, and I kind of liked it!"

For the rest of the evening, I teased some of my companions by occasionally inserting the phrase "I readily agree" at appropriate conversational moments.

During the next day's filming, the big moment arrived, with Frayling sitting on the ledge and declining to descend the cliff while I set up the anchors and rope. There were several ears anxiously awaiting my response, in hopes that the obnoxious phrase would not be uttered. "I wholeheartedly concur!" I replied instead. In the aftermath it's truly a shame that some program reviewers suggested that Frayling was less than sporting by not descending the cliff. I can attest that he was quite willing, although I think more viewers can identify with his feigned reluctance than if he had actually tried such a stunt.

Making a film can be tedious business. Every desired camera angle requires a separate setup, and our director and cameramen were perfectionists. Views from above, from across, from the side, and from below laboriously filmed over several days are eventually combined in the editing process into one connected sequence sometimes lasting but a few minutes. Lighting, sound, camera stability, and crew safety were of utmost importance on our project as Towers carefully supervised everything. Eventually I descended all the way to the tomb while filmed from the opposite hillside.

Our return again to the top of the cliff, the moment long anticipated by the film crew, eventually arrived. They, too, must descend to the cliff tomb, and none had any significant mountaineering experience. And what an absolutely horrible and terrifying place to learn! I taught them how to rappel while I protected each with a separate rope. Derek Towers led the way, and everyone remained surprisingly unperturbed. I reassured them that they were well secured, even if panic should overtake them, but by the end of the day some even professed to enjoy the experience. Donkeys laden with equipment were brought below the cliff, and I hoisted each package of gear up to the mouth of the tomb. It wasn't long before it became clear that our daylight hours were short in number and it was time to quit to return on another day. Darkness comes amazingly quickly in the Theban mountains, and we descended to the ground while several of the crew packed up and led our cast of many down the wadi to the awaiting vehicles. It had been an unusually long, hot, and tiring day.

Earlier that afternoon Frayling had almost met his doom. Having climbed back up the cleft and hiked back down to our base, he accidentally strayed onto one of the ephemeral trails that can be found here and there in desert terrain. The result left Frayling stranded and barely hanging on above a large drop. Despite our urgent calls to the porters to assist, no one came to his rescue. I quickly rigged my gear to descend rapidly and deal with the situation, and Christopher barely managed to return to safety. Now the day was closing, and I insisted on retrieving the climbing gear while the others hiked out. Being responsible for the safety of my friends was both a personal and a professional obligation, and I felt very uncomfortable with the idea of leaving the ropes out overnight in an environment where they could potentially be damaged by gnawing creatures or other natural forces.

With a cameraman in tow, we literally ran up the slope yet again to the cliff top and sprinted along its edge as the day's brightness dimmed with each second. Approaching the cleft, I jumped in and speedily maneuvered downward. As I reached a tight section, I felt a tremendous strike to the top of my head. Accompanied by a flash of light in my skull and a horrible thud, the blow left me temporarily stunned and disoriented, and I nearly let go. The cameraman in hot pursuit had accidentally knocked loose a grapefruit-size rock as he ran along the edge directly above the cliff. It fell at least ten feet before meeting its unintentional target. In our haste I had neglected to put on my helmet.

I wedged myself in the crack and numbly gathered the courage to investigate my injury. My fingers felt a deep gash, and my hand returned covered with blood. The cameraman was extremely concerned and severely apologetic. Had I been dislodged from my holds, I might have tumbled down through the cleft, onto the sloping ledge, and over the big edge, perhaps hitting the lip of Hatshepsut's tomb as I hurtled to the ground. It was an accident, I assured him, and more pressing matters were at hand.

I asked him to check my eyes, and he reported that one of my pupils was dilated, suggesting a concussion, a skull fracture, or some similar injury. Still intent on accomplishing our mission, I insisted on collecting the gear and making a best effort to get out. It would be better to lose consciousness, a distinct possibility, on a trail than to be wedged at night in a crack on the edge of a remote cliff in the desert.

With the anchor dismantled and the ropes coiled, we slithered back up to the cliff top. In the dimness of the encroaching darkness, we carefully made our way down to the wadi. I wasn't feeling particularly well but was still walking, and we made steady progress in the blackness, eventually reaching our waiting and concerned colleagues, who had their own problems. Our porters had decided that they should be paid at least double the agreed amount. It was the BBC, after all, and they surely must have deep pockets! "Could you help us settle this matter, Don?" asked Towers, unaware of my situation. I silently replied by shining a flashlight at the gash on the top of my head, and my requested services were immediately excused.

Returning across the river, I cleaned up the gash while a couple of my teammates generously located a big bag of ice, which I applied in an attempt to reduce the swelling. I had to make a crucial decision. Should I rush to a nearby hospital and possibly disrupt this wonderful television adventure? Or should I try to treat things myself and hope for the best? I nervously chose the latter, and eventually I drifted off to sleep but then awoke with a start, disoriented and feeling nauseous. Beset by panic, I raced out of the hotel through Luxor's dark streets in a groggy attempt to find the only doctor I knew in town. Amazingly, I actually found his clinic, but all my desperate knocking was in vain, as the office was closed. The following day, which we were taking off for some reason or other, is a patchy memory at best. Somehow I crossed the Nile, made my way toward the desert cliffs, only to awake from my dream state to find myself descending a small trail in an obscure desert wadi parallel to the road leading up to the Valley of the Kings. I had no recollection of how I reached that spot, but I continued down to the green of the Nile Valley and returned to Luxor. My tenuous condition quickly improved that evening, and I felt ready and able to carry on with filming the next day.

Returning to the cliff, the film crew performed like seasoned mountaineering professionals as they confidently descended to the tomb and the gear was once again hauled up the cliff. Now that we were finally filming inside the tomb, I was able to explore its interesting features. A sloping corridor led down where it makes a sharp right turn that leads to the room where Carter found the sarcophagus. The walls bear evidence that this tomb had been nearly filled to the ceiling with water-deposited debris. From this room a small tunnel leads down to a tiny chamber, which I was surprised to find flooded to an unknown depth with clear water. I hesitated to clamber on and wade, as the presence of bats within suggested that the water might be rather polluted. This little chamber in this isolated tomb provided dramatic evidence that rain surely does fall in the Theban mountains and can accumulate in ancient structures. The cleft and the gully down which we rappelled serve as natural conduits for the delivery of water, and the whole phenomenon dramatically illustrates the threat to similarly situated tombs in the Valley of the Kings and elsewhere in the region. We revisited the tomb in April, and there was still a significant quantity of water left from the winter despite the processes of heat and evaporation.

The rest of the filming within the tomb proceeded rather uneventfully, and we were relieved to be finished with it. All that remained was for me to rappel down to Christopher Frayling waiting at the bottom, who would interview me about Carter as I dangled from the rope. When I reached the ground, I removed my helmet and disengaged from the rope. "Thanks, old chap!" I replied to Frayling as he handed me my hat, a hat that covered a nearly fatal souvenir I still carry in the form of a dent and a scar.

Several little scenes we filmed in the Theban mountains sadly never made it past the cutting-room floor. Presented with the spectacular cliffside desert scenery, my alpinist instinct demanded that I stand on a precipitous promontory and yodel in the best mountaineering tradition. As the somewhat out-of-place sounds echoed off the steep canyon walls, Frayling calmly surveyed the surrounding arid landscape. "Switzerland it isn't!" he concluded. Another scene had me running at the very edge of the cliff in order to promptly report to Frayling that we were indeed properly situated above the Hatshepsut cliff tomb. "He's running!" proclaimed a surprised Christopher. "It's too hot to walk!" I explained à la Clint Eastwood. Snip! Snip!

There were many other memorable incidents working with the project—for example, a staged outdoor party that nearly turned into a riot. The scene was to illustrate Howard Carter's affinity with the local people, and we invited some of the village workmen who had helped us. The setting was dramatic, with the darkness of night illuminated by the uneven light of flaming pots of kerosene. I arranged for a singer and some drums, and Frayling and I thoroughly enjoyed the dancing and other frivolities. Things took a bizarre turn for the worse, however, when the roast goat arrived. It caused quite a bit of excitement, and the table where it lay was rushed by several hungry guests with outstretched hands. With the cameras rolling, the "chef" swung at the interlopers with a large knife, no harm intended other than to shoo them away until all was ready. But then out of the darkness emerged an elderly man wearing a black robe and brandishing a whip, who then proceeded to beat the eager goat-grabbers. This provoked quite a stir, and although I'm not sure if the chef thanked him, I do know that Mr. Whip afterward approached me and asked me for some money for his services. I rejected his suggestion, and the party carried on to become strange yet again.

At one point not long after, I turned around just in time to see a small child toddling toward one of the fire bowls with a plastic cup full of liquid. A moment later a large fireball erupted, which nearly singed the clothes off my back as the little fellow ran off giggling. These kinds of incidents certainly weren't suitable for the television program we envisioned, and the worst was yet to come. Someone began to throw rocks at us, perhaps someone who was disgruntled at not being invited to the party (or was it something arranged by the unrewarded whip man?). With our little lighted area surrounded by the black of night, it was impossible to see their source, and that was the final straw. "Enough!" declared Derek Towers, and we quickly shut down the show. Two smiling anonymous local men approached me and introduced themselves as guards, declaring that they had been working for us all evening. I showed them the bruise on my arm from one of the flying rocks. "Nice job!" I commented sarcastically as I walked away.

Still, there were many wonderful moments on this first foray into television, including fine Luxor evenings with new friends and afternoon interviews in the Theban necropolis. Frayling and I can still joke about "the curse" in relation to my bashing from a rock and his subsequent horrifying plunge in a Cairo elevator when its cables snapped. Aside from the scars and memories, perhaps the most notable thing I gained from the whole experience was a sincere respect for Howard Carter. Having had the opportunity to literally walk in his footsteps, I realized that the man with the bow tie was tough, bold, driven, and a true explorer. *The Face of Tutankhamun* nicely portrays the Howard Carter not many people knew. Though his abrasive personality won him few true friends in his lifetime, he surely led an amazing life, and most Egyptologists no doubt envy his accomplishments. From then on I felt that I understood the man and could relate to his personality and circumstances.

The Face of Tutankhamun debuted as planned on British television in November 1992, just in time for the seventieth anniversary. I was in London for the occasion, and the British Museum celebrated with a wonderful exhibition entitled Howard Carter: Before Tutankhamun. I attended its opening reception with Derek Towers, Christopher Frayling, and some of my other filmmaking colleagues along with an interesting selection of prominent Egyptologists, including Harry James, Carter's biographer. On this same trip, I also planned an excursion out to Putney Vale Cemetery to visit Carter's grave. I had written a review of James's book for *Archaeology* magazine, and the magazine inserted a little sidebar by archaeologist Paul Bahn pointing out the dilapidated state of the grave site. Bahn and I got together (a trip that became quite interesting for other reasons) and visited the cemetery, and indeed it was a pathetic sight. As the opening scenes of *The Face of Tutankhamun* indicate, Carter's funeral was attended by few, and here the grave of the best-known archaeologist of all time remained obscure and mostly neglected, the sparse words engraved on its headstone barely legible and continuing to fade.

Paul and I decided to begin a fund to rehabilitate the site and at least replace the headstone with one that was worthy. At home I set up a bank account in which I placed some of my own funds, and it wasn't long before I learned that the British Museum itself had announced that it was going to restore dignity to Carter's grave. There was no need to compete, and I turned my money over to the British Museum as a gift from my infant son. In a year or two, I was delighted to learn that a beautiful new gravestone had been produced and that young Samuel's name was noted during its dedication.

With its large budget and superb production qualities, *The Face of Tutankhamun* serves for me as a high standard of comparison for all other programs in which I have been involved, some more successful than others. One that proved particularly bad was a show about mummies. I was to be the featured archaeologist, and the show would begin with the royal mummies in the Egyptian Museum in Cairo, then proceed down to the Valley of the Kings, where I was working. I got the idea that there was trouble afoot when a friend of mine who was facilitating the program in Cairo sent me a fax in Luxor. It was a copy of the crew's travel schedule, in which their arrival was noted as "will probably be met at the airport by Don Ryan, a thirty-something Indiana Jones wannabe."

"Watch out for Gigi, the director," warned my friend. "She's a bit of trouble."

This "wannabe" business was both rude and wrong, and the Indiana Jones reference tiresome. With all the fascinating work and discoveries of archaeologists worldwide for at least a century and more, it's interesting that a fictional movie character has become the primary archaeological frame of reference for many Americans. Nearly any archaeologist who has received any sort of press has been called the "Indiana Jones of [fill in your town—Poughkeepsie, for example—or the name of your school—Farm Town Community College]. The allusion that there exists some sort of dangerous, swashbuckling life for the typical archaeologist is ridiculous. You see Indiana Jones neither spending hours on his hands and knees tediously revealing or documenting artifacts in the earth, nor spending hours in a laboratory or in a library preparing reports.

No, what you actually see is a kind of grave robber, snatching high-value objects while pursued by various thugs with accents. "Yeah, archaeologists are just like Indiana Jones," I have often commented sarcastically. "Let me show you the scars on my chest where I've been dragged behind a truck by Nazis!"

Still, I've known some who love to play off the image and will milk it for all it's worth. One archaeologist of my acquaintance even made great efforts to support the myth in hopes that it would help him meet women. The hat and the talk might initially have impressed, but the faux swagger and whip would eventually scare nearly anyone off. I've heard of others who claimed to have been the inspiration for the Jones character, including an amateur American archaeologist whose actual last name is Jones and another who claimed that the stories were based on his own lost diaries. From what I've heard, though, Indiana Jones is very much a fictional character, a creation of the imagination of screenwriters. His original name was to be Smith, and Indiana was the name of George Lucas's dog.

Is there adventure in archaeology? Sure, such is often the case. Especially working in places like Egypt, but it certainly doesn't require Nazis in hot pursuit, fistfights, or gun battles. Indiana Jones, as entertaining as the films are, is essentially a cartoon; archaeologists such as myself are real, and archaeology is even more fascinating *because* it's real.

Gigi and her film team eventually arrived in Luxor, and my informant was correct. I was immediately told that they had been denied permission to film what they wanted in Cairo, so she didn't have a show. "Hmmmm," I replied. "I thought *I* was the show." She was obviously new to working in Egypt and easily frustrated, especially with the notion of having to adapt to evolving circumstances. In the next few days, things became very silly. At one point the crew lacked a vehicle, so I ran alongside a moving truck and hopped onto a railing on the back to be taken up the hill to the house of my driver, who could be hired for the job.

"That jumping on the truck thing," commented Gigi. "Let's get that on film."

I shrugged my shoulders at the suggestion. "Okay, if that's what you want!"

We found someone who would be willing to drive his truck by for me to jump on, and each time, as the cameras rolled, another vehicle, donkey, or other obstruction would appear to block the proceedings. I was filmed here and there, making my way to the valley, even solo climbing a cliff in the process. The whole farce was annoying, but the greatest offense involved keeping my Egyptian assistants after hours in the heat, which resulted in one of them becoming ill.

Gigi finally left, and the Cairo Museum sequence was substituted with scenes of a mummy being examined using modern technology in an American hospital. It took me months to be paid for my work, and I sent a complaint about my awful experience to the production company. The only response was from the company's kindly phone receptionist, who apologized for the lameness of her coworkers.

Another memorable program involved my demonstrating an ancient Egyptian skill, making rope from papyrus. My participation began at an evening reception in the Los Angeles County Museum of Art. A friend informed me that someone he had just met was producing a program on the topic of "great builders of Egypt." He pointed out a tall, bushy-haired fellow, and I introduced myself. "I hear you're doing a program about Egyptian construction, and frankly," I jokingly claimed, "you don't have a show unless you've got rope." I explained the importance of the technology, and the producer, Joshua Alper, seemed almost convinced. I sent him some articles on the subject, and it wasn't long before I was flown from Seattle to Los Angeles to make a little cordage, Egyptian style. The setting was at a rock-climbing area named Stony Point, where I was filmed ascending a rock wall as an explanation for my interest in rope. I brought with me some stalks of papyrus, which I prepared by pounding with a hammer before placing the strands between my bare toes and twisting them in the proper fashion. It was similar to the techniques I had seen on the walls of ancient tombs and witnessed in rural Egyptian villages. Joshua thought it was great, and I heard many comments that it added much to a program that could have so easily defaulted to the usual fare of befuddling pyramids and forests of sacerdotal stone columns.

The increasing quantity of archaeology- and history-themed shows, many cheaply produced or playing to the sensational or fringe, is also a bit disturbing. Mummy curses, intergalactic aliens involved in ancient cultures, lost continents, and Martian pyramids are regular viewing fare, seducing the public with a heap of nonsense and giving such notions an air of credibility. After all, "I saw it on television!" More than one channel that began with noble educational intentions has sold out to this kind of sadly appealing programming. Fortunately, conscientious TV addressing the past can still be found and tends to stand well above the rest. The best of the genre serves to excite, delight, and educate viewers and enhance private and public support for archaeology and other scholarly endeavors.

ELEVEN

PYRAMIDS IN
THE ATLANTIC

WHEN I WAS TEN YEARS OLD, I used to fantasize that I was
a member of the crew aboard a strange raft adrift in the
ocean:

> The sky began to darken as another wave broke over
> the bow. Only an hour remained of my watch with the
> steering oar before I could take a well-deserved break.
> Fearful thoughts of an impending storm dissipated as the raft
> glided over each swell like a buoyant cork—after all, this
> vessel was made from balsa, and any water crashing aboard
> would seep back into the sea through the cracks between the
> lashed logs. It had been a busy day. Knut and Eric caught
> a few sharks, grabbing the sandpapery tails with their bare
> hands and tossing them up on the deck. It was a crazy kind
> of sport, born of a search for novelty on a voyage that had
> already lasted over three months. "Stay away from the end

*that bites!" yelled a cheery Norwegian voice from within
the cabin. The voice belonged to the raft's captain, Thor
Heyerdahl, who came up with the wild idea of floating
across the Pacific on an experimental replica of a prehistoric
South American raft.*

There's a lot of provocative evidence suggesting that there were
people from the New World in Polynesia, perhaps even before the
Polynesians themselves. It was a heretical idea for sure in the world
of anthropology, and critics often cited the notion that the seafarers
of South America, as well noted by the Spanish conquistadores,
were shore huggers and that their sea vessels were incapable of surviving the rigors of an ocean voyage. "There's one way to find out,"
Thor challenged the critics. Build one, launch it into the ocean,
and see what happens. Experimental archaeology, one could call
it. Not only would the voyage prove possible, but it was relatively
easy, as the winds and currents of nature's conveyor belt can readily
transport one to beautiful island destinations.

Every day aboard the raft named Kon-Tiki *was an
adventure. Yesterday Torstein found a strange, unknown fish
that hopped from the ocean onto his sleeping bag, and we
were still talking about the whale shark that passed below
the raft last week, a terrifying yet utterly fascinating creature
whose power and mass rivaled those of even our hefty
collection of floating logs. Our friend from Peru, a parrot
named Lorita, provided constant amusement, as did the
sprays of flying fish that would spontaneously erupt from the
sea, a couple even landing in our frying pan. Thor emerged
from the cabin and glanced at the sky. A few seagulls flying
above caused a smile to break across his face. "Land is near,*

*young man!" he confidently assured me. Since I was the
youngest member of the* Kon-Tiki *expedition, Thor went out
of his way to make sure I was comfortable, informed, and
busy. "Climb the mast and give us a report," he encouraged
as he took over my position at the oar. I gingerly climbed
up toward the crossbar and blocked the sun with my hand
over my eyes. Scanning the horizon, I caught a glimpse
of something curious: a thin line of green that broke the
monotony of the seemingly endless sea. "Land ahead, Thor!"
I yelled exuberantly. "Land ho!" Terra firma at last and,
more important, a successful test of a radical idea.*

"Donald!" called the female voice from nowhere. "Donald!
Time for dinner!" At that moment the illusion was shattered and
the *Kon-Tiki* yet again reverted to a pile of crudely assembled lumber
perched on a Southern California hillside, the ocean transforming
back into a sea of long green grass. Thor and the crew all vanished as
the sun began to set behind the avocado groves and I answered my
mother's call to return to the house. It was a great voyage that would
resume the next day and the day after that. It all started with a little
paperback book placed in a child's Christmas stocking. A paperback
called *Kon-Tiki,* selected by a Santa who resembled my father, a man
who knew the sea, having served as an officer on a battleship and
captained his own sailboat. Why that book? I can never answer; he
had no doubt read it himself and thought it would be a fine treat for
his bookish son. He was right. Thor Heyerdahl and his *Kon-Tiki* lit
in me a fire for adventure that has never been put out.

The voyage of the *Kon-Tiki* expedition took place in 1947, ten
years before I was born, but with millions of copies published in
over fifty languages, the wonderfully written book about the expedition was an international phenomenon. An obscure Norwegian

with a background in zoology quickly became a world celebrity and a symbol of bold adventure. Thor's shaky home movies of the voyage, accompanied by a wildly compelling story, brought him an Oscar for Best Documentary in 1950, while anthropologists cringed at his ideas and the methods of pursuing them. Thor, as both his fans and critics would learn, was just beginning, and would spend the next fifty-five years challenging traditional scientific dogma, backing up his notions with scholarly publications and lectures, and appealing to the common sense of the public with books that served to question and inspire. A few years after the famous expedition, Thor published an impressive, competently written scholarly explanation of the scientific theories behind the *Kon-Tiki* voyage, called *American Indians in the Pacific*. This impressive tome, with over eight hundred pages of closely spaced print and hundreds of bibliographic references, was barely read then and even still remains practically unknown. Inside, Thor presented a wealth of information supporting his notions, which suggested that the history of the Pacific was a far more interesting one than most could imagine.

During the mid-1950s, Heyerdahl led the first major scientific expedition to explore the archaeology of Easter Island. This remote island in the Pacific, known for its iconic giant stone heads, poses many questions, and, like Egypt, it's been fertile ground for both scientific and fringe ideas. The expedition's impressive work and publications continue to serve as a foundation for all further work on the island, and Thor's popular account of the whole adventure, *Aku-Aku,* was another bestseller. Apart from *Kon-Tiki* and a couple of my dinosaur books, it was a real favorite of mine and still is.

In 1969, Heyerdahl built another experimental boat, this time from papyrus. Proceeding on his belief that the oceans weren't obstacles but manageable highways, he noticed that a lot of ancient people in different parts of the world used what can be generically called "reed boats." These vessels were typically constructed out of bundles of naturally buoyant reeds or sedges and could be made in a variety of sizes. There seem to be many depictions of reed boats in pre-pharaonic rock found in Egypt's deserts, noted by their upturned bow and stern. As with *Kon-Tiki,* Thor wanted to test the seaworthiness of an ancient type of boat, and he did so by building the *Ra* near the base of the pyramids at Giza. The boat was then transported to Morocco, where it was launched into the Atlantic for a voyage to the Americas, complete with Thor and his remarkably diverse crew. For a variety of reasons, the boat began falling apart well short of its goal, and *Ra* had to be abandoned.

The following year Thor built another, christened *Ra II,* and the crew's easy and successful crossing took fifty-four days. I excitedly followed the story of the *Ra* expeditions as they happened, and when the documentary film came to the theater, I enjoyed every minute of it. Thor had done it again!

As I learned years later, there was a lot of confusion about what Thor was doing. The public certainly loved the adventures, but what was he trying to prove? Some believed that he was trying to prove that the ancient Egyptians came to America before Columbus. The style of the boat, its name, and the location of its construction were suggestive. The fact was that evidence from ancient Egypt provided the best models from which to reconstruct what was meant to be a testable generic model of a reed ship. For several reasons Egypt was a good location for putting it all together. In reality Thor never believed that the Egyptians had come to the New World, and at least during the time of the pharaohs they didn't seem to venture much away from the shores of the eastern Mediterranean and the Red Sea coast. But others might have and probably did, and I'd venture to say that someday there will be conclusive evidence that will rewrite the history books.

A third reed boat, named *Tigris,* was built in 1977 with the intention of connecting three locations of ancient civilization that seemed to have developed around the same time: Mesopotamia, the Indus Valley, and Egypt. There's evidence to suggest that all three areas had such boats and might have been in contact during the formative years of their cultural development. The *Tigris* was afloat for months, sailing from Iraq through the Persian Gulf and the Indian Ocean, to Pakistan and into the mouth of the Red Sea, where it was burned in protest against the wars taking place in that region.

After *Tigris* there would be other Heyerdahl expeditions, including archaeological excavations in the Maldive Islands, in Peru, and a return to Easter Island. Through these years of provocative expeditions, he became a beloved figure, not only in his native Norway but throughout much of the world. He also became a major international spokesman for global cooperation and environmental issues, the latter especially in matters involving the world's oceans. The man's adventurous spirit and "thinking out of the box" mentality continued to inspire me and my archaeological work, and I followed his work to the extent I could.

I finally met Heyerdahl, and I can thank both Howard Carter and Giovanni Belzoni for the privilege. I was in London in November 1992 for the exhibition at the British Museum, discussed in the previous chapter, celebrating the life of Howard Carter on the seventieth anniversary of the discovery of Tutankhamun's tomb. During my weeklong visit, I hoped to accomplish a little of this and a little of that, including the excursion to Howard Carter's grave and a visit to the headquarters of the Royal Geographical Society. The society is a distinguished organization, established in 1830, and its members are a veritable who's who of exploration during the last two centuries. In days gone by, its lecture halls hosted reports of searches for the sources of the Nile and expeditions to the poles, and it remains a prominent institution to this day, addressing all aspects of geography. The society also houses a vast archive of material relating to various and sundry geographical projects, and I found, much to my surprise, some items related to Giovanni Belzoni.

I spent an afternoon scrutinizing this interesting stuff, and as closing time for the archives approached, I packed up my notebooks and headed for the door. Nearly out of the building, I was startled by the approach of a large entourage heading inside, consisting of what appeared to be journalists, photographers, and a host of other people. At its center was a man whose visage I immediately recognized. It was Thor Heyerdahl himself. The one man in the world I would choose to meet if I were ever presented with such an option. Thor was in London to give a lecture, a fact of which I was unaware, and now here he was—confident, charismatic, and a few feet away. I joined the surrounding crowd, and after a few moments I decided to make a bold, spontaneous gesture totally against my nature. I rudely pushed my way through the throng and stretched out my hand. "Thor Heyerdahl!" I exclaimed. "I'm an archaeologist, and I've wanted to meet you my entire life." Thor, I would later learn, was rather embarrassed by his fame and probably took advantage of the moment to escape from his adoring fans. I was one, too, of course, but at least one who claimed to be an archaeologist. On top of that, there was only one of me versus dozens of the others.

Thor excused himself, and we were directed to a small, comfortable room, where we sat and began to chat. I was terrified of making some sort of mundane, starstruck comments, and no doubt I did, but Thor set me at ease and made me feel as if I were at least as interesting as himself. He was also accompanied by a beautiful woman, Jacqueline Beer, a former Miss France and television/movie actress who would become his wife a few years later. The details of the conversation are hazy because I was so overwhelmed. I did mention that I had once sent him a copy of an article I'd written on the subject of papyrus, and in response he had sent me a lovely postcard, which I kept as a treasure. Again the details escape me, but I do recall the conclusion: "Thor," I offered, "should you ever need some guy with a Ph.D. to carry your water bottle on a future expedition, I'm your man!" Thor graciously handed me his card with an invitation to "stay in touch." I wasn't sure what to believe. "Stay in touch . . . " Why would this international celebrity want anything to do with a pipsqueak like me? Nonetheless, I exited the Royal Geographical Society walking on air and couldn't wait to return to my hotel to call Sherry and tell her what had just happened. "Guess who I just met!" I yelled into the phone. Naturally, she couldn't guess . . . another Egyptologist, perhaps? "Mighty Thor! I met Mighty Thor!" She had of course heard of the man for years and was impressed. The very next day, strangely, would bring me a completely unexpected counterpoint to the whole experience.

The following morning I had an appointment to meet archaeologist Paul Bahn, who shared a mutual interest in Carter's grave site. We met at the appointed hour in the morning and I immediately found him to be a friendly, bright, witty fellow. His academic credentials were impressive: an author and editor of many archaeological tomes (including the textbook I myself used in teaching), a protégé of the esteemed British scholar Lord Colin Renfrew, and an expert on, among other subjects, the enigmatic Easter Island. Our initial interaction was quite pleasant, and I enthusiastically described my own work in Egypt. Sometime within the conversation, I excitedly announced that I'd actually met the world-famous explorer Thor Heyerdahl the previous night. Paul's demeanor immediately changed to one enraged with anger. "That man," he announced, "is a fraud and a liar," and the vitriol continued despite my attempts to moderate it. Didn't everyone love Thor? I thought naïvely. Did he not command the respect of even those who disagreed in detail? Apparently not. My encounter with Paul was a reality check. In less than twenty-four hours, I had met not only my boyhood hero and the foremost inspiration for my archaeological career but, coincidentally, the one individual, as I would learn, who could justly claim the title of Thor's most aggressive opponent. The subject was abruptly dropped, and we focused on the cemetery visit. Just a few years later, Paul would write a book about Easter Island, with a whole chapter—and then some—dedicated to "debunking" the *Kon-Tiki* expedition and Thor's ideas about Polynesian prehistory.

Welcome to the world of Thor Heyerdahl: beloved global celebrity, explorer, author, and occasional academic pariah! Some of his ideas were just too radical for the mainstream, many of whom objected to the dramatic nature of his experiments or were envious that his unconventional theories were better known and more appreciated by the public than theirs were. Paul Bahn was not alone, just the latest in a series of critics who'd attacked Heyerdahl for over five decades. I would meet many academicians, however, who would come up empty when pressed to articulate what it was that Thor was actually doing; they really didn't know and might have been merely holding a negative opinion that had been passed on to them by their colleagues or former professors, who themselves might have known little. Yes, Thor represented a volatile mixture of science, adventure, and controversy, but for those who took a careful look, there was much to appreciate.

In 1994 my proposal to work in Egypt was dismissed by a high antiquities official whose reputation for being difficult is still clearly remembered. I had requested permission to reopen one of the best-known yet most poorly documented sites in Egypt, the famous Deir-el Bahri royal mummy cache. The cache was a well-hidden tomb used to secrete the bodies of the New Kingdom pharaohs when the Valley of the Kings fell out of use. Local robbers discovered the tomb around 1871 and quietly looted it for several years. When the cache was made known ten years later, the antiquities authorities quickly emptied it of its many mummies, coffins, and other leftovers from royal burials. Very few notes were taken in the process, and I knew that much could be learned from examining the site of this great discovery. The tomb's deep entrance shaft eventually filled in, and no one had been inside in many decades. I would have greatly enjoyed the challenge of revisiting the cache and seeing what might remain to help reconstruct its history. Alas, "Dr. No," as he was known, rejected my proposal. An annual expedition to Egypt was something I so much looked forward to, even during the summer with its oppressive heat, and with permission denied I felt a sincere frustration and was anxiously looking for a way to fill the void. (The tomb has since been reexamined.)

I fumbled Heyerdahl's calling card between my fingers. Should I really take him up on his "stay in touch" offer? Surely I must be just another one in a million to whom he kindly extended wishes. I mulled over the idea of contacting him constantly in my mind and eventually decided to act. Why not? The worst that could happen was that I would hear nothing from him or be given some sort of generic negative reply. If so, I was back at square one, and if not, perhaps the great explorer would share at least a kind word. Nothing ventured, nothing gained, I concluded. I would contact Thor, for better or worse.

I didn't dare call him on the telephone, as I was intimidated by the prospect of having a meaningful conversation, stuttering my way through a "remember me?" introduction. Instead I decided to call the Kon-Tiki Museum in Norway, an institution that displayed Thor's work (including the actual *Kon-Tiki* and *Ra II* vessels), in hopes that I could talk my way into obtaining Heyerdahl's fax number. They graciously provided the information, and I composed a carefully worded message of inquiry. I gingerly fed the letter into my fax machine, making sure that everything was in order before carefully dialing the number and listening for the characteristic screech sound indicating that some sort of analogous machine on the other side of the world was ready to receive whatever I had to offer. The paper fed its way through, successfully emerging out the other end, and the waiting began.

It was only a day or two afterward when I returned home to see the message light blinking on my phone answering machine. The usual mundane stuff, I assumed—a dentist-appointment reminder, some junk solicitation for installing vinyl siding on my perfectly adequate home, or other such nonsense. I pushed the button and was utterly startled. The voice that emerged from the depths of the phone was unmistakable, its thick, Scandinavian accent readily identifiable. "This is Thor Heyerdahl. I received your fax, and maybe you'd like to come out and visit me and we can talk. Please contact me, and we can discuss the details." I couldn't believe it. Thor Heyerdahl himself was calling me at my little house in Tacoma, Washington, expressing an interest in meeting me. I was stunned and played the message back over and over again. Sherry, too, was somewhat excited, and I immediately set about constructing a reply indicating that yes indeed I would come out to visit; I just needed a place and time. Needless to say, the message on my phone was not erased for many weeks.

As I continued to communicate with Thor, I was quickly informed that he currently lived on the island of Tenerife in the Canary Islands, a place whose name I had heard of yet had no idea of its location. A perusal of an atlas indicated that this cluster of eight volcanic islands was located several dozen miles off the African coast of Morocco and was politically considered to comprise two provinces of Spain. What a curious place for a Nordic man to live, but I concluded it did make sense. Thor loved warm climates and islands, whether it was in the South Pacific or South America or the Canary Islands. Before moving to Tenerife, in the early 1990s, he had been living in Peru, where he spent several years excavating at the magnificent mud-brick pyramid complex known as Túcume.

Looking for a change of pace and a fresh venue, he was lured to the Canaries by some photographs sent by a Norwegian friend, Fred Olsen, which depicted what appeared to be seven stone step pyramids situated improbably in a large vacant lot in the middle of a rural town named Güímar. Thor paid a visit and was impressed. The Pirámides de Güímar, as they became known, were impressive and puzzling, and if one were shown a picture of these structures without the accompanying context, one's first guess might be that they were ruins located in Mexico. Given Thor's belief in the probability of contacts across the oceans in antiquity, these pyramids were in fact strategically located where the currents will sweep a seagoing vessel across the Atlantic Ocean from the Old World to the New. Even Columbus had stopped in the Canaries for supplies before making his way west to transform the world forever, and the *Ra* expeditions watched these islands pass in their wakes.

I managed to find enough money for a plane ticket and flew to Tenerife, not knowing what to expect on the other side. To my surprise, Thor and Jacqueline both were waiting for me at the airport, and I'm sure if I had not waved, they wouldn't have recognized the obscure archaeologist they had briefly met two years before. Once again I tried hard not to sound too much like a groupie, which required considerable restraint, and I was taken to a small apartment in the village of Güímar and given instructions as to where to meet the following day. Thor at the time was living in a temporary house while a small, walled estate was being restored nearby.

Our first full meeting together was remarkable. While Thor discussed his many projects, our conversations were occasionally interrupted by Jacqueline reporting the latest news from the seemingly unending series of arriving faxes. "It's Gorbachev, sending Christmas wishes" or "Fidel says 'Happy Holidays.'" It was truly a different world I was entering, with Thor being the consummate global citizen, admired, and well liked by all manner of world leaders and other movers and shakers, including European royalty, Nobel Peace Prize winners, and dictators from both the left and right.

Nearly every sentence out of Thor's mouth was fascinating, and he had plenty of questions for me. What I didn't realize then was that I was essentially being interviewed for a job, and as I found out at the end of that first wonderful week I spent in Tenerife, I passed the test. Over the years I had unintentionally accumulated the proper and necessary skills to work with Heyerdahl. I had a broad knowledge of ancient history and archaeology, abilities with several modern and ancient languages, experience as a director of field projects, and a record of both scientific and popular writing. Very importantly, I had a substantial knowledge of, and appreciation for, Thor's own research and philosophy.

Indeed, the entire first trip to Tenerife was a real eye-opener. The Thor Heyerdahl I imagined from my youth was just as impressive in real life. There is a fear, I suppose, that we might meet our heroes or idealized role models and find ourselves disappointed, reality not matching expectations. I had no expectations as to how we might get along and merely hoped that Thor would somehow tolerate me for a week. As it turned out, we became nearly instant friends. He was amazing, and he continually impressed me with his insights, born of an unconventional mind, decades of travels matched by few, and a persona unafraid to confront dogma. He was a gentleman and a gentle man, with a wonderful sense of humor that was clever and never vulgar and, as I would learn, a true humanitarian, just as much at home—if not more so—sharing a simple meal on the floor of a mud hut in an impoverished country as he was at a state dinner with a king or a queen.

I was very curious as to how Thor organized his life, and as I was interested in writing, Sherry suggested that I take a good look at his office and see how he was logistically set up to write his many wonderful books. At least I knew that I would return home with some useful tips. Thor, I found out, was a disciplined man. He was usually at work at 8:00 A.M., answering correspondence and writing. A leisurely lunch, typically at the seaside, was followed by a busy afternoon, a short power nap of about fifteen minutes, a leisurely dinner, and then to bed by around 10:00 P.M. or so. Thor worked six days a week, but Sunday was for rest and quiet thought. On that day he preferred to commune with nature, usually enjoying a ride into the mountains or along the sea.

At over eighty years old, Thor didn't know how to drive a car. He was certainly capable, but chose not to, perhaps preferring to spend his time thinking rather than concentrating on controlling a fume-spewing machine around countless curvy roads. Thor's lack of automotive skills was actually to my advantage. Many times over the several years I would work with him, I had the privilege of being the chauffeur on his Sunday escapes, driving to beautiful places while we chatted about an incredible breadth of topics, from his previous expeditions to our present work to future projects and global politics. Wonderful meals were always part of the schedule, and then on Monday it was back to work.

Thor not only didn't drive a car, but he refused to learn the ways of the modern computer or own a cell phone. A multilingual secretary could deal with some of that, and Thor could type with two fingers at best on a manual typewriter. He actually preferred to write on yellow lined legal pads, and on many visits to Tenerife I brought with me packs of these pads, which he greatly appreciated. (Most were presented as gifts from young Samuel, who was rewarded in return with a nice postcard of thanks.) Despite the fact that his thick old-school Norwegian accent had become something of a joke among his present-day countrymen (it is sometimes referred to as "the Heyerdahl accent"), Thor's command of the English language was better than my own, and he was fluent in German, French, Italian, and Spanish and conversational in several others.

I worked with Heyerdahl as his right-hand man for about seven years, setting aside my attempts to work again in Egypt until he passed away in 2002. My many adventures with Thor could fill a book of their own. Thor had several ideas in mind when he brought me aboard his research raft. First, he wanted an able coauthor to write an updated, condensed, and popularized version of *American Indians in the Pacific,* his scientific explanation for the *Kon-Tiki* expedition. The book, we decided, would be titled *Lost Wakes in the Pacific* and would be accessible to both scientists and lay readers alike. Second, Thor had ambitions to pursue a couple of new archaeological projects, including excavations at a site on the northwest coast of Morocco and investigations into the pyramids of Güímar, which lay within a short walking distance of his own home on Tenerife. Both projects were linked to his long-standing belief that the oceans of the world were not barriers between ancient cultures but natural conveyances whose winds and currents readily enabled people to move about and perhaps spread culture and ideas.

"Boundaries?" Heyerdahl provocatively asked. "I have never seen one, but I hear they exist in the minds of most people."

The Moroccan proposition involved Thor's interest in Lixus, the ruins of a settlement with a port that was utilized at various times by the Phoenicians, the Carthaginians, and the Romans. Located on the Atlantic coast and perfectly situated to take advantage of currents running east to west to the New World, Lixus might perhaps offer clues to possible contacts across the oceans over many centuries, if not a couple of millennia, prior to Columbus.

The author (*right*) and Thor Heyerdahl during a lecture appearance.

I accompanied Thor to Lixus twice, traveling first to Casablanca and then traveling north up the coast. It's a marvelous and complex site, which had already been partially probed by a few earlier expeditions. Finding the location of the ancient port would be a major goal, and modern technology such as ground-penetrating radar could be put to use to outline its contours. Morocco would be a splendid place to work, too. Here, unlike the crowded confines of the Nile Valley, there were miles and miles of wide-open spaces. Thor had been to Morocco a few times before, having launched the *Ra* expeditions from the port of Safi, and he had subsequently been awarded one of the country's highest honors by the king himself.

We needed to obtain formal permission to excavate at Lixus, and eventually a meeting was arranged with Moroccan antiquities authorities to approve our proposal so that we could immediately begin work. A small group of us, including a colleague of Thor's from Norway, traveled to Morocco for this meeting in the country's capital, Rabat. Anticipating a congenial welcome, we were instead treated to a long-winded lecture in French about our arrogance in wanting to excavate at such a site as Lixus, and our intentions were questioned. Although my French listening skills weren't perfect, I was readily getting the gist that something was seriously wrong by the growing look of irritation on the faces of my colleagues. Thor finally had had enough and spoke up, addressing our honest intentions and commenting on the unexpected rudeness. We got up and left, and I quickly called home to inform an American member of our team, airline ticket in hand, to by no means come to Morocco, and certainly not with the expensive and sophisticated equipment he had arranged for us. Thor, though, was somewhat defiant and insisted that we drive up to the site of Lixus the very next day. There we were greeted quite cordially by the local archaeologists, who seemed to be well aware that we'd be coming. Perhaps the friendly reception at Lixus was the result of a fear that the antagonism shown us at our original meeting had gone way overboard and that Thor, with his international clout, might offer a bad report. We were never quite sure of all the dynamics involved, and the speculation regarding our reception is full of intrigue but unproved.

With strange things occurring around us, I departed to the

airport to return to Tenerife while Thor and Jacqueline kept their plane tickets but decided to quietly take a ferry to Spain. The ferry was delayed, and upon arrival on the opposite side of the straits, Thor was surprisingly greeted by a "journalist" who inquired as to how he'd enjoyed his trip to Morocco. With that, the strange Lixus affair never improved much. Despite his royal connections and repeated overtures, Thor's efforts to excavate at Lixus were thwarted and eventually abandoned.

We would have somewhat better luck in Tenerife itself with the Güímar pyramids. Thor was convinced that these curious structures were the work of the indigenous people of the Canaries called the Guanches. With their probable origins among the Berber people of North Africa, the Guanches settled the islands during the first millennium B.C. Their culture is fascinating, and their language is extinct, but a number of words survive, especially in place-names. They raised sheep and wheat, and some lived in the countless caves that dot the volcanic landscape. Most curiously, the Guanche practiced mummification.

Through the efforts of Thor, Fred Olsen, and others, the site of the Güímar pyramids was preserved, and I watched and occasionally advised as the area was turned into an "ethnographic park." A research foundation with the acronym FERCO (Foundation for Exploration and Research on Cultural Origins) was formed, and one of our first projects was a program of excavation that we hoped would help us solve some of the fundamental questions the pyramids posed: Who built them, when, and for what purpose? A local archaeologist, Tito Valencia, and I started by excavating a small natural cave that seemed to penetrate underneath one of the smaller pyramids. There had been local legends that perhaps it led to secret chambers, perhaps containing Guanche mummies, but a bulldozer associated with a sewer project had used the cave entrance as a convenient place to shove loose debris. The entrance was small, and when I first took a look at the spot, Thor suggested I crawl inside and see what I could see. The volcanic rocks were sharp against my chest, and I inched my way in a body length or two. Within moments I was struck by an eerie tingling feeling on my skin and in my hair that became increasingly uncomfortable, to the point where I decided to quickly extract myself from the tunnel. As I returned to daylight, Thor began to laugh. I was covered from head to toe with fleas; the cave had served as a refuge for some of the local feral dogs, who enjoyed its cool interior.

The Pyramids of Güímar on Tenerife in the Canary Islands are enigmatic structures and an archaeological challenge.

We excavated much of the cave and found that after a couple of short bends it ended with no secret rooms to be found. We concluded that there was no particular evidence to suggest that it was even related to the pyramid above it. Near its entrance, though, we found some of the distinctive pottery and stone tools of the Guanche, with radiocarbon dating providing a date of about A.D. 1000.

The Pyramids of Güímar are a complicated site, and altogether we conducted four field seasons of excavations there. The latter three involved interesting combinations of volunteers and archaeological professionals who worked together to mostly dig test pits and make maps. A lot of our digging indicated that whatever this curious place was, it had been heavily used and reused, and we often found a jumble of material from different eras, including rusty nails mixed in with old Guanche artifacts.

One of our major goals, of course, was to determine the true nature of the pyramids themselves. Old Spanish records suggested that these were indigenous constructions, and it's possible that they were used for solar worship by the Guanches. Stairways up their western sides leading to flat summits seemed to support the notion that such approaches would indeed be suitable for greeting the rising sun. There also seemed to be deliberate orientations along walls of two adjoining pyramids, which accurately aligned to the setting of the sun through notches in the mountains to the west during the summer solstice. There were some, however, that weren't buying the idea that Pirámides de Güímar were either old or native. Alternate theories included the idea that they were Spanish agricultural terraces or were piles of rocks from farmers of the last few centuries clearing their fields.

Thor found these ideas ridiculous. Building three-dimensional terraces with large stone corner blocks would be an absurd waste of time and energy, and as far as their being mere rock piles, there were plenty of examples of those, some even across the street from the site, which resembled, as one might suspect, piles of rocks. No, there was something very strange about the Pirámides, and during our investigations we visited other sites with similar structures, including some in utter ruins on other islands in the Canaries.

To solve some of these outstanding questions, a deep probe into the pyramids bore the possibility of providing some answers. Would digging shafts to penetrate their interiors reveal secrets of their building history? If we reached the original building surface and found organic remains that we could carbon-date, perhaps we could gain an idea of their antiquity, or lack thereof. Could there even be burials inside?

Digging within the pyramids proved a very intimidating challenge. We brought in one of the best American engineers we could find and quickly learned how difficult the task would be. The pyramids consisted primarily of small, coarse volcanic stones mixed with loose soil, which presented a veritable nightmare in terms of maintaining the archaeological integrity of the digging and, more important, the safety of the archaeologists. Our talented engineer attempted to address the problem using traditional mine-shoring methods, placing beams in our initial shaft's walls to prevent the dreaded cave-in. While well suited for mining, the method failed to keep the upper stuff from mixing with the lower stuff, thus violating our need to maintain a clean record of potential strata as we dug deeper. The situation was very frustrating.

I took the issue to Thor, who with his busy schedule could visit the site only for brief periods every day or so. He thoughtfully considered our dilemma, and in short order removed an old envelope from his shirt pocket and drew a little sketch with a pencil. "Try this," he said. The drawing illustrated a set of square boxes that, like nesting Russian dolls, could fit one within the other. We would set the first and largest box on top of the pyramid and excavate inside, the box dropping down with us as we dug, preventing stratigraphic contamination and at the same preserving our lives. When the top of the box reached the surface, we could then insert another, just slightly smaller in size, and add more as necessary.

When I presented the idea to our engineer, he was extremely skeptical but was ultimately willing to give it a try. We built our first box out of reinforced wood right on top of the pyramid, about one meter square and two meters tall and in some ways resembling a phone booth—minus the phone, of course. We slipped the curious device into our shallow mine shoring, crawled inside, and began to excavate. It worked like a charm. Once again, as I had grown accustomed, Thor's genius was reliable. The following year we returned, but this time we had ordered a set of nesting boxes made of steel that would allow us to dig a shaft whose beginning dimensions were two meters square. With a wonderful crew of very experienced archaeologists, including an incredible amateur nicknamed "Termite," we were able to reach bedrock in two shafts dropped down through the center of two different pyramids. The results were disappointingly inconclusive. Datable material was ultimately not forthcoming, nor were Guanche burials encountered. On the other hand, our efforts were a mere sample, and theoretically it's possible that we could have missed a burial by inches and a continued search for datable material could prove worthwhile.

Working for Thor was always an adventure, and I made regular trips to the beautiful Canaries for work sessions. Thor was constantly on the move, and occasionally we met in such places as New York City for events like the formal Explorers Ball or a press conference, or perhaps in British Columbia to investigate a possible Northwest Coast Indian connection to Polynesia (it's not as weird as it sounds). Twice he graciously agreed to visit my university, Pacific Lutheran, conveniently an institution founded by Norwegians and a regular stop on the tour of Scandinavian royalty and cultural luminaries.

Being Thor's right-hand man never ceased to be a fun challenge. Modern technology enabled our full-time cooperation, and many a night would be interrupted by the sound of my fax machine going off with the latest news and requests for information or advice that would be a daunting challenge for anyone. I, however, was usually prepared. Trying to anticipate anything and everything that Thor might possibly need, I regularly collected relevant information, and with advanced library skills and a knowledge of Internet search engines I aimed to deliver answers in the shortest possible turn-around time. The 3:00 A.M. faxes were by no means annoyances (to me at least—I can't speak for my wife) but were an exciting call to action. I couldn't believe I was actually being paid to do this; it was just too much fun and too wonderful!

Working for Thor did have its downside. I had to deal with some of his uncivil opponents, who occasionally resorted to name-calling or other degrading behaviors. Thor did not take kindly to meanness and preferred his opponents from earlier in his career, who were stridently opposed to his theories but could express themselves without the degree of viciousness that often came with the later attacks. Thor was his own best ambassador and his opponents tended to moderate themselves when they met the man in person, when the idea of Thor came face-to-face with the reality of Thor.

Thor reluctantly accepted the role of celebrity that had been imposed upon him but recognized that it enabled him to conduct his life and work in the manner he chose. He recognized, too, that in public, he was *the* Thor Heyerdahl and a Norwegian, and should he be seen in public with a dirty shirt or rebuffing his fans, the word would be passed on. Many a restaurant meal was interrupted by autograph and photograph seekers, and there were times—especially on Tenerife, where there are loads of Europeans vacationers—when Thor preferred to hide and relax while his wife and I hit the streets shopping. And then there were those who came to seek Heyerdahl on Tenerife, confident that he harbored the elusive answers to some of life's and history's most profound questions. It wasn't always easy being Thor Heyerdahl, but he took it all in stride and lived life to its fullest.

On April 18, 2002, Thor Heyerdahl passed away. He had been diagnosed with a brain tumor the previous year but told no one. With decades of dangerous adventures behind him, he was a survivor, and I suspect that he felt he would somehow even overcome this daunting challenge to his very existence. There had been a report of his diagnosis in the Norwegian press, but I dismissed it as yet another celebrity rumor. Thor would have told me, I concluded. I called him up and asked him, and he confidently assured me that he felt fine, which to me meant that the story was false. In retrospect, he hadn't denied it.

The last time I saw Thor alive was in Oslo just about a month before his final days. I had traveled to Norway to attend a board meeting of FERCO. I arrived earlier than the other committee members, and my first encounter with Thor left me shaken and distraught. I had last seen him vital, strong, and in good spirits just a few months previously in Tenerife. Now he looked gaunt, and his physical persona seemed to have aged, as if his eighty-seven years had quickly caught up with him. Usually tough and resilient, he walked the cold winter streets of Oslo uncharacteristically bundled up. I reported back to my recently arrived colleagues and announced that something was seriously wrong with Thor. When we all met, the group agreed. Thor was his usual jovial and charismatic self, but he seemed to have seriously physically deteriorated. In characteristic fashion, Thor took command of our business meetings, during which he addressed several contentious issues.

It was indeed fortuitous that Sherry and Samuel planned a visit

to Norway while I attended my meetings. Sherry was looking forward to seeing her ancestral homeland for the first time, and we
felt that Samuel, at nine, was finally old enough to travel easily and
generally appreciate the experience. Despite the ominous signs of
Thor's failing health, it was a wonderful experience. Samuel was
able to visit the *Kon-Tiki* raft itself accompanied by its celebrated
captain, while Sherry genuinely enjoyed the Norwegian experience.
Within a few days, I would see Thor for the last time. He had
recently written a couple of books about the origins of the Scandi-
navians. ("They just didn't appear out of the ice!" he liked to say.)
Never claiming to be an expert on the subject and playing the role
of a wide-eyed, unbiased investigator, he joyously let whatever clues
he found take him wherever they might lead.

Extensive travel, an excavation in Russia, and visits to many
museums, libraries, and archives produced conclusions that were
controversial and mostly at odds with accepted ideas. Among his
proposals was that the Norse god Odin was once a historical per-
sonage and that place-names from Norse mythology could be found
in the Caucasus region. The books were heavily criticized by the
scholarly world—how dare Thor, with his eager public audience,
step into a world in which they felt he was ill equipped?

Thor's last stand, as one might call it, took place in an auditorium at Oslo University. At a table in front of a large attentive
audience sat Heyerdahl, pleasantly smiling and exuding his usual
confidence. After an introduction he calmly read a summary of
this thesis. On its conclusion, and as expected, the attacks began
immediately. One Norwegian scholar stood up and read a painfully
long and detailed critique that tested the endurance of even those
who agreed. At some point the critic was informed that his time
was up, and he reluctantly halted. Another scholar stood up and
praised Thor, and so it went.

Thor's rebuttals were short, clever, and delivered with a laugh that infected much of the audience. After the lecture he was surrounded by various well-wishers, and I last saw him leaving the auditorium, standing tall with his wife and anxious to retire for the evening to prepare for travel the next day.

No one could anticipate what would transpire. My family trip to Norway was splendid and was followed up by a few days in London, where Samuel was able to visit the British Museum and meet some of my scholarly friends, including Harry James, Nick Reeves, and Christopher Frayling. Thor went to spend a few weeks with his family at their estate in northern Italy. Back at home it was business as usual until around the second week of April, when I received news that Thor had suffered a devastating stroke. The news was spread far and wide. With a dire prognosis, he refused treatment and left this world on his own terms. Thor passed on, and a living legend was gone.

TWELVE

A RETURN TO AN
ANCIENT VALLEY

THOR'S DEATH LEFT a huge vacuum in my life. He had been a best friend, a mentor, a real-life hero, and, only incidentally, my boss. After much thought and conversations with his son, I decided not to attend Thor's funeral, an elaborate state affair held in Oslo's beautiful cathedral, the Domkirke. I wanted to remember Thor as the joyous living man I had seen just a few weeks before, not a motionless figure in a wooden box surrounded by the sorrowful. There was much unfinished work to do, and I decided that the life and legacy of Heyerdahl would be better served if I returned to Norway a few months later when things had calmed down.

Armed with a nicely organized dossier detailing our ongoing projects, I traveled to Oslo to meet with the board of the Kon-Tiki Museum in an effort to gain a continuation of my salary for at least a couple more years. The proposal was turned down, as the board claimed an uncertain future without Thor aboard the ship, so to speak. In reality the captain had died and the raft was adrift. Thor's son, however, was fully supportive of my interests and at one point stated as much publicly. The museum's director, along with Thor's daughter, Bettina, and his wife, Jacqueline, were likewise behind me, but unfortunately neither of them had a vote in such matters. And I, too, was set adrift.

Lying awake at night counting pennies in my head, I wondered what would come next. I applied to teach at a couple of schools. One of them lost my application materials, and the other, a small community college, probably viewed my extensive résumé with the suspicion that I was actually looking for something better. One day, feeling depressed and unambitious, I received an out-of-the-blue e-mail from an adventure cruise ship asking if I'd be interested in lecturing on a monthlong cruise in the South Pacific, beginning at Easter Island and terminating at Tahiti. I would be able to see parts of Polynesia that are hard to visit, including the Marquesan island of Fatu Hiva, where Heyerdahl got his start, and the Tuamotus, where the *Kon-Tiki* finished its amazing voyage.

I was in no particular mood to do anything other than look for work, but Sherry encouraged me to go. Maybe it would cheer me up, she argued, and perhaps I might even meet some people who would be interested in my research. Besides, I would be paid a hundred dollars a day, so I'd be making a little money along the way. I reluctantly agreed and soon found myself on Easter Island, where a ship rocked in the rough waters offshore. With a crew of about one hundred and approximately 150 German and American passengers, the ship was small enough to navigate in waters where few of the large boats can venture, and its little fleet of inflatable Zodiac rafts facilitated landings on many obscure islands.

Each of the passengers on the cruise was paying a substantial amount of money for the privilege of participating in a marvelous itinerary. There would be no cabaret singers, disco dancing, or midnight buffets on this voyage. Instead the likes of myself would be the entertainment, plus an anthropologist, a geologist, a botanist, and an ornithologist, who would present regular evening lectures and accompany and advise the travelers on shore. Some of the passengers were a bit eccentric, and on my first morning on Easter Island I was stopped by a woman who posed the amusing question, "Where are the men?"

I knew exactly what she was trying to ask and pointed in the direction of the coast, where one of the island's famous *moai* statues could be seen standing on its ancient stone platform. "Yonder," I stated, "and there's more where that one came from."

The woman was an accomplished interior designer named Dottie, and when she found out about my Egyptological background, she was thrilled. "Why don't you lecture about Egypt? I'd much prefer that," she joked with a hint of seriousness.

"No, ma'am, I've been contracted to discuss Polynesian archaeology."

She had been to Egypt twice and had fallen in love with the place. Although I answered questions now and again about Egypt when I dined with different guests, as we were required to do, the focus was to be Polynesia.

The ship went to amazing places, including uninhabited isles such as Ducie Atoll and Henderson Island. Most excitingly, we successfully landed on Pitcairn Island, whose difficult waters have often thwarted even the swift and maneuverable Zodiacs. Here live the descendants of the famous *Bounty* mutineers, who seized their ship in 1789, setting their notorious Captain Bligh adrift and sailing about Polynesia seeking safe haven with their Tahitian girlfriends. They found remote Pitcairn, burned the *Bounty* offshore, and weren't discovered for years. Other highlights of our remarkable voyage included a trip to Mangareva, where the tyrannical Father Laval essentially enslaved the population and built a beautiful cathedral from coral, decimating the natives in the process. We visited several islands in the Tuamotus, where coconuts as food and as exportable commodities were central to the natives' existence.

And then there were the spectacular Marquesas Islands, including Fatu Hiva where Thor Heyerdahl spent a year with his first wife and gathered the inspiration that would motivate the *Kon-Tiki* expedition and much of his life. I swam with wild dolphins, saw the graves of Jacques Brel and Paul Gauguin, hiked into narrow jungle valleys, and met a good number of interesting people. In all, the weather had been exceptional, and we had successfully accomplished every one of our fifteen island landfalls.

Within a few weeks of returning home, I received a letter from Dottie and was invited out to visit her in the Florida Keys. I timidly carried a revised dossier describing a variety of archaeological projects I hoped to pursue in Egypt and elsewhere, including a return to the Valley of the Kings. Dottie's response was, "Why not?" Due in large part to her generosity, I was back in business, so to speak, and then began to investigate the new realities of gaining permissions. Things had changed since I was last in Egypt ten years previously. For one thing, the Antiquities Service, now called the Supreme Council of Antiquities (SCA), was directed by a veritable human dynamo, Dr. Zahi Hawass.

With an engaging personality and quickly growing international recognition, Hawass became an articulate Egyptian spokesman for the archaeological heritage of his own country, something not accomplished before. For much of the previous two centuries, Egyptology had been dominated by foreigners who came and picked the plums, and I would venture that if asked to name a prominent Egyptian archaeologist or discovery, the vast majority of the American and European public wouldn't have an answer.

Indeed, there was plenty of good work being done by Egyptians in Egypt, but the news wasn't well dispersed. Passionately dedicated to his own country, Hawass enthusiastically and colorfully presented to the world what his nation was most famous for, and in doing so he has become perhaps the most recognizable living Egyptian citizen next to Omar Sharif and President Mubarak.

Zahi came from a small town in the Nile Delta, and though he originally intended to study law, switched to archaeology instead. Eventually he became director of the vast ancient cemeteries of Sakkara and Giza, where he was actively involved in a variety of innovative and state-of-the-art projects. His archaeological accomplishments are numerous, and it was no real surprise that this ambitious man ultimately became director general of the SCA in 2002. The world of Egyptian archaeology would never be the same. Much due to his efforts, the old Antiquities Service was greatly professionalized, rules against corruption were established and enforced, and an increasing number of competent Egyptian archaeologists were being trained and working in the field. At the same time, Hawass was regularly keeping Egypt in the international headlines, with announcements of new discoveries and bold demands that stolen objects be repatriated to Egypt.

I had first heard of Zahi Hawass back in the late 1980s, and in 1989, on day two of my first field season in the Valley of the Kings, my antiquities inspector bluntly reported that "Zahi Hawass doesn't know who you are."

"He's the pyramids guy," I responded with a shrug. "Why would he be interested in what I'm doing?"

As I later learned, Zahi was interested in everything and everybody archaeological in Egypt, including the new guy working in the Valley of the Kings.

In 2003 it became clear that if I wished to return to Egypt

I needed to meet with the formidable Dr. Hawass to explain my intentions. The opportunity came soon enough. A California chapter of the American Research Center in Egypt was hosting Zahi for a lecture, and I offered to introduce him in hopes of finding a few moments to meet with him before or afterward. He arrived in style, and a reception in his honor held before his presentation offered me a chance to have a word. Much to my surprise, Zahi was well aware of my work—in fact, very well aware, leaving me extremely impressed, especially given the sheer quantity of work conducted in Egypt over the decades, including the ten years of my absence. He stated that he had no objections to my returning, only that I add more Egyptologists on my staff, not an unreasonable request since it is the Valley of the Kings.

I gave my introduction, and Hawass eagerly approached the podium and presented a fascinating and appealing lecture, to the delight of the audience. Zahi the showman was at his best, and one could easily see the side of his personality that charmed the public. When he was finished, he solicited four random questions from the audience. Ironically, and to my great horror, two of the questions from anonymous audience members were directly related to my work. One fellow stood up and asked Zahi if "he had ever heard of this Thor Heyerdahl guy who built this papyrus boat and crossed the ocean like an Egyptian?" I couldn't believe it! If Hawass went off on Heyerdahl, I would probably have given up on working in Egypt. To my relief, Zahi gave a very sensible and nondisparaging answer. Potential crisis averted, or so I thought, but no, another random question addressed Hatshepsut.

"Dr. Hawass? You know that woman Hatshepsut, the female pharaoh? Do you know what ever happened to her mummy?"

How could this be? I shuddered. Once again Zahi gave a reasoned answer and then pointed to me in the front row. "There is a tomb in the Valley of the Kings that contains a mummy some think might be hers. Dr. Donald here knows a lot about it." And so it went. Zahi departed, and I began to fill out the paperwork to resume my work in the royal cemetery.

There was at least one false start, but in October 2005 everything looked in order. My new team was small but outstanding and included my longtime friend the archaeologist Brian Holmes and Egyptologists Larry Berman, from the Museum of Fine Arts in Boston, and Salima Ikram, from the American University in Cairo. Sadly, my original colleague from my first days working in the valley, Mark Papworth, had passed away just a couple of years before. I'm sure he would have been delighted to know that we were back in action and would have enjoyed coming along. The goals of this new season were somewhat modest, but becoming reestablished in Egyptian archaeology would be satisfying in and of itself.

Having been absent from Cairo for twelve years, I was both amazed and dismayed at some of the changes. The city was as crowded as ever, and the traffic was worse, although new bypasses skirted some of the busier areas. Construction had continued at a high pace, and where there was once desert, new communities had sprung up. The air was notably more polluted, and sometimes my eyes burned as soon as I went outside, my visibility limited by a brown fog. On the positive side, the American Research Center in Egypt, which had once been a very limited affair, was now a bustling facility, serving as a valuable resource and a cultural center for foreigners and Egyptians alike. I was particularly impressed by the improved professionalism of the SCA. In previous years one would have to travel to that tall, chaotic building in Abbasia for a process that could sometimes involve repeated visits over several days. Now the offices had been relocated to a sophisticated part of the city, and I was delighted to learn that I had an appointment at a fixed time to have my official papers signed. The friendly and efficient formalities were over in less than half an hour, and I was on my way.

It was exciting to be once again on the night train to Luxor, and I eagerly awaited seeing the sunrise illuminate the countryside and the approaching sight of the Theban mountains. We were back! Like Cairo, Luxor, too, had undergone a few changes. The sheer number of tourists and river cruise boats was startling, and the unmistakable logo of the Golden Arches could be viewed through the columns of the Luxor temple. Across the river one could see a series of large rectangular police posts perched on the cliffs and hillsides, a response to terrorist activities that struck the area in the late 1990s and brought tourism to a halt for a while. Luxor was now well guarded, and a police presence was everywhere, with convoys required for travel to parts north and south of the city. As in Cairo, I found that the Luxor antiquities offices were especially efficient and helpful.

The Valley of the Kings, too, was dramatically different. A master plan for better protecting the area was well under way. The entrance to the valley had been moved far back, and a huge parking lot for buses was located in a place where their impact would be minimized. A new visitors' center had been built, with the numerous souvenir stalls centralized and their vendors banned from the valley proper. I should say "technically banned," as the valley was crawling with athletic young men who confronted tourists with postcards for a bargain price in between running from the police, who exhausted themselves chasing the rascals over the hillsides. Sadly, our once-obscure and quiet part of the cemetery now had a major trail passing through it, although compared to the central part of the valley it receives relatively sporadic traffic. Two fascinating nearby tombs were now open to the public, that of Thutmose

IV (KV 43) and Montuhirkhopeshef (KV 19), our former "office" from our first two field seasons.

After a couple of days of formalities and organizing logistics, we were able to begin work. We were assigned a smart young inspector, and the valley electricians installed the lights again in KV 21, in whose burial chamber we once more set up our tables and chairs. First on our agenda was to review the state of our tombs. How had they fared in the last dozen years, especially in the wake of the great flood of 1994? We were particularly interested in viewing the crack monitors we had installed in 2003, and we were delighted with the results. There were no signs of any shifting in the cracks, the fine crosshairs still aligned as when we left them. That's not to say that cracks might not be expanding for whatever reasons elsewhere in the valley, but at least our tombs, in the short term anyway, appeared to be stable. Although we found no evidence of major flooding in any of our tombs, there was evidence of some water entering Tomb 21, leaving a very fine layer of silt on the floor of the burial chamber, apparently the result of rainwater pummeling the exterior stairs and running down the corridors and steps below.

I was anxious for Larry to take a look at the objects stored in Tomb 60, and it was exciting to reopen the tomb. I was aware that the tomb had been entered at least once in the last year or so. I saw as much on a *National Geographic* television program during which Zahi Hawass and company explored its interior and marveled at the mummy housed in a wooden case we had built. The tomb, as expected, was much as we had left it, although we were surprised to find something that resembled a human body covered with a sheet lying atop the mummy's box. "Darn that *National Geographic*!" I yelled. "They were too lazy to put the lady back into her box!" Much to my surprise, though, such was not the case. When I pulled back the sheet, there lay another mummy, that of a bald young boy whose battered chest lay ripped open. I recognized the fellow. He used to reside in the nearby tomb of Thutmose IV, where I had seen him in a couple of different chambers in previous years. Apparently he was moved to KV 60 for safekeeping with the opening of KV 43 to tourists. Our royal woman was still inside, and *National Geographic* was absolved.

The 2007 field camp outside the entrance of KV 21. The canopies provide shade and a nice fresh-air working environment.

Larry scrutinized many of the artifacts from Tomb 60 and the others, with the informed eyes of a curator who has had a lifetime of experience with a wide variety of Egyptian objects, and Brian was helpful in examining and cataloging our many previous finds. Perhaps the biggest highlight of our new field season was the arrival of Salima Ikram, whose effusive personality has made her the darling of many an international lecture or television appearance. Salima wrote her Ph.D. dissertation on the topic of meat and butchering in ancient Egypt, a surprisingly fascinating subject with many tangents. She was naturally interested in the several small wrapped mummy packages we had recovered from Tomb 60, whose contents remained unknown. Salima suspected that they were "victual mummies": preserved birds and chunks of meat that served as food provisions for a tomb's occupant. There was one way to find out. Salima had brought with her a portable X-ray device, which she and an assistant set up with practiced efficiency in the burial chamber of KV 21. True to form, she bubbled with enthusiasm as she knelt down clad in her protective lead apron to position each object and plate of film.

We did not have to wait long for answers. The kind scholars at Chicago House assisted in the development of the X-ray film, and within a day Salima came to my hotel room bearing the results. Holding the exposures up to the light streaming through a sliding glass door, we could see that Salima's suppositions were correct. Revealed there were the little desiccated remains of small birds, wrapped in oval packages, and substantial chunks of meat, still attached to the bone, including an impressive rack of beef ribs.

The return to the Valley of the Kings proved a wonderful success with only a few drawbacks, including some health issues. Much to my surprise, I experienced twelve different afflictions during the month we worked, including the typical predictable illnesses, along with headaches and even a sprained ankle. Apparently, some of the immunity I once believed I possessed had worn off in the years since my last visit. On the bright side, we were working in the fall rather than the summer. It was a very welcome and sensible change from the brutally hot conditions we had experienced during our first four field seasons.

Egyptologist Dr. Salima Ikram operating her portable
X-ray unit in the burial chamber of KV 21.

In the more hospitable season of fall, there were plenty of other archaeologists around from all over the world working on tombs, temples, and other projects. There was even a bit of a social life, featuring occasional parties, dinners, and lectures, along with informal get-togethers with other Egyptologists. Very generously, Chicago House made its wonderful library available for use by visiting scholars. Overall, I returned home encouraged and excited, with hopes of future field seasons to come. Not only had my dreams of returning to Egypt been fulfilled, they had far exceeded my expectations.

Just a few months after I left, a startling announcement came out of Egypt. A new tomb had been found in the Valley of the Kings, the first since Howard Carter's discovery of Tutankhamun in 1922. I knew it was coming. My friend Otto Schaden had told me as much the year before. Otto had been working for years clearing the debris out of the lengthy corridors that constituted the Twentieth Dynasty tomb known as KV 10, which belonged to the Nineteenth Dynasty ruler Amenmesses. While digging outside the tomb's entrance, Otto uncovered what appeared to be the edges of a pit and very much looking like the top of a tomb shaft. In what seems to be almost a cosmic tradition in archaeology, the discovery was made just a few days before he was finishing up his field season. A new tomb would surely be an incredible discovery, but there was also an excellent chance that this was just a shallow pit full of rubble, perhaps a false start to a shaft leading to nothing. With such tantalizing prospects, it must have been an agonizing year of anticipation while he waited for the next field season, when the truth would be learned.

A shaft it was, leading to a sealed single chamber packed with seven coffins and numerous sealed white jars. It was an amazing scene to behold, but opening tombs of course soon leads to the reality of dealing with their contents. In the case of this new KV 63, Otto was presented with the horrifying fact that most of these wooden coffins had been chewed nearly to sawdust by termites and were seemingly held together by their painted surfaces. And, incredibly, the coffins held no mummies but contained a strange variety of mummification materials, ancient stuffed "pillows," floral wreaths, and other funerary equipment.

The situation with the artifacts was a conservationist's nightmare. Otto remained in Egypt for months until the tomb was properly documented with everything in situ. As was the case with the discovery of Tut, official and unofficial visitors, including the press, were a constant distraction, but the tomb's contents were successfully removed to the nearby KV 10 to await further study. What did Otto find? Is it actually a tomb if no bodies are found? Or is it more proper to see it as a cache of funerary objects? Can these objects be associated with individuals known or unknown? Like so much in archaeology, the extent of the answers we seek might never meet our expectations, but even so, mysteries can keep us interested and motivated.

It was another long year of anticipation for me, too, as I prepared my application for another field season. This time I would include archaeologist Paul Buck, who taught me how to wield a trowel during our formative first field experiences in Egypt as graduate students. Paul, unable to accompany me on my very first year in the valley, was now a professor and researcher in Las Vegas, and he was eager to participate. With his vast field experience in Egypt and elsewhere and his hilarious sense of humor, Paul was a very welcome addition to the team. Additionally, Denis Whitfill, a longtime adventure buddy who had worked with me and Thor Heyerdahl on Tenerife, would serve as our photographer and archaeological technician. Larry and Salima would return, and our team would be rounded out by Barbara Aston, whose expertise in interpreting ancient pottery was extremely desirable.

Our focus in 2006 would be the rubble-choked Tomb 27, a daunting task that at least superficially guaranteed no great results from what would be our substantial efforts. It was an intimidating process. Although we had earlier removed some of the upper layers of flood debris in a couple of the tomb's four chambers, there were literally tons more before we would reach the floors where we expected to uncover whatever was left of the original burial.

On the day we were to begin, our local work crew's documents had not been completely processed, and, anxious to start, Paul, Denis, and I decided to commence excavations without them. A couple days of moving rocks and buckets up a ladder extending down the shaft left us with sore backs and an even greater appreciation for the hard work of our employees who would soon arrive. Eventually the shaft was completely cleared, and we found at its bottom the remains of mud bricks that had originally sealed the tomb's door. The first chamber that followed was reminiscent of the sole room constituting KV 28. There was plenty of modern garbage about, and soot tarnished the doorway and ceiling. Surprisingly, we found very little here, although a suspicious layer of plaster in the floor brought temporary excitement with thoughts of a sealed shaft having escaped the destruction wrought upon the rest of the tomb. Alas, it turned out to be a sort of floor repair squaring up a short ramp leading to a large adjacent chamber we designated C.

Even though encumbered with flood debris, Chamber C was curiously interesting. A channel dug through the dirt leading to a pit nearly reaching the tomb's floor remained from either Mariette's initial probe or from subsequent tomb robbers. Our own test pits in the room's corners to determine its architectural plan had already revealed a small collection of pottery and the skeletal remains of a headless torso. Against one wall, too, was a tall, wide niche with no discernible function, resembling an unfinished start to what in other tombs would be a staircase.

Chamber C would prove to be quite a challenge as we systematically brought the level of debris down to the floor. Here we expected to find whatever might be left of the room's contents, and in this we were more than well rewarded. Our careful excavation revealed a great mass of pottery, all shattered into a jumbled mess, many of the pots being similar to the large white jars we had examined in the side chamber of Tomb 21. It seemed impossible to determine how many there once were, but by counting the surviving hard mud jar stoppers, we were able to arrive at a number for at least the large pots. There were other types of pottery as well, including little plates and bowls. Though damaged, they would prove to be the key in dating KV 27's use.

The huge quantity of shards was imposing, and we hoped to be able to match up a few vessels at least as a sample. A thick cluster of broken ceramic bits and pieces was examined and collected from a pile against the wall in hopes that we might find a complete collection of joining fragments. To our disappointment, this little deposit contained an almost random selection of shards from several different vessels, but this in itself was quite instructive. It now became easy to imagine what had happened here. The room had been used to store a large number of vessels, including perhaps thirty white pots containing embalming leftovers or grave goods. Piles of dishes, some perhaps loaded up with food for sustaining the deceased, were likewise placed or stacked on the floor. One day a catastrophe happened, on a date that remains undetermined. Either the force of a massive flood broke down the tomb's door or, more likely, the tomb had already been breached, pilfered, and left open, and churning brown water poured down the tomb's shaft, carrying with it rocks and boulders.

The powerful surge was not kind to any of the tomb's four chambers. The ceramic contents of Chamber C, for one, were violently slammed against the floors and walls and buried deeply in the muck during the first of what would be many flood events to damage the tomb. Whatever else that might have been in this room suffered a similar fate. Anything organic had scant chance of long-term preservation. The skeletal torso we had previously uncovered represented a mummy whose wrappings had likely rotted away quickly. Like the pottery, it, too, had been slammed against the wall, probably losing its head in the process. We found very little of the rest of it, other than a few small skull fragments, and we even entertained the notion that perhaps the mummy had washed in from another chamber in the tomb.

The pottery provided us with an Eighteenth Dynasty date, but unfortunately no names or any other sort of writing was attached to them. The tedious removal of the debris from Chamber C continued, and one day a nice surprise was discovered: a fragment of a limestone canopic jar with two lines of inscriptions. I was off working on a television program, and Denis could hardly wait to report the news. This is exactly the sort of information we had hoped for that might tie the tomb to actual individuals who lived and died in Egypt around thirty-four hundred years ago. That night Denis brought the images up on a laptop computer, and I could see the clearly cut hieroglyphs, but excitement soon turned to disappointment. There were two lines of inscriptions, all right, with a funerary inscription. Such inscriptions, though, often contain four lines, ending with the name of the deceased, and the essential part was missing from our fragment. So close, I thought, but so typical of our experience working in these undecorated tombs, as they don't give up their secrets easily.

Lucky for us, it would be only a few days until an adjoining piece of the canopic jar was recovered—with the missing two lines of text! And yes, there was a name, that of "the god's father, User-het." "God's father" was probably an interesting job in the New Kingdom. Although it sounds as if it could be applied to the father of a pharaoh, it actually seems to be a kind of priestly title for one with specific religious duties. The name Userhet is certainly known for several high-ranking individuals of the Eighteenth Dynasty, but there was something oddly familiar, if not suspicious, about this particular combination of name and title.

Pottery restorer Mohammed Farouk holds a reconstructed pot from KV 27, the result of weeks of work sorting through innumerable fragments.

I checked some images on my computer. Yes, I knew this User-het. His name and title were found on the three canopic jars that Howard Carter had excavated in the ruins of KV 45, just around the corner from Tomb 27! We had found pieces of the fourth jar! Rather than finally having achieved the satisfaction of matching tomb to owner, we were instead met with a puzzle. Obviously, the jars belonged together, and something was clearly amiss. Was KV 45 indeed the original burial place of Userhet, with one of his jars taken elsewhere by tomb robbers or others? Could KV 27 actually be Userhet's original tomb? Given a score of three to one, KV 45 versus KV 27, one might assume by sheer numbers that 45 wins. Perhaps, but the simplest explanations are not always the most accurate. Could the canopic jars have been washed from elsewhere into one or both tombs by the floodwaters that devastated each of their original burials? Maybe, but it seems far-fetched. Nonetheless, I prefer the explanation that the jar fragments in KV 27 are intrusive, and thus we are left where we were before, searching for answers that continue to elude us.

Meanwhile our study of the artifacts from all six tombs in our concession continued. When we again reopened KV 60 to retrieve a few objects, we were met by a surprise: The wooden box holding the female mummy was gone, and so was the mummy. She had recently been taken to Cairo for study by Zahi Hawass and his team of experts. The questions concerning the death of Hatshepsut and the whereabouts of her mummy were still unanswered over fifteen years after the press had announced that I had in fact rediscovered her mummy. I maintained my position that the KV 60 mummy appeared royal to me, and I suppose Hatshepsut could be a candidate for its identity, but we had no way of telling.

Zahi must have been thinking about Hatshepsut for some time, and identifying her mummy would be a worthwhile project that he was certainly capable of organizing. He was well aware of the mummy in KV 60 and was apparently very impressed when he first laid eyes upon her. She would certainly need to be included in any serious study.

The author holds a fragment of an inscribed canopic jar from KV 27 belonging to Userhet.

At the Egyptian Museum in Cairo, Hawass gathered together four unidentified female mummies, each of whom he believed had circumstantial reasons to be included in a short list of contenders who could possibly be the female pharaoh. Among them were the two mummies originally noted by Howard Carter in Tomb 60: the nurse named Sitre, still in her coffin that had been removed to Cairo around 1906, and the mummy we encountered when we rediscovered the tomb.

The mummies were CT scanned in search of evidence that could provide any sorts of clues. The possibility of making a solid identification was slim, but it was at least worth a try. Along with the mummies, a few surviving objects related to Hatshepsut's burial were brought out for examination, including a small wooden box bearing the pharaoh's name. It had been found over a century before in the famous Deir el-Bahri mummy cache and had been used like a canopic jar, containing a mummified liver, presumably that of Hatshepsut herself. When the box was scanned, it was found to contain something else, something unprecedented. It was a tooth, and it must have been put into the mix during the mummification process. If it had fallen out during embalming, I can't imagine that such an integral part of a pharaoh would be merely thrown away. So here apparently was Hatshepsut's tooth, a revelation with profound implications. In reviewing the CT scans, it was found that there was one mummy missing the appropriate tooth, and, like Cinderella's slipper, the tooth exactly matched the mummy I'd rediscovered from the floor of KV 60. It was the sort of rare discovery that will likely happen only once.

In June 2007, Zahi announced the news that the mummy of Hatshepsut had been identified, and it was a media sensation. My phone rang constantly for days, with reporters from all over the world asking my opinion about the discovery. As I wasn't directly involved in the project, there was not much I could say, other than that from what I knew, the identification was very compelling, if not completely persuasive, and I continue to believe that. A new state-of-the-art DNA laboratory exclusively for the examination of mummies has been set up in the basement of the Egyptian Museum, and Zahi hopes to bolster Hatshepsut's identity by comparing genetic materials from the mummy with those of her relatives.

Along with the identification, the CT scans revealed some fascinating information about Hatshepsut's death. Some Egyptologists had suggested the possibility that she could have been murdered by her stepson and the rightful heir to the throne, Thutmose III. However, murder would have been unnecessary. Hatshepsut's state of health was a disaster. She was extremely obese and had serious dental issues and cancer, all three of which might have caused or contributed to her demise.

I've often been asked how I felt about my role in all this. Howard Carter originally discovered a tomb, I rediscovered it, and Zahi Hawass identified the mummy. In some ways I'm cynically happy that Carter showed such disinterest in KV 60 that he walked away from it, unintentionally leaving for me the excitement of its rediscovery many decades later. Elizabeth Thomas's speculation about the tomb and Hatshepsut inspired us to consider certain possibilities, and Zahi's interest and ingenuity have apparently solved for us what had long been a genuine mystery.

With our enthusiasm bolstered by the recent news, we returned to Egypt again in the fall of 2007. There was a lot of unfinished business: Two chambers remained to be cleared in KV 27, and our catalog of all objects from the six tombs needed to be reviewed for accuracy and completeness. Much of my team returned, as did Brian Holmes. Paul Buck wasn't able to join us, but we gained an enthusiastic helper in the form of Lisa Vlieg, a recent graduate in classics and anthropology from Pacific Lutheran University. It was her first trip to Egypt, and we saw to it that she immediately ventured to the Giza pyramids and the Egyptian Museum.

It would prove to be another great field season. One day, for example, Denis was involved in photographing all the artifacts from KV 60, and one of the larger objects from the tomb was set up on his table. It was a sizable piece of curved wood from the head end of a coffin. Most of its surface was covered with a black, resinous substance that had been applied in ancient times. We could even see the brush marks. There are many known coffins from the Eighteenth Dynasty, along with a number of other funerary items that are coated with this black stuff, and the explanations for it are varied. One idea argues that the coating is related to a transition to the netherworld, and another suggests that whatever decoration might lie beneath was not intended to be seen by the living. Regardless of the how and why, the black substance was there.

While the coffin fragment rested on the photography table, our inspector, Abu Hagag, with his usual healthy curiosity, studied its surface carefully. "Dr. Ryan," he called, "I think I see something here...a hieroglyph under the surface!" I took a look, and sure enough, in a tiny spot where the resin had chipped away, there appeared to be a hieroglyph depicting a human arm. Perhaps there might also be an interesting inscription beneath, but how to reveal it?

Abu Hagag suggested we request a local conservator, and in a couple of days a bearded, robed gentleman by the name of Sayeed arrived. After a brief look, he quietly commented that he felt he could deal with the situation, and he returned the next day with a small box of equipment. Laying the coffin piece on a woven grass mat, he wrapped cotton around a scalpel, dipped it into an acetone solution, and carefully applied it to the wooden surface. The black substance turned to goo, clinging to the cotton, and our suspicions were immediately confirmed. There were indeed hieroglyphs underneath.

Our excitement mounted as Sayeed worked with amazing patience and caution, even refusing to take breaks. He seemed at least as interested in what was being revealed as we were, and we couldn't help but check back on him regularly. What was eventually revealed astounded us. Beneath the black coating was a beautiful painting of the protective goddess Nephthys, standing on a multicolored basket with her arms raised. Surrounding her were funerary texts bearing a name and a title. The name belonged to that of a chantress, that is, a temple singer, and her name was Ti. Who was this Ti? We had never heard of her, but, more interesting, what were the smashed remains of her coffin doing in Tomb 60?

A large piece of the head end of a coffin from KV 60.
The fragment had been mostly covered with black resin,
but upon being cleaned it surprisingly revealed decoration and texts.

The author examines the reconstructed face
from a shattered coffin lid recovered from KV 60.

Along with this exciting question was our realization that we
had many, many more coffin fragments similarly covered with the
black substance that might likewise bear decoration. They had long
been stored by us in KV 60, where we had considered them of little
interpretive value. We retrieved a couple of the larger pieces that
could be joined together and asked Sayeed to continue. Underneath

the coating he revealed an image of the goddess Isis, likewise with upraised arms and coming from the foot end of the same coffin. The revelation was a genuine surprise, but there was certainly not enough time to clean all that we had. It would have to wait.

Meanwhile, back in KV 27, we were gradually working our way down in the last of its chambers. With just about a week left in our field season, we were confident that we would finally complete the clearance of this final tomb in our concession. There were but a few inches of flood debris remaining on a portion of the chamber's floor when something was encountered in the solidified mud. Very careful digging soon revealed a face staring up at us. It was a skull, and two more would be found nearby. In the corner Brian Holmes revealed very ephemeral evidence of a coffin tilted at an angle. Nothing much was left of it but a powdery black stain. Maybe this was the actual burial chamber, and these bones and the shadowy coffin were all that survived of what once were wrapped and boxed mummies.

The newly discovered skeletons in KV 27 would require a great amount of care to release them from their hard surroundings, and we had no time left to finish the job properly. We protected them from further damage and closed up the tomb. The revelation about the blackened coffins with their artistic secrets, too, left us with much unfinished work. We would need once again to return to the Valley of the Kings—the wonderful and amazing archaeological gift that keeps on giving.

The face of one of the occupants of KV 27 is gradually revealed as it is
unearthed from hard, compact sediment on the tomb's floor.

CONCLUSION

Reis Omar Farouk stood at the edge of the deepening shaft, yelling orders to the workmen in a tone that mixed fear and praise. One man sat precariously on a thick wooden plank poised above the hole, hauling on a thick hemp rope that ran through a huge, antiquated pulley affixed to a sturdy beam. The distinct ringing tone of hoes striking against limestone chips was followed by a short pause as the rubber basket full of debris was hooked to the rope and then hoisted to the surface.

The shaft belonged to a tomb last opened in 1906 by Edward Ayrton, working for Theodore Davis. Inside, Ayrton encountered the mummy of "a man, tall and well built . . . unwrapped and thrown on one side." His name was confirmed by a few remaining objects in the ransacked tomb's sole chamber. He was Amenemope, a "vizier"—second-in-command, that is—to the Eighteenth Dynasty pharaoh Amenhotep II, and as in reports of so many other, similar tombs in its time of discovery, the tone here is almost dismissive. When we reopened it in 2008, we encountered much of the tomb's contents still intact, minus the mummy—a provocative quandary. Meanwhile, at worktables situated outside Tomb 21, black coffin fragments were being cleaned and examined and shattered ancient pots were being reconstructed. Nearby, three skeletons were carefully unearthed in a subterranean chamber of Tomb 27 while a protective wall was built around its entrance. All in a day's work in this most exciting of archaeological sites.

Back in 1817, Belzoni thought there was nothing left to discover in the Valley of the Kings, and even Theodore Davis with all his discoveries concluded in 1912, "I fear the Valley of the Tombs is now exhausted." Of course they were both mistaken. King Tutankamun's tomb, arguably the best of the best, was discovered ten years later. And here we were, even decades beyond, in the Valley of the Kings, discovering new things. Anyone who thinks exploration is dead but for the planets and stars is shortsighted. Right here on earth there is plenty to discover and even more to learn. Sometimes it can be right under your nose or in places previously unappreciated. In my own archaeological work, I looked at "boring" or neglected subjects and found them to be both exciting and worthwhile. Each time we come across something new, whether artifacts from the past or ideas from the mind, it's a discovery.

Exploration is alive and well, as the many active members of groups such as the Explorers Club and the Royal Geographical Society can attest. Whether it's in the realm of zoology, geography, oceanography, or any number of other fields, one can argue that only the obvious stuff has already been found. In terms of the prospects of archaeology, Thor Heyerdahl once said, "For every minute, the future is becoming the past," and as a result there will always be something to study. When I was a boy, I dreamed of adventure and exploration. Now that I'm an adult, some of those dreams are still alive, and I truly feel blessed to have done much, yet at the same time I feel that I'm only just getting started!

PHOTOGRAPH CREDITS

166 Donald P. Ryan
170 PLU Valley of the Kings Project
173 PLU Valley of the Kings Project
179 PLU Valley of the Kings Project
188 PLU Valley of the Kings Project
190 PLU Valley of the Kings Project
193 Denis Whitfill/PLU Valley of the Kings Project
245 Richard Londgren
248 Denis Whitfill/2000 Excavation at the Pirámides de Güímar
265 Denis Whitfill/PLU Valley of the Kings Project
267 Denis Whitfill/PLU Valley of the Kings Project
273 Denis Whitfill/PLU Valley of the Kings Project
275 Denis Whitfill/PLU Valley of the Kings Project
279 Denis Whitfill/PLU Valley of the Kings Project
280 Denis Whitfill/PLU Valley of the Kings Project
282 Denis Whitfill/PLU Valley of the Kings Project